COMMUNICATION ETHICS TODAY

C·O·M·M·U·N·I·C·A·T·I·O·N E·T·H·I·C·S

The Teaching and Practice of Communication Ethics
John Strain and Simon Robinson (eds.)
1-905237-33-2

COMMUNICATION ETHICS TODAY

edited by

Richard Keeble

C·O·M·M·U·N·I·C·A·T·I·O·N E·T·H·I·C·S

Troubador Publishing Ltd
9 De Montfort Mews
Leicester LE1 7FW, UK
Tel: (+44) 116 255 9311 / 9312
Email: books@troubador.co.uk
Web: www.troubador.co.uk

C·O·M·M·U·N·I·C·A·T·I·O·N E·T·H·I·C·S

Series Editor: Richard Keeble, School of Jouirnalism, University of Lincoln, UK

ISBN 1 905237 68 5

Typeset in 11pt Stempel Garamond by Troubador Publishing Ltd, Leicester, UK

Contents

Introduction

Journal with a difference

RICHARD KEEBLE

Ethical Space is an academic quarterly with a difference. These were the opening words of the journal's first editorial and the issues in the volume which make up this book certainly live up to that statement.

In the first instance, the journal, as the voice of the Institute of Communication Ethics, set itself the distinctly difficult task of drawing together contributions from an eclectic range of disciplines in the field of communications. So among the areas represented are philosophy, public relations, alternative and mainstream journalism (both on and off-line), media regulation, law, corporate social responsibility, education, information studies, peace studies and counselling. There is a danger here of superficiality. Yet the benefits clearly outweigh the disadvantages – and through mixing viewpoints from a range of perspectives the journal has promoted a uniquely rich and exciting intellectual debate.

Too many academic journals dwell in the land of esoteric and obscure theorising far away from the dilemmas and challenges of practitioners. In contrast, *Ethical Space* has carried contributions in a range of genres to celebrate the work of both internationally-acclaimed academics and practitioners. "Views" such as those in this volume by Nicholas Jones on the Hutton aftermath and Roy Greenslade on journalistic ethics are lively, often controversial and always topical "think pieces" of around 1,500 words. "Articles" are more substantial pieces, referenced, and around 3,000 words – but they are without the theoretical underpinnings and structural conventions of the academic paper. Here Michael Foley's article on journalists' dilemmas over confidential sources, Anne Gregory's assessment of the Phyllis Report on government communications and Richard Orange's analysis of the Hutton report are excellent examples of this genre.

And "Papers" are those 5,000-word academic papers (all rigorously peer-reviewed) which form the intellectual backbone of the journal. The international focus of the journal has been particularly evident here with outstanding, original contributions from England, Ireland, Scotland, Holland, New Zealand, the United States, Finland, Norway and Germany. Moreover, *Ethical Space* is also extremely fortunate in having an editorial board of such academic and professional eminence with universities in Spain, Australia, the United States, Scotland, England, Wales, Finland, Germany, Israel, France and Holland among those represented.

Journalism is the discipline at the heart of all ICE's activities. Thus, not only is there a topical flavour to all the contents of *Ethical Space*. But each issue begins with a few news items. Thus in the first volume, for instance, Mike Jempson reported on the launch of MediaWise, a new ethical forum to promote continuous dialogue between the public and media professionals, while Claude-Jean Bertrand highlighted a new innovative website containing the largest collection of media codes of ethics in cyberspace. Alongside all of this were updates on ICE activities – so news of conferences and calls for papers were carried regularly.

Another distinct feature of the journal are the interviews conducted by Kristine Lowe with eminent figures in the world of communication ethics. The Question and Answer format allows for a searching exploration of viewpoints and, indeed, the interviews with Fareena Alam, the new editor of Europe's leading Muslim magazine, Johan Galtung, the eminent peace researcher (included here), and Philip Hodson, chief spokesman for the British Association of Counselling and Psychotherapy, all proved fascinating.

Finally, the journal ends (conventionally) with reviews of books and websites. Yet, out of all the many communication ethics texts we read, one often holds a special place. So in Vol 1 No 4, *ES* did something different and had six academics revealing their favourite books (and there were a few surprises there!).

Ethics is about reflection (cultivating that ethical space) and action. *ES*, in its first volume, proves itself committed to inspiring rigorous and lively reflection on international communication issues — and ultimately to promoting ethical action.

Richard Keeble is Professor of Journalism at the University of Lincoln. From 1984–2003, he was a lecturer at City University, London. He was a sub-editor on the *Nottingham Guardian Journal* and *Cambridge Evening News* before becoming editor of *The Teacher* (1980–84). His publications include *The Newspapers Handbook* (Routledge, fourth edition 2005), *Secret State, Silent Press: New Militarism, the Gulf and the Modern Image of War* (John Libbery 1997) and *Ethics for Journalists* (Routledge 2001). He is currently writing a history of war reporting for the Open University Press.

Contact: University ogf Lincoln, Main Campus, Brayford Pool, Lincoln LN6 7TS, UK; tel: 01522 886 940; email: rkeeble@lincoln.ac.uk

Preface

CLIFFORD G. CHRISTIANS

This book is a search for truth. There are a number of crucial issues in communication ethics today, but certainly a believable concept of truth is indispensable. As the norm of justice is to politics and stewardship to business, so truth-telling sets the standard in communications. Truth is communication's master principle, and the writers here demand it for themselves, and from the media professionals and academics their chapters represent. Rather than the news media lurching along from one crisis to another with an empty centre, the authors of this book seek for credible variations on truth. These chapters *en masse* promote truth-telling as the over-arching ethical framework for understanding the media's mission and practice (cf. Christians 2002). Rather than merely identifying the issue of truth as important for twenty-first century professional ethics, truth and its nuances are elaborated in terms of communication institutions, technologies, regulation, theory, and practices.

Communication Ethics Today lives out of Aristotle's legacy. "Falsehood is itself mean and culpable, and truth noble and full of praise" (Aristotle 1925, bk.4, ch.7). Truth and lying are permanently imbalanced. We ought not grant them equal status and then merely calculate the best results. Lying must be justified while telling the truth does not need to be. In Sissela Bok's elaboration, only in a monumental crisis, or as a last resort, can lying even be considered for moral justification. "Deceit and violence — these are the two forms of deliberate assault on human beings" (Bok 1999: 18). Those who are lied to are resentful, hostile, and suspicious. "Veracity functions as the foundation of relations among human beings; when this trust shatters or wears away, institutions collapse" (ibid: 31).

While Aristotle's predilection is Greek in its cadence, he speaks to the world and across history. For Hinduism truth is the highest dharma and source of all other virtues. In Serbo-Croatian the true is justified, as with a plumbline in carpentry. The Truth and Reconciliation Commission in South Africa demonstrated that sufferings from apartheid can be healed through truthful testimony. In the Talmud, the liars' punishment is that no one believes them. Rhetoric for Augustine does not produce knowledge nor opinion but is *aletheiac* (truth-producing). For the former secretary general of the United Nations, Dag Hammerskjold, "the most dangerous of all dilemmas is when we are obliged to conceal the truth to be victorious" (Jensen 2000: 7). In Gandhi's *satyagrapha* the power of truth through the human spirit eventually wins over force. The fundamental norm of Islamic communication is truthfulness. For the Shuswap tribe in Canada, truth as genuineness and authenticity are central to culture.

PROMOTING A ROBUST AND HEALTHY VERSION OF TRUTH
But truth's pride of place in human intelligence does not make our work easy nor our burden light. Living up to the truth-ideal is virtually impossible, even for those who idolise it. Every case elaborated in this volume is complicated and some issues are serpentine. Solutions are elusive, though there may be moral discernment among veteran practitioners. In industrial societies, human values are increasingly sacrificed to technocratic efficiency. In the epistemology of virtual reality, the meaning of disembodiment is still unclear. Agreeing on visual accuracy in a digital world has been almost impossible, even among competent professionals of good will. And even if we could get our thinking straight, sophisticated electronics bury us with unceasing information and little time to sift through the intricacies of truth-telling.

Despite its luminosity and catharsis, truth is dissentient. For J. L. Austin (1961), truth is an illusory ideal; there is no "truth, the whole truth and nothing but the truth about, say, the battle of Waterloo or the Primavera". In Nietzsche's terms, "there is only one world, and that world is false, cruel, contradictory, misleading, senseless....We need lies in order to live" (1967: 461). But rather than be entangled in complexity or demoralised by confusion, this volume opens up a pathway from truth in conventional journalism to a robust, healthy version of it here. Moving beyond the traditional view of truth as objectivity, the authors put particulars in their milieu. The moral dimensions of truth are made explicit. In fact, the book's trajectory needs elaboration in order to appreciate its immense value in media ethics today.

Historically the mainstream press has defined itself in terms of an objectivist worldview. Centred on human rationality and armed with the scientific method, the facts in news have been said to mirror reality. The aim has been true and incontrovertible accounts of a domain separate from human consciousness. In Bertrand Russell's formula, "truth consists in some form of correspondence between belief and fact" (Russell 1912: 121). Genuine knowledge is identified with the physical sciences, and the objectivity of physics and mathematics sets the standard for all forms of knowing. For Quine (1953) philosophical inquiry is natural science reflecting on itself. In the received view, truth is defined in elementary epistemological terms as accurate representation. News corresponds to context-free algorithms, and journalistic morality is equivalent to the unbiased reporting of neutral data.

Attacks on this misguided view of human knowledge originated already in Giambattista Vico's *fantasia* and Wilhelm Dilthey's *verstehen* in the counter-Enligtenment of the 18th century. The assault has continued with hermeneutics, critical theory in the Frankfurt School, Wittgenstein's linguistic philosophy, Antonio Gramsci, and Lyotard's denial of master narratives, until the anti-foundationalism of our own day indicates a crisis in correspondence views of truth. Institutional structures remain Enlightenment-driven, but in principle the tide has turned currently towards restricting objectivism to the territory of mathematics, physics, and the natural sciences. In reporting, objectivity has become increasingly controversial as the working press's professional standards, though it will remain entrenched in our ordinary practices of news production and dissemination until an alternative mission for the press is convincingly formulated.

The demise of correspondence views of truth has created a predicament for the notion of truth altogether. However, instead of abandoning the concept, truth needs to be relocated in the moral sphere. Truth is a problem of axiology rather than epistemology. With the dominant scheme no longer tenable, truth in *Communication Ethics Today* becomes the province of ethicists who reconstruct it as the media's ideal.

A CONCEPT OF TRUTH AS DISCLOSURE

These chapters speak in concert about credible language as pivotal to the communications enterprise. But they recognise mutually that the mainstream view of truth as accurate information is too narrow for today's social and political complexities. They together argue for a more sophisticated concept of truth as disclosure. Already in 1947, the famous Hutchins Commission report on *A Free and Responsible Press* called for this alternative. It advocated a deeper definition of the press's mission as "a truthful, comprehensive and intelligent account of the day's events in a context which gives them meaning" (ch. 2). Dietrich Bonhoeffer contends correctly that a truthful account takes hold of the context, motives, and presuppositions involved (1995: ch. 5). In his terms, telling the truth depends on the quality of discernment so that penultimates do not gain ultimacy. Truth means, in other words, to strike gold, to get at "the core, the essence, the nub, the heart of the matter" (Pippert 1989: 11).

To replace newsgathering rooted in the empiricist methods of the natural sciences, fiction and fabrication are obviously not acceptable substitutes. In terms of disclosure and authenticity, this book seeks what might be called "interpretive sufficiency". This paradigm opens up the social world in all its dynamic dimensions. The thick notion of sufficiency supplants the thinness of the technical, exterior, and statistically precise received view. The contributors recognise that no hard line exists between fact and interpretation; therefore, truthful accounts entail adequate and credible interpretations rather than first impressions. The best journalists weave a tapestry of truth from inside the attitudes, culture, and language of the people and events they are actually reporting. Their disclosures ring true on both levels; that is, they are theoretically credible and realistic to those being covered. The reporters' frame of reference is not derived from a free-floating mathematics, but from an inside picture that gets at the heart of the matter. Rather than reducing social issues to the financial and administrative problems defined by politicians, the media disclose the subtlety and nuance that enable readers and viewers to identify the fundamental issues themselves.

The interpretive sufficiency demonstrated in *Communication Ethics Today* takes seriously lives that are loaded with cultural complexity. Within social and political entities are multiple spaces that exist as ongoing constructions of public life. The authors of this book understand that our selves are articulated within these decisive contexts of gender, race, class, and religion. They insist that empirical and theoretical work reflect a community's polychromatic voices through which participatory democracy takes place. They recognise that one of the most urgent and vexing issues on the civic agenda at present is not just the moral obligation to treat ethnic differences with fairness, but giving an authentic voice to explicit cultural groups politically.

Telling the truth is not aimed at informing a majority audience of racial injustice, for example, but offers a form of representation that generates a critical consciousness. Interpretive sufficiency in its multicultural dimension locates persons in a non-competitive, non-hierarchical relationship to the larger moral universe. It imagines new modes of human transformation and emancipation, while nurturing those transformations through dialogue.

TRUTH THE IMMOVABLE AXLE

Throughout the episodes, theories, and historical accounts articulated here, the issue is how the truth works itself out in community formation. The concern is not first of all what the authors themselves declare to be virtuous. Instead of limiting the writers' perspectives to their own morality or to neutral principles, they engage the same moral space as the people they analyse and represent. In this perspective on truth as divulgence, the concern first of all is not experimental robustness but vitality and vigour in illuminating how the communication arts can flourish. Truth as authentic disclosure gives the contributors intellectual leverage; it responds to the human yearning for a lever long enough to move the earth.

It is far from settled whether a credible version of normative values in general, and of truth-telling in particular, can be established for cross-cultural ethics. But this is a worthwhile goal, even an essential one, given the centrality of truth to communications as a scholarly field and professional practice. In the powerful wheel imagery of the Buddhist tradition, truth is the immovable axle. While other issues must continue to be researched and resolved, this book is one way to reinvigorate truth as the axis of a new model of communication ethics.

REFERENCES

Aristotle (1925) *Nicomachean Ethics*, ed. Ross, W. D., Oxford, UK, Oxford University Press

Austin, J. L. (1961) "Truth", *Philosophical Papers*, Oxford, UK, Clarendon Press

Bok, Sissela (1999) *Lying: Moral Choice in Public and Private Life*, New York, Vintage Random House

Bonhoeffer, Dietrich (1955) *Ethics*, trans. Smith, N. H., New York, Macmillan

Christians, Clifford (2002) "Social Dialogue and Media Ethics," *Ethical Perspectives* 7: 2-3 (September) pp 182-193

Commission on Freedom of the Press (1947) *A Free and Responsible Press*, Chicago, University of Chicago Press

Jensen, Vernon (2000) "Bridging the Millennia: Truth and Trust in Human Communication", Sixth National Communication Ethics Conference, Gull Lake, Michigan, USA, May pp 6-7

Nietzsche, Friedrich (1967) *The Will to Power*, ed. Kaufmann, Walter, New York, Random House

Pippert, Wesley (1989) *An Ethics of News: A Reporter's Search for Truth*, Washington, DC, Georgetown University Press p 11

Quine, W. V. (1953) *From a Logical Point of View: Nine Logico-Philosophical Essays*, Cambridge, MA, Harvard University Press

Russell, Bertrand (1912) "Truth and Falsehood", *Problems of Philosophy*, New York, Henry Holt

Does dumbing up mean duller?

Roy Greenslade

Roy Greenslade questions whether ethical journalism is an oxymoron

Does ethical journalism inevitably mean dull journalism? Are those who criticise the morality of the tabloid agenda just killjoys eager to erase humour and human interest from our newspapers? Anyway, why shouldn't people be free to read whatever they like?

Those who seek to ensure that papers abide by an ethical code often confront questions like these because, taken at face value, many of our arguments are underpinned by what might be deemed to be prescriptive arguments. We are, however unfairly, cast in the role of fundamentalist preachers.

Our critics, who number among them most tabloid journalists, see us as either naive (namby-pamby do-gooders) or political meddlers (bitter old leftists). In either case, we are damned because we are imbued with political correctness (a term originally conceived as the embodiment of enlightened understanding and good manners which, as we know, has been successfully transformed by the right into a term of abuse).

Indeed, it is the press's ability to turn rational thought on its head, spinning away day by day against all who threaten their supposed right to do as they please, which lies at the heart of the problems we consistently face.

If we are to make out a case for ethical journalism we have to explain that there doesn't need to be a contradiction between the exercise of freedom and the exercise of responsibility. They are not mutually incompatible. The proper function of democracy depends on the tempering of freedom with responsibility because the people are more likely to make sensible decisions if they are told the truth about what is being done in their name by their state. Trying to tell the truth, no matter how hard to discover, no matter how difficult to accomplish, should be the core reason for a newspaper's existence.

For so many British national newspapers, of course, that isn't why they are published all. They are commercial entities, embedded in the market in order to return profits, and largely owned or controlled by people who also wish to use them as propaganda vehicles. Given those conditions, it is remarkable – and not without merit – to have forced them to accept the need to work to an ethical code of any kind. There is much to be done, but the drawing up of an editors' code of practice in 1990 was a significant start, despite being too rarely observed in spirit and too often breached in letter.

The code, and its often illogical policing by the Press Complaints Commission (PCC), has not changed the culture which has long infected popular papers and which is spreading to the so-called quality press. One central problem concerns the way in which papers shy away from the straightforward telling of stories. They are terrified of boring readers. Most editors, tabloid and broadsheet, subscribe to the view that readers must be wooed: they won't read unless they are, for want of a better word, entertained.

Every story must therefore be made "accessible" to the greatest possible number of people and this is most usually achieved through transforming purely factual "policy" or "issue" stories into human interest stories. A subjective, personal experience is always regarded as more readable than an objective, general report.

Humanising stories may be understandable but it has led to the distortion of the news agenda because stories are therefore chosen for their entertainment value rather than their information worth. If one studies the content of the tabloids this state of affairs is blatantly obvious: news selection is slanted deliberately towards stories laden with entertainment values, such as the bizarre, the humorous, the sentimental, the sexy, the lurid and, needless to say, the star-studded. Picture choice informed by the same mind-set is even more conspicuous.

With the accent on telling an entertaining story, what is lost is context because, filtered through the reporter and sub-editor's inevitably convoluted prose, we receive only a fragmented version of the truth. And, anyway, the story itself may well be of only marginal importance once weighed on the scales of public benefit values.

Worse, much worse, is the retailing of prejudice, such as the false stories published in 2003 in the *Sun* and *Daily Star* respectively about asylum-seekers eating swans and donkeys. This was racism dressed up as entertainment, an example of the reactionary political agenda pursued by almost all tabloids (though not the *Daily Mirror*). We are not killjoys for wishing to kill off trash such as this. There is no responsibility in proclaiming press freedom to publish stories likely to incite hatred against minority groups.

Stories which cannot be "sexed up" are continually overlooked by the popular press, regardless of their merits to society. So overt is this tendency that the more candid – or maybe cynical – owners and editors don't even try to conceal it. Rupert Murdoch, owner of four national titles, has said: "We're in the entertainment business." Richard Desmond, owner of three nationals, once remarked: "We're a branch of showbiz, aren't we?" Note that his *Daily Star*, the fastest-rising title, hardly reports any news at all.

Piers Morgan, former editor of the *Daily Mirror*, who made much of his Pauline conversion to serious journalism after September 11, soon reconverted to a staple diet of entertainment-based editorial. Fun is the tabloid editorial watchword and, to paraphrase a now-unfashionable philosopher, I think it's fair to say that celebrity, rather than religion, is now the opium of the people. The strength of modern celebrity culture cannot be blamed on papers alone, but their editors obviously feel they dare not struggle against it lest sales are affected. So they are now forced to go on producing, and reproducing, the famous: they have therefore become both the fame-pushers and the fame addicts.

The serious broadsheet press has also been attracted by the showbusiness magnet. Rarely is there a day when the broadsheets don't carry a picture of a famous person on their front pages, often in blurbs specifically designed to appeal to casual news-stand buyers. There is also some evidence that, at *The Times* at least, the adoption of the compact format, will lead it further down the celebrity road. Its tabloid-sized version promotes entertainment articles at the expense of policy stories.

But this situation is not cast in stone. There is no reason — as the *Guardian*, *Independent* and *Times* tabloid sections have illustrated — why serious subjects cannot be made entertaining without distorting the truth. Many of the contributions are far from dull. I agree that people ought to be able to read what they like. But do newspapers, organs of information, have to publish only that which slavishly panders to the baser appetites of the lowest common denominator?

Some measure of prescription about what is for the greater public benefit should inform every newspaper's editorial values. In other words, it's a matter of exercising press freedom for the overall good of society. To do that, all those people who wish to further the cause of ethical journalism have to pressure owners and editors – which includes harrying them by making them stick more closely to the editors' code – in order to punch home the message that too much of what they publish is unacceptable.

We must create a situation in which they have to ask themselves the most basic question of all: Why do we exist? What's journalism for? They can no longer point to their circulation figures to justify what they do because overall sales have been in decline for 30 years and have been accelerating downwards in recent times. Pandering to the public doesn't appear to be working, does it?

Roy Greenslade is Professor of Journalism at City University, London. This is a re-working of the talk he gave at the launch of *Ethical Space: The International Journal of Communication Ethics* at City University, London, on 26 November 2003. Formerly media commentator on the *Guardian*, he wrote a regular media column for the *Daily Telegraph* for a few months. Since this "View" was published in 2004, Piers Morgan has quit the editorship of the *Daily Mirror* after he published fake photographs of British soldiers abusing Iraqi prisoners. *The Times* is now entirely tabloid while the *Guardian* has adopted the Berliner format.

The Hutton aftermath:
is the age of spin over?

Nicholas Jones

Nicholas Jones, for 30 years a BBC political and industrial correspondent, argues (in ES *Vol 1 No 3 in 2004) there is a 'window of opportunity' to change the way the government communicates with the media*

Almost a year has passed since the death of the weapons inspector Dr David Kelly, an event which was to set in train the Hutton Inquiry and which hastened a fundamental shake-up in the way the British government communicates with the news media and therefore hopefully with the public. Lord Hutton's investigation and subsequent report were traumatic events not only for the BBC but also for many senior figures in Tony Blair's administration. Under forensic examination, and the glare of publicity, were the ethical standards of BBC journalists, the intelligence services and numerous Downing Street and Whitehall information officers.

Alastair Campbell's ignominious resignation, within days of giving his evidence to Lord Hutton, was a seminal moment, the occasion for a dramatic gear change by the Prime Minister. Blair announced almost immediately that strategic control over the flow of information from the state to the public should never again be in the hands of a political propagandist. Slowly we can see that post-Campbell structure taking place: a new senior civil service position has been created, that of permanent secretary for government communications, and the first holder of that post is Howell James, an experienced public relations practitioner.

Another senior civil servant, Godric Smith, formerly one of the Prime Minister's official spokesmen, has taken over control of the strategic communications unit. Blair's new director of communications, David Hill, has been stripped of the executive power exercised by Campbell and has been doing more on the political front. This has resulted in the political appointees, the ministerial special advisers, being required to take a step back.

Over the summer and autumn of 2004 it should be possible to determine whether there is a chance of repairing what Bob Phillis and his review team concluded was a "'three-way breakdown in trust between government and politicians, the media and the public". We shall soon be able to see whether this new structure is delivering what is needed and whether it will allow Blair to honour his much-repeated undertaking that his administration has turned its back on spin and stopped chasing tomorrow's headlines. The brief for the new permanent secretary is to become head of profession for government information officers, provide "strategic leadership" and establish a central unit that should become the "centre for excellence" across the information service. This new structure, and Howell James' appointment, does deserve to be given a try. Will he have sufficient authority? Will he be given full support? This does present a timely challenge to the cabinet secretary, Sir Andrew Turnbull: can civil servants regain the influence which they lost to the political appointees in the wake of Labour's 1997 general election? Indeed does the Prime Minister stand any chance of stemming the damage done to his own reputation for trust? Will it be possible to restore the credibility of government statements?

Before I set out what further action I think the government and parliament should be taking perhaps I should deliver a health warning about my own remarks. Last month I outlined a checklist of what I considered was the damage which had resulted from the Campbell regime in Downing Street. I contended that Campbell and Co. had taken advantage of commercial pressures in the media and driven down journalistic standards, especially when it came to the ethics of political reporting. He exploited the demand for exclusive stories by offering access and interviews in return for favourable coverage; he encouraged the trade in off-the-record tip offs and encouraged others to trade confidential information on an un-attributable basis; he destroyed what remained of the trust between the lobby and Downing Street; and he sidelined the House of Commons and undermined the authority of the Speaker by blatantly trailing ministerial statements before they were announced to Parliament. Campbell has refused a request by myself — and the National Union of Journalists — to debate these issues. Instead he gave a pithy response last month to the Commons Public Administration Select Committee when MPs put my checklist to him. "That," said Campbell, "is self-serving nonsense from someone who has unhealthy obsession with his subject." But there, despite that rebuke I still maintain that Campbell is in denial; that he does not see nor wish to discuss the ethical points which I have raised.

What struck me about Campbell's appearance before the committee was that he saw it all in terms of a battle between the government and the press. The newspapers were to blame for all the cynicism and negativity, for treating all politicians in a bad light, for de-legitimising communication between government and the public. Ninety per cent of spin was down to the press not Downing Street. Unless the newspapers were ready to "buy into" a process of change then there wasn't a chance of improving the way politics were reported. As one MP said, Campbell seemed to be preaching a gospel of despair. However, he did say he wanted the good journalists to stand up against the bad and to be fair he accepted that some broadcasters were anxious to drive up standards. That's the point of my checklist.

When Campbell was with Blair in Downing Street he had a chance to drive up the ethics of our trade but in my opinion he blew it. What I wanted him to do was to be far more open; I know it's a cliché, but to give all journalists a level playing field, so that whenever possible, there is equal access to all of the news for all of the journalists at the same time. Let's be frank about it, journalists aren't going to make the first move. Our industry is far too competitive for that. It is the state that controls the flow of information and it is the state that must make the first move. So why is No. 10, under pressure from newspaper reporters, still holding back from allowing the lobby briefings at Westminster to be televised? That was one of the principal recommendations of the Phillis review, that arrangements should be made immediately to allow the televising and recording of all government briefings and for publishing an immediate transcript on the No 10 website.

Why can't the government understand that at Westminster journalists from the electronic news media, by which I mean television, radio, news agencies, websites and so on, now outnumber those working for newspapers. Through the Internet it is now possible, as we saw with Lord Hutton's inquiry, to provide vast swathes of official documents on line and almost instant transcripts of who said what. Why doesn't the government drive a wedge between the print and electronic media? Is it because British governments — I'm not making a party point here — remain too close to media proprietors and, just as with issues of privacy and intrusion, are fearful of taking on the tabloids.

I would contend that by and large our standards of accuracy, by which

I mean in television and radio and on in Internet web sites, are far greater than in many newspapers. The speed with which we transmit news is so fast that often there is no hiding place; our mistakes are spotted immediately and have to be corrected or we lose our credibility. What televised lobby briefings would achieve is a bedrock of official information; information that was always on the record and available for instant replay. The briefings could even go out live on the Downing Street web site and be seen not just here but around the world. Increasing that flow of information, sweeping away Whitehall's culture of secrecy which Campbell exploited, will put some of the responsibility back where it belongs, on the shoulders of the journalists. That would do more than anything to explain and expose what the tabloids are up to. How the popular papers treat the news to suit their own agendas.

Frankly it's time that instead of bleating about this that the likes of Campbell and Co. started encouraging the government to take some positive action. Thankfully, to a degree, it is happening almost by default. Often you can hear ministers with their backs against the wall, for example, being interviewed on Today or Newsnight telling viewers and listeners to check it out for themselves. "It's on the website," they say. "That's where you can see what I really said." Perhaps it's time that the government woke up to what's happening and looked at the ways Islamic and Arab protest groups choose to communicate. They know all about using video, television and the Internet: just look at the Arab station, Al Jazeera or the web sites of Osama Bin Laden's supporters. When Bin Laden sat outside a cave, cradling a kalashnikov, enthusing young Muslims to become suicide bombers, he didn't need a Peter Mandelson to tell him what to do.

It is because we in western countries must find ways to defend and uphold our democratic values, when challenged by the Islamic and Arab world, that I believe our governments should make the best use of the very latest communications techniques. I am not against that. But we have to decide on what ethical basis we should operate. Do we want to go down the American path and have a politicised system where the top 5,000 jobs in each administration will be political appointments depending on whether the Democrats or Republicans are in power? Or do we want to retain the British model whereby strategic control over the flow of information, and the ethical considerations governing that flow, are in the hands of neutral civil servants capable of serving whichever government is in power.

My feeling, having just heard Alastair Campbell giving evidence, is that he still thinks that political control is the answer, that Blair will have to rely on political appointees. Where does that leave us? In my opinion, if the Conservatives got back, they would probably follow the Campbell route. Can you see an incoming Conservative administration turning down the chance to bring in 80 or so political activists, right to the heart of government, bearing in mind it's the taxpayer who picks up the £5million annual wage bill? That might mean — as happened in 1997 — that there is another clear-out of civil service directors of information. This time the heads of information would be seen as having been tainted by their service for a Labour government. So I finish by saying we are in some ways at a crossroads. There is a window of opportunity to change the way the government communicates with the media; there are opportunities to raise the ethical standards of political journalism; and we will find out whether Britain is moving inexorably towards a presidential system where, as in the United States, the top jobs in the information service of the state are automatically considered to be political appointments.

The communications crisis
and the Iraq invasion

Kristine Lowe interviews Johan Galtung

At a time when the war on terrorism dominates the news agenda, Kristine Lowe talks to the eminent peace researcher, Johan Galtung, about some of the major communications ethics issues involved.

Galtung has had an impressive international academic career spanning 40 years, five continents, over 30 visiting professorships, 70 books and more than 1,000 published monographs. He is a consultant to several UN agencies and a constant travelling lecturer. In addition to being one of the founders of peace research, his early work includes one of the main texts on imperialism and so-called dependent development, "A Structural Theory of Imperialism", published in the *Journal of Peace Research* Vol. 8, 1971. The theory presents a "centre-periphery" model of power and development. In communication terms, this implies that the world is divided into either dominant central or dependent peripheral lands, with a predominant news flow from the former toward the latter.

Originally presented as a model to explain power in international relations, this model has frequently been used to explain the flow of international news and the structure of international media organisations. It is associated with the New World Information and Communication Order (NWICO) and the debate over western media imperialism raised by third world countries through UNESCO during the 1970s. Imperialism is, however, far from an outdated model of explanation according to Galtung who is currently working on a major new work entitled "On the coming Decline and Fall of US Imperialism". He explains:

I have gone through the fall of 25 empires: they end in demoralisation —

rarely military conquest. The British Empire ended in demoralisation.... The US now behaves like a wounded elephant, lashing out in all directions. This is the boiling stage of demoralisation, with emotions impeding rational thinking. Demoralisation is oscillating before it stabilises. Like individual pathologies, healing is related to the ability to come on top of the pathology rather than the other way round... But, the hypothesis is not that the fall and decline of the US empire implies a fall and decline of the US Republic (continental USA). On the contrary, relief from the burden of empire control and maintenance when it outstrips the gains from unequal exchange, and expansion increases rather than decreases the deficit, could lead to a blossoming of the US republic. I admit to an anti-empire bias because of enormous periphery suffering outside and inside the republic; and a pro-US republic bias because of the creative genius and generosity of the USA. "Anti-American" makes no such distinction between the US republic and the US empire.

How does he view the breakdown of dialogue and international diplomacy in the run-up to the Iraq war?

Of course there was no dialogue. This was a classical colonial war by the leading colonisers in human history, the Anglo-Americans. In 1800 India and England were at the same level economically. A hundred years later India was made into a slum — with some wealth on top. They are aiming for the same in Iraq, with the same pretext of liberation. The way to deal with such people is not only through dialogue, but through Gandhi's way: determined, decisive and massive non-violent resistance, like an economic boycott of all Anglo-American firms making profits out of the spoils from the aggression and occupation.

As for the war on terrorism, Galtung holds few hopes for any positive outcomes:

The war against terrorism can only backfire. They [the terrorists] have a cause, and that cause has potentially 1.3 million adherents as all Muslims have pledged to defend, not to spread, their religion with the sword. And they have been trampled upon in Saudi-Arabia, in Afghanistan, in Iran, in Iraq, in Indonesia by Christian penetration and particularly by a market capitalism totally against the Koranic understanding of business as a holistic human relation. The West does not even dare to understand that exchanging goods for money without even eye contact is a sin, not only the many military interventions. The two buildings hit on 9/11 were, in my interpretation, executed in public space for their sins against Allah.

No wonder then that Galtung, who in recent times has focused on comparative civilisation theory, exploring the underlying implications for peace and development of occidental and oriental civilisations, thinks the mainstream western media can be parochial in their outlook. In his seminal essay, "The Construction of News Values" with Marie Holmboe Ruge in 1965 — reprinted in Tumber, Howard (1999) (ed) *News: A Reader*, Oxford, Oxford University Press pp 21-31 — Galtung defined the central values in foreign news reporting. The basic thesis was that events would become news the more they fitted certain organisational, cultural and ideological criteria. They also identified socio-cultural influences that derive from Northern European culture. From this perspective, news values tend to favour events which are about elite people, elite nations and negative happenings. When commenting on the way in which cultural affinity has impacted on news values in the war on terrorism, Galtung said:

To mention only one factor: the lack of understanding of the most elementary aspects of Islam and of Arab history. I was once to be interviewed on a key BBC programme and there was the usual pre-interview. I said something about the Sykes-Picot treason in 1916 — the Anglo-French foreign ministers who had promised the Arabs freedom if they would rise against the Turks but gave them colonisation instead. The interviewer did not ask me to explain, but had never heard of the names — known to anyone in the Arab world, alluded to in bin Laden's first declaration. They know so much more about the West than vice versa. So there was no interview.

With so many predictions of doom, I asked Galtung what hope he sees for the future, and what role, if any, could or should the media play in conflict resolution?

There should be less violence and war journalism, more conflict and solution journalism. The journalist should always ask what the underlying conflict is about and what the possible solution is. Not only who threw the bomb but how can we stop it. For much material on peace journalism see www.reportingtheworld.org and www.transcend.org.

In earlier interviews Galtung has commended the role former CBS anchor Walter Cronkite played in the conflict between Israel and Egypt, saying he combined his role as a journalist with that of a mediator. Is this a type of journalism he would like to see more of?

No, I don't believe that media should do mediation, leave that to mediators. Media should give material and they will achieve a lot just by asking the questions above. I think journalists should stick to their task to make the world more transparent and also ask hard questions whenever somebody has a peace plan. But they should not conceal what the conflict is about and the many efforts to arrive at solutions.

Does the Internet with its increased opportunities for interaction have any potential to play a role in conflict resolution?

The Internet is very important as a better source of adequate news than the usual Murdoch propaganda and a marvellous instrument for dialogue.

Since I located Galtung in Australia — the heartland of Rupert Murdoch — I asked him if he had any thoughts about Murdoch's dominant role in the media industry. For instance, with virtually all of Murdoch's 156 newspapers globally taking a pro-war stance, would it be fair to speak of a limiting of the range of opinion or a narrowing of concepts?

The moment media are known to be part of the Murdoch empire they are already stigmatised as too predictable, too autocratic, too incompatible with democracy. They are not as important as people think, as they are too stupid, too badly informed and too obvious.

Ethical issues in alternative journalism

Chris Atton

Alternative media have been examined in terms of their significance for the mobilisation of campaigns through activist information, political education and the critique of dominant ideologies (for example, Atton 2002a; Downing 2001 and Rodriguez 2001). However, little attention has been paid to the ethical bases on which the journalism of alternative media is produced. This paper is, I believe, the first attempt to address questions of ethics and morality in alternative journalism. Some of these questions are not dissimilar to those facing journalists in the mainstream, whilst some are particular to alternative media, resulting from those media's specific, intellectual, political and moral standpoints. The latter largely centre on issues of representation and objectivity, particularly developed from the structural and cultural characteristics of radical media, and the radicalising of journalistic practices through notions such as the "native reporter" and "active witnessing".

Keywords: alternative, journalism, ethics, objectivity, "native reporter", "active witnessing"

INTRODUCTION

First we need to identify some key characteristics of alternative media organisation and production. There has emerged a consensus amongst scholars in the field that alternative media organisations privilege non-hierarchical, often collective modes of organisation that are coupled with radical political agendas. These agendas would often, as Downing (2001) has argued, be played out in a prefigurative politics of communication through which radically democratic aims (his focus is on leftist, progressive media, rather than what he has later termed the "repressive" media of the far right) could be actualised within radical media formations. Such alternative media are also distinctive in terms of their content: accounts of political struggle and the socio-political contextualisation of such accounts by those actively involved in them are presented through lateral, non-hierarchical modes of organisation, mostly run on a non-commercial basis.

Alternative media projects tend to be edited, written and run by non-professionals, by groups that are primarily activist for progressive, social change. From a leftist perspective, Downing has highlighted a general political perspective of social anarchism that informs and drives such media practices. Downing explicitly places the organisation of radical media and their journalistic practices in opposition to a construction of mainstream media that is largely monolithic, centred on profit-making, hierarchical organisation and a practice of journalism that, by dint of its routinisation and codification as a profession, is implicitly exclusive. Against this he presents an ideal type of radical media, one that is radically democratic in terms of access and political aims, which Rodriguez has valuably termed "citizens' media" (Rodriguez op cit).

This is not, however, to perpetuate a binary opposition between alternative and mainstream media. Recent studies of alternative media have begun to illuminate the complex, hybrid nature of alternative media in relation to its mainstream counterparts (Downing op cit; Atton 2002b; Hamilton and Atton 2001; Hamilton 2003). Conspicuous features of alternative media practices have not simply broken with mainstream practices, they have often sought to radically redefine them. These studies emphasise the central role of individuals and groups normally considered to lie outside the professionalised media in terms of contributors, editors and owners. Hybridity can also been found in the form and content of alternative media reporting. It can be argued that, far from alternative media establishing ways of doing journalism that are radical to the extent that they mark dramatic ruptures from existing practices of journalism, their work may draw from existing forms (such as tabloid journalism) and methods (such as investigative journalism).

Atton (ibid) has argued that the use of tabloid forms of address (colloquial language, humour, the apparent trivialisation of subject matter, the brevity of texts) presents radical opinions in a populist manner that subverts the existing models of tabloid journalism (normally employed to maintain conservative news agendas). These radical forms connect historically with earlier, radical forms of journalism that predate the commercialised and capitalised forms of journalism that are normally considered as the originating sites of tabloid journalism (Williams 1970). In the UK, the radical press of the eighteenth and the nineteenth centuries may be considered as a precursor of current radical news sheets such as *SchNEWS*. These styles of radical journalism developed from social movements and thus represent "social" media that emphasise a communicative democracy based on a "media commons" rather than on a segregated, elitist and professionalised occupational activity. Hamilton (op cit) has taken this argument still further, finding examples of these participatory media as far back as early-modern England.

In the contemporary media landscape there are many candidates for inclusion as "alternative media". Whilst many of these do draw on mainstream journalistic practices, many map less easily on to the idealised notion of alternative media as springing from radical social movements. Some, such as the monthly social justice magazine, *New Internationalist*, organise their editorial activities on an explicitly collective basis, at the same time as they function as commercial ventures. The work of the investigative and satirical British fortnightly *Private Eye* is run on more traditional lines, seeking advertising largely from suppliers of goods and services targeted at a high-income audience. Many of their contributors are professional journalists "moonlighting" anonymously, finding in the magazine a place for stories they are unable to publish elsewhere (often for legal reasons).

There is an enduring socialist press in the UK, including such publications as *Socialist Worker* and *Tribune*. As the media of specific political movements or parties they combine editorial hierarchy with a desire to involve readers (activists) as contributors to their pages (see Allen 1985 for a critical examination of *Socialist Worker*'s attempts to achieve this). The radical, local community press of the 1970s (documented, for example, in Minority Press Group 1980 and Whitaker 1981) has largely vanished. In its place we have seen the rise of publications targeted not at geographic communities but at communities of interest. These include newspapers and magazines produced by and for specific ethnic and sexual communities: the black and Asian press, the gay and lesbian press, for example. Most of these survive through traditional, commercial means (advertising) and preserve editorial hierarchies of organisation, at the same time writing for and from within the communities they serve. A publication such as the *Big Issue*, founded on capital from Gordon Roddick of the Body Shop, similarly combines editorial hierarchy, advertising as a funding mechanism and contributions from both young, professional journalists and non-professionals.

In the space of an essay such as this, it is impossible to explore this heterogeneity of approaches. However, it is possible to isolate a set of ethical practices which, in differing ways, we may find at work across the field of alternative media. In what follows I have chosen to draw largely on examples from what we might consider as grassroots, social movement media. This is in order to throw these practices into sharper relief against the background of the dominant, mainstream versions of these practices. Whilst studies of alternative media have increased in frequency, depth and insight in recent years, there has been little sustained work on the practices of journalism, still less on the ethical dimensions that such radical practices might entail.

THE REJECTION OF OBJECTIVITY AND IMPARTIALITY

The professional ideal of objectivity, understood as the separation of "facts" from "values", may be considered as the key ethical dimension of journalistic practice. Allan (1999) and Schudson (1978, 2001) locate the emergence of this normative practice in the American press of the 1920s and 1930s. It was due, they argue, to two separate, but linked social forces. The first was rooted in "popular disillusionment with state propaganda campaigns" and "a wariness of 'official' channels of information" (Allan op cit: 24). If "reality" could no longer be reliably constructed from officialdom, then a more "rational" method was needed. This was found in the second social force, that of scientific rationalism.

Journalism at this time was aligning itself as a profession alongside science, the law and medicine, thus it appeared "natural" that it should draw for its rigour on the scientific method employed by those professions. The results, as Allan emphasises, were swift and enduring. Specialised "beats" emerged and with them came the expert journalism and the by-lined report. Investigative reporting and interviewing flourished; "'impersonal', fact-centred techniques of observation" (ibid: 25) informed these practices, with the consequent rise of the columnist whose work was clearly separated from "the news", and who was allowed the freedom to engage in value-driven writing.

Though as Schudson reminds us, the rise of objectivity as an ideology was never a merely technical exercise, not

> *just a claim about what kind of knowledge is reliable. It is also a moral philosophy, a declaration of what kind of thinking one should engage in, in making moral decisions. It is, moreover, a political commitment, for it provides a guide to what groups one*

should acknowledge as relevant audiences for judging one's own thoughts and acts. (Schudson 1978/1999: 294)

Practitioners of alternative journalism have both recognised the moral and political nature of objectivity and have directed their work to challenging its central assumptions: that it is possible in the first place to separate facts from values and that it is morally and politically preferable to do so. Such challenges are not the sole province of alternative journalists, neither are they new. The Glasgow University Media Group's (GUMG) work stands as a significant project exploring the concatenation of facts and values in television news reporting that still considers itself objective and impartial (Eldridge 2000).

Workers within alternative media, however, seek to challenge objectivity and impartiality from both an ethical and a political standpoint in their own journalistic practices. Amongst practitioners in the US and the UK at least, the power to do so in recent decades has come not from the critical media studies of such as GUMG but from American scholars whose prime expertise lies elsewhere. The radical political essays of American dissidents such as Noam Chomsky and Edward Said (especially Chomsky) continue to be cited in alternative media as the major demystifiers of the objectivity of the US corporate media.

From these accounts (for example, Chomsky 1989; Said 1981) alternative journalists have begun to finish the story, so to speak. Convinced by and sympathetic to such notions as Chomsky's "worthy and unworthy victims" and the systematic and longstanding pro-Zionist coverage in the American media at the expense of Arab (specifically notably Palestinian Arab) voices, these journalists have sought to expose the moral claims of their mainstream counterparts. This stance can be considered as a supremely ethical one for it seeks to present through radical journalistic practices moral and political correctives to the "fact-centred techniques" found to be just as value-laden as the "pre-objective" journalism they sought to replace. But what ethical issues do these radical practices bring with them? What does being an alternative journalist mean in ethical terms?

ALTERNATIVE ETHICS

Alternative media are characterised by their explicitly partisan character. In the language of ethics, they exhibit clear biases, yet they proclaim their selectivity and their bias, and generally have little interest in "balanced reporting". What may we find in such practices that makes them different from, say, the tabloid newspaper that exhibits clear and consistent bias against asylum seekers or the gay and lesbian communities, as many British tabloids continue to do? The dominant moral argument within alternative media has two aspects. First, alternative media projects tend to be set up to provide a counter to what alternative journalists consider an already-biased set of reports. Sceptical of what counts as balance in the mainstream media, they seek to set up their own counter-balance. Hence, the argument runs, the viewpoints already dominant in the mainstream media do not need repeating. What appears as bias and the absence of balance in the alternative media is to be considered not as a set of absolute truths; instead it comprises a set of accounts told from different perspectives.

The practice of alternative journalism thus enacts Edgar's (1992: 120) claim that "journalism cannot be objective, for that presupposes that an inviolable interpretation of the event as action exists prior to the report". These stories might well use official or semi-official sources in the public domain that have been ignored by mainstream journalism, such as the investigative journalism of *CovertAction Quarterly* in the US and the "parapolitical" journal *Lobster* in the UK. For example, in 1995 the US journal, *CovertAction Quarterly*, published an extensive feature on British military tactics to target Republican teenagers in Northern Ireland for harassment and even death. *Lobster* was the first to break the story about Colin Wallace and "Operation Clockwork Orange", the MI5 plot to destabilise the Wilson Government.

Second, alternative journalism seeks to invert the "hierarchy of access" (Glasgow University Media Group 1976: 245) to the news by explicitly foregrounding the viewpoints of "ordinary" people (activists, protesters, local residents), citizens whose visibility in the mainstream media tends to be obscured by the presence of elite groups and individuals. Langer (1998) has shown how a limited set of narratives and character-types within mainstream narratives operate forms of cultural closure that prevent other forms of story-telling and other representations (whether oppositional or contradictory) from being essayed. In the case of ordinary people, dominant story-types deal with overturning expectations — there is an emphasis on how the "unremarkable" individual may be capable of extraordinary achievements (such as through adversity or lack of cultural and material resources).

Ordinary people are also encountered as subject to the control of external forces ("fate"), in which Langer locates stories of human tragedy (such as accidents, deaths and bereavements). In both cases, such stories and their actors tap into mythic representations of heroes and victims, from which derive their cultural-symbolic power and their resonances with audiences. The representation (and, as we shall see, the self-representation) of ordinary people in alternative journalism seeks not to set them apart as either heroes or victims but as a set of voices which have as equal a right to be heard as do the voices of elite groups. In so doing a further division is erased, that of "fact-based" reporting and "value-driven" commentary. Story-telling by those who are normally actors in other people's stories conflates these emblematic types of journalism and challenges the expert culture of both the news journalist and the "expert" columnist.

The alternative media emphasise a humanistic set of journalistic values that are far removed from either the attempts at objective reporting or the persistence of the ideological necessity of objectivity. Alternative journalists enact social-responsibility journalism with an important difference. Unlike the social responsibility journalism attempted in the US, culminating (for the present) in the public journalism movement, alternative journalists do not inhabit the mainstream – where public journalism seeks to effect change from within current practices and organisational regimes; alternative journalism seeks to do so freed from the constraints that limit the development of social responsibility in mainstream journalism (Davis 2000; Woodstock 2002).

We have already noted that alternative media is not simply about doing journalism differently, it is also about organising differently. This holistic approach to radicalising media practices offers freedom for journalists from many of the constraints that typically face mainstream journalists and that can present an array of often conflicting loyalties that interfere with daily practices of doing journalism. There is a strong ethical dimension to the organisation and production of alternative media. Advertising is largely rejected, for fear of publications being influenced by external forces (though many publications do take advertising for products and services they approve of, such as those for similar publications and the products of ethically-trading companies).

The notion of proprietorial influence is quite foreign to alternative media, given that most are run democratically and co-operatively by the media workers themselves. If the loyalties we find in mainstream media tend to be absent, in their place we find loyalties that centre on "community", whether a community of interest or an "actually lived", local community. The journalists place themselves firmly within such communities, espousing a loyalty that proceeds at the same time from specific causes or ideologies and from the particular, activist communities in which they are actors. Such loyalties are increasingly established on a trans-national scale (as we find in the global Indymedia network).

As Harcup has pointed out in his examination of journalism ethics within the mainstream, this is a significant loyalty that can often be overlooked: "the journalist as citizen, with a sense of loyalty to other citizens" (Harcup 2002: 103). It is this loyalty, this concern with the citizen and especially with making the voices of those citizens heard that drives much alternative journalism and has resulted in a particular ethics of representation, through the practice of "native reporting" (Atton 2002: 112).

NATIVE REPORTING AND ISSUES OF REPRESENTATION
If, as Fursich (2002: 80) argues, "most reporting is a form of representing the Other", then the most powerful journalistic method employed to counter Othering within alternative media is surely that of "native reporting", where social actors, instead of being subjects of the news become their own correspondents, reporting on their own experiences, struggles and ideas. This has become a common method of alternative journalism and finds its most developed forms in the "active witnessing (Couldry 2000: 37) journalism of the new social movements, such as those produced by the British video magazine Undercurrents and the international, web-based news service Indymedia. Both privilege a journalism politicised through subjective testimony, through the subjects being represented by themselves: "native-reporting situates the activist in both the texts they produce and in the sociopolitical contexts in which they place them (and are themselves placed)" (Atton 2002: 113).

An illuminating instance of this practice is a video report produced for Undercurrents by "Jen", an activist for the Campaign Against Arms Trade (ibid: 113-114). Her piece presents her as advocate for arms control, an activist campaigner, a commentator and an investigative reporter, emphasising the hybrid nature of much alternative journalism. Here, explicitly partisan accounts are constructed from a personal, ideological commitment that deals with the emotive and the rational through a radicalisation of journalistic technique. Bias and selectivity apart, though, what ethical issues does this approach raise? It is clear from Jen's report that she is not a professional journalist, nor does she pretend to professionalism. Her interview with Robin Cook (then Foreign Secretary for the British government) is opportunistic, unplanned, hurried and brief. I have shown Jen's report to many postgraduate journalism students and have found a striking consensus.

Whether finding themselves either already sympathetic to the cause being advocated or, if previously ignorant of the issues, finding themselves satisfactorily informed about those issues, almost all the students found Jen's lack of conventional journalistic expertise worrying and at times embarrassing. Is this an example of the threat to professional values that access to technology can bring, where "anyone with Internet access [or access to a camcorder or a minidisc recorder] can, in theory, set up their own media operation" (Keeble 2001: 12)? Does this threaten standards to such an extent that it undermines trust in the profession of journalism? Perhaps this is the wrong question to ask. Instead, we may identify different, more beneficial ethical dimensions.

First, such reports are about mobilising public opinion. In this respect, they are no different from the campaigning journalism of the mainstream media. The presence of explicit mobilising information is an enduring characteristic of alternative media, the aim of which is to suggest possibilities for social action to audiences (Bybee 1982; Lemert and Ashman 1983). Second, deprofessionalised approaches to doing journalism have been found to encourage audiences to start their own media projects, to become their own reporters (Atton 2002: Ch. 5). Together these may result in the "de-naturalisation" of media spaces, encouraging audiences to rebalance the differential power of the media and to consider how "the media themselves are a social process organised in space" (Couldry op cit: 25). Media audiences may thus become media activists, having available to them methods for the de-naturalisation of the media, for re-imagining and renaming media power in their own locales, in their own words.

But we must not consider this one example as typical. The value of acquiring conventional training in journalism has been recognised by many alternative media projects and journalists (indeed, some of those who work for the alternative media are "moonlighting" from day jobs in the mainstream). The writing styles in US publications such as *CovertAction Quarterly* and *Z Magazine* strongly resemble those found in investigative journalism within the mainstream. Undercurrents offered camcorder training to activists and strove to produce broadcast-quality footage. The British alternative political newspaper, *Squall*, was staffed by activists who had or were undergoing journalism training (say, at night classes) and some of their reporters and photographers have produced work that has accorded so well with professional standards that it has been published in more mainstream publications (such as Gibby Zobel's work in the *Big Issue* and the *Guardian*).

These differences are simply the result of producing journalism for different audiences. Despite Undercurrents' desideratum of broadcast-quality footage, it also celebrated the performativity of "underproduction": "turn your weaknesses (few resources, little experience) to an advantage by keeping your feature simple but powerful" (Harding 1997: 149). The primary audience for such work, it was assumed, would be the activist community itself. *Squall*, on the other hand, was more interested in "talking to the bridge" and celebrated the diversity of their readership (which included British Members of Parliament). The paper operated its own house style in order to preserve its standards.

The radical news sheet *SchNEWS*, produced weekly in Bristol, England, also has a house style of its own, yet its espousal of tabloid conventions sets it quite apart from the alternative journalism we have so far considered. In its employment of pun-filled headlines (such as Terror Firmer, Chinese Horrorscope, Water Disgrace!) and its colloquial and irreverent copy style *SchNEWS* might be considered as the British tabloid of alternative journalism. It takes the ethical stance of native reporting and places it in a framework derived from right-wing newspapers whose ideologies could not be further from its own. In so doing it both inverts the hierarchy of access to the media at the same time as it subverts media conventions through which familiar prejudices (racism, homophobia) are communicated.

The representation of, for example, ethnic minorities and of gays and lesbians is rarely an ethical issue for alternative journalists, since they are already operating from within a morally "progressive" environment where discriminatory practices largely do not arise. Where biased representation may arise is, ironically enough, as a result of a politically progressive notion of free speech. Apparently influenced by Noam Chomsky's dictum that "if you believe in freedom of speech, you believe in freedom of speech for views you don't like" (cited in Achbar 1994: 184), some alternative media projects have relinquished what has been an abiding ideology of "no platform for fascists/racists/homophobes" in favour of an "open platform" approach. This is in part a libertarian impulse, but has also been the result of "open publishing" software used by Internet-based media such as the Indymedia network.

Open publishing software enables any individual or group to upload ("publish") material onto a web site without editorial approval. Intended to encourage native reporting and democratic access to the media, it has predictably been used by racists to post offensive material to Indymedia sites. Indymedia's IMC-Global website (www.indymedia.org) responded to this by removing such material, as well as removing its "open newswire" from its front page. A communique from the editorial team explains this: "While we struggle to maintain the news wire as a completely open forum we do monitor it and remove posts" (www.indymedia.org/publish.php3). Indymedia do, however, still make these posts available in a separate page titled "hidden stories" (http://www.indymedia.org/search-process.php3? hidden=true). Whilst censorship and editing does take place, it does not prevent voices from being heard, nor prevent users from accessing that content. Neither does this quasi-editorial function of the core group extend to the editing of individual pieces of work. These limits apart, Indymedia enable any activists to contribute their work.

What began as a technical advance, though, has developed into a political issue. Activist and Indymedia contributor ChuckO (2002) has called for "aggressive action against racist and anti-semitic posts [which have] damaged Indymedia's reputation with Jewish people and people of color". The loyalty to communities is once again present, though here it is part of a dilemma: to support free speech but to denounce hate speech. The issue is complicated further by the independence of Indymedia sites. Each of the 70-odd sites that comprise its international network is editorially independent from the rest. As Sara Platon (2002) notes in a reponse to ChuckO, "each one of them has its own editorial policy and its own way of dealing with racism or other 'unwanted' articles and comments in the main newswire. Some are more pro free speech, and some are more restricted in what they 'allow' on the website".

Just as there is a range of hybridised approaches to doing alternative journalism, there is also an array of ethical responses, often apparently in conflict with those prevalent across mainstream media. Whilst alternative journalism has no written code of ethics (nor is it likely to, given its heterogenous and libertarian nature), its ethical practices are explicit. Platon argues that "unlike as in more traditional forms of mass media, disagreements within the Indymedia news network are often out in the public domain". However alien the ethical practices of alternative journalism might appear from within the mainstream media, the various methods and techniques it has developed to address bias, impartiality, representation and professionalism are similarly out in the open. At the very least we may attend to them. We may find in them a range of practices and also challenges to those practices. We may also find in them challenges to dominant journalistic practices that, some might argue, are long overdue.

REFERENCES

Achbar, Mark (1994) *Manufacturing Consent: Noam Chomsky and the Media,* Montreal, Black Rose Books

Allan, Stuart (1999) *News Culture,* Buckingham, Open University Press.

Allen, Peter (1985) "Socialist Worker - Paper with a Purpose", *Media, Culture and Society,* 7 pp 205-232

Atton, Chris (2002a) *Alternative Media,* London, Sage

Atton, Chris (2002b) "News Cultures and New Social Movements: Radical Journalism and the Mainstream Media", *Journalism Studies* 3 (4) pp 491-505

Atton, Chris (2003) (ed) What is 'Alternative' Journalism? Special issue of Journalism: *Theory, Practice and Criticism* 4(3)

Bybee, Carl R. (1982) "Mobilizing Information and Reader Involvement", *Journalism Quarterly,* 59(3) pp 399-405, 413

Chomsky, Noam (1989) *Necessary illusions: thought control in democratic societies,* London, Pluto Press

ChuckO (2002) "The sad decline of Indymedia". Available online at www.infoshop.org/inews/stories.php?story=02/12/08/2553147

Couldry, Nick (2000) *The Place of Media Power: Pilgrims and Witnesses of the Media Age,* London, Routledge

Davis, Steve (2000) "Public Journalism: The Case Against", *Journalism Studies* 1(4) pp 686-689

Downing, John (2001) *Radical Media: Rebellious Communication and Social Movements,* Thousand Oaks, Calif., Sage

Edgar, Andrew (1992) "Objectivity, bias and truth", *Ethical Issues in Journalism and the Media,* Belsey, Andrew and Chadwick, Ruth (eds), London, Routledge pp 112-219

Eldridge, John (2000) "The contribution of the Glasgow Media Group to the study of television and print journalism", *Journalism Studies* 1(1) pp 113-127

Fursich, Elfriede (2002) "How can global journalists represent the 'Other'? A critical assessment of the cultural studies concept for media practice", *Journalism: Theory, Practice and Criticism* 3(1) pp 57-84

Glasgow University Media Group (1976) *Bad News,* London, Routledge and Kegan Paul

Hamilton, James (2003) "Remaking media participation in early modern England", *Journalism: Theory, Practice and Criticism* 4 (3) pp 293-313

Hamilton, James and Atton, Chris (2001) "Theorizing Anglo-American Alternative Media: Toward a Contextual History and Analysis of US and UK Scholarship", *Media History* 7(2) pp 119-135

Harcup, Tony (2002) "Journalists and ethics: the quest for a collective voice", *Journalism Studies* 3(1) pp 101-114

Harding, Thomas (1997) *The Video Activist Handbook,* London, Pluto Press.

Keeble, Richard (2001) *Ethics for Journalists,* London, Routledge

Langer, John (1998) *Tabloid Television: Popular Journalism and the "Other News",* London, Routledge

Lemert, James B. and Ashman, Marguerite Gemson (1983) "'Extent of Mobilising Information in Opinion and News Magazines", *Journalism Quarterly,* 60 (4) pp 657-62

Minority Press Group (1980) *Here is the Other News: Challenges to the Local Commercial Press* (Minority Press Group Series No. 1), London, Minority Press Group

Platon, Sara (2002) "Re: The sad decline of Indymedia" pers. comm (email).

Rodriguez, Clemencia (2000) *Fissures in the Mediascape: An International Study of Citizens' Media,* Cresskill, N J, Hampton Press

Said, Edward (1981) *Covering Islam: How the Media and the Experts Determine How We See the Rest of the World,* New York, Pantheon

Schudson, Michael (1978) *Discovering the News,* New York, Basic Books

Schudson, Michael (1978/1999) "Discovering the news: a social history of American newspapers", *News: A Reader,* Tumber, Howard (ed), Oxford, Oxford University Press 1999 pp 291-296

Schudson, Michael (2001) "The objectivity norm in American journalism", *Journalism: Theory, Practice and Criticism* 2(2) pp 149-170

Whitaker, Brian (1981) *News Limited: Why You Can't Read All About It* (Minority Press Group Series No. 5), London, Minority Press Group

Williams, Raymond (1970) "Radical and/or Respectable", *The Press We Deserve,* Richard Boston (ed), London, Routledge and Kegan Paul pp 14-26

Woodstock, Louise (2002) "Public Journalism's Talking Cure: An Analysis of the Movement's 'Problem' and 'Solution' Narratives", *Journalism: Theory, Practice and Criticism* 3(1) pp 37-55

Dr. Chris Atton is Reader in Journalism, School of Communication Arts, Napier University, Craighouse Road, Edinburgh, Scotland EH10 5LG; Tel +44 (0)131-455 6127; Fax +44 (0)131-455 6193; email: c.atton@napier.ac.uk. He is the author of *Alternative Literature* (Gower 1996) and *Alternative Media* (Sage 2002) and the editor of a special issue of *Journalism: Theory, Practice and Criticism* on alternative journalism (2003). He is co-editing a special issue of *Media, Culture and Society* on alternative media and is researching the use of the Internet by far-right political groups in the UK. His third book, *An Alternative Internet,* was published in the spring of 2005 by Edinburgh University Press.

Press Complaints Commission: Privacy and accuracy in ten years of self-regulation of the British press

Chris Frost

The Press Complaints Commission (PCC) is the self-regulatory body established by the UK newspaper industry to adjudicate readers' complaints. Its tenth anniversary presented an ideal opportunity to conduct a statistical analysis of the commission's performance in dealing with readers' complaints. The study reveals that although the PCC had handled almost 23,000 complaints from 1991 to 2001, it adjudicated on only 707, upholding approximately 45 per cent (321). In a detailed examination of the PCC's performance in adjudicating on accuracy and privacy, the two most significant areas of complaint, this study finds that not only has the PCC adjudicated relatively few such cases, negating the PCC's claim to be raising standards through its adjudications, but that complaints from celebrities play a much more significant role in the PCC's work than the commission suggests. The study also finds that the PCC's rate of upholding such complaints, particularly accuracy, has reduced significantly over the ten-year period. There is little empirical evidence that standards have been raised or that the culture of British newspapers and magazines has changed in that period as has been claimed by the PCC.

Keywords: PCC, Press Complaints Commission, self-regulation, press, complaints

CONTROVERSY DOGS PCC SINCE FOUNDING
The PCC was set up in January 1991 in the wake of growing concerns about the invasive nature of some of the media and the falling reputation of the

Press Council, the previous self-regulatory press body. The commission was proposed by the Calcutt committee set up by Margaret Thatcher's Conservative government in 1989 to examine privacy and related matters. (see Frost 2000: 190; O'Malley and Soley 2000: 89; Shannon 2001: 35) It was a time of growing public concerns over the intrusive nature of some news media and the seeming inability of the Press Council to deal with it (Robertson 1983).

Several controversial invasions of privacy over the past few years, including reports about entertainer Zoe Ball, model Naomi Campbell, footballer Gary Flitcroft and the Catherine Zeta Jones and Michael Douglas v Hello court case, have highlighted the issues of invasions of privacy and journalistic sensationalism. A report in June 2003 by the culture, media and sport select committee of the House of Commons examined the performance of the British press and the PCC and while it did not recommend replacing the PCC, proposed a number of changes and recommended the introduction of a privacy law (House of Commons 2003 vol 1 pp111).

The PCC has attracted criticism from politicians, media critics and the public almost from the outset and Sir David Calcutt QC was asked to examine its performance in 1993. He reported that the commission was failing and should be replaced by a statutory press tribunal (Frost, 2000, O'Malley and Soley 2000) The appointment of Lord Wakeham as chairman in 1994 reduced the number of attacks on the PCC from media commentators (Shannon 2001: 165-167) as he handled the continuing rows about intrusion into the lives of celebrities (and royalty, in particular) with more subtlety than his predecessor, refusing to be drawn into making reckless comments about apparent breaches of the code (ibid: 186-196).

A SHORT HISTORY OF PRIVACY IN THE UK

The Judicial Proceedings (Regulation of Reports) Act 1926, was one of the first pieces of UK legislation outlining what could be written about people's personal lives (Frost op cit: 122). Journalism organisations agreed to condemn methods of news-gathering which caused distress to private persons in 1937. Bills were presented before parliament in 1967 and 1969 to limit intrusion into privacy. The Nordic Conference on the Rights of Privacy in 1967 kept the subject topical but it was not until 1970 that there was a serious attempt to introduce a law on privacy by the justice committee (ibid).

The 1972 Younger committee on privacy concluded: "Privacy is ill-suited to be the subject of a long process of definition through the building up of precedents over the years since the judgements of the past would be an unreliable guide to any current evaluation of privacy" (committee on privacy 1972: 206). The Sexual Offences Act (1976) introduced the concept of anonymity in to UK law, making it an offence to name victims of rape. It also gave anonymity to the accused in such cases, a protection later removed by the 1988 Amendment Act, but once again suggested by the government following several high profile cases.

The Data Protection Act (1984) gave some right to privacy and this was strengthened by the 1989 Data Protection Act and the introduction of the concept of sensitive personal data. Several MPs attempted to introduce a right of privacy during the early 1980s but the government finally agreed to investigate the problem in 1989 with the appointment of the Calcutt committee. It recommended against a statutory tort of infringement of privacy but called for a criminal offence of physical intrusion and the placing of surveillance devices. Calcutt advised that the taking of photographs and bugging without consent should also be offences.

The second Calcutt report in 1993 recommended a tort for infringement of privacy and the Heritage committee later in the year also asked for a protection of privacy law, with a public interest defence. However, the government announced in 1994 that it had postponed plans for privacy laws indefinitely. The Lord Chancellor proposed a law of privacy in 1998. However, the Human Rights Act of 1998 granting a right of privacy in the UK for the first time, meant that there was no likelihood of statutory change while everyone waited to see what effect the new law would have. The present government has announced its intention not to introduce a privacy law in its response to the culture, media and sport select committee report on "Privacy and Media Instrusion":

> ...the committee also make the case for introducing a privacy law. The government does not accept that case, and considers that existing legislation is capable of dealing adequately with questions of privacy (Department of Culture, Media and Sport 2003: 1.4).

The other big area of concern for the public in general and those who are written about is accuracy. Accuracy raises more complaints than all the other issues put together accounting for an average 60.5 per cent of complaints to the PCC. Many of these are easily dealt with and the number dealt with to the satisfaction of the complainant after the early intervention

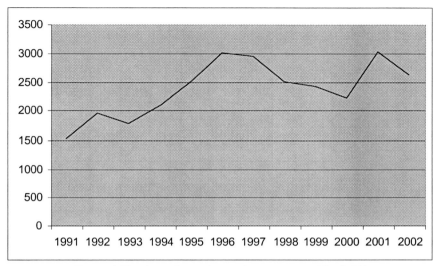

Figure 1: Total number of complaints received by PCC

of the PCC leads one to wonder why the newspaper concerned did not arrange a correction or apology in the first place, bearing in mind that the PCC will not take complaints unless the publication is approached first.

Throughout its brief history the PCC has issued regular reports of its adjudications. From 1993 it has also issued an annual report. The total number of complaints received each year rose to a peak of 3,023 in 1996 although there are more typically 2,500 a year (see Figure 1). This means that during the first ten years, there were 22,988 complaints. Of these the commission adjudicated only 707. An examination of these complaints and the decisions made by the PCC provides an insight into the workings of the PCC and, perhaps more significantly, how press self-regulation is intended to change the ways in which journalists work. It should also illustrate the areas in which the PCC actually works (rather than those where it claims to work) and where it fails, as many of its critics believe.

THE PCC, PRIVACY AND ACCURACY: ANALYSING THE DATA

The method applied provides a statistical analysis of the PCC's regular reports, usually issued quarterly but occasionally, in the early years, either monthly or six-monthly along with the commission's annual reports issued from 1993. The annual reports show the total number of complaints received and the percentage of complaints made under each clause of the code of

Table 1: Fate of complaints made to PCC

Year	1991	1992	1993	1994	1995	1996	1997	1998	1999	2000	total
Complaints received	1520	1963	1782	2091	2508	3023	2944	2505	2427	2225	22988
No breach	347	584	704	914	1026	897	914	954	942	857	8139
Third party	0	107	114	87	77	146	335	205	0	0	1071
Resolved	72	182	231	356	413	393	514	555	650	544	3910
Unreasonable delay	46	64	97	85	91	110	93	112	0	0	698
Outside remit	137	232	447	427	800	1125	593	689	0	0	4450
Adj upheld	32	31	40	34	28	27	34	45	26	24	321
Adj rejected	28	49	57	54	35	54	48	41	23	33	422
Complaints concluded	662	1249	1890	1957	2470	2752	2531	2601	1641	1458	19011
All figures from annual reports of the PCC											

practice (see Table 1). The quarterly or monthly reports give the adjudications on each complaint investigated by the PCC.

Investigated complaints are the only cases adjudicated but form only a small portion of the total number of complaints received; they are the only cases that illustrate the PCC's thinking on ethical matters. Each adjudicated complaint as reported in the quarterly/monthly bulletins was entered in a database. The database listed the name of the complainant, whether they were well-known, the name of the newspaper, the substance of the complaint, any particular comments made by the PCC and the number of the report in which the complaint was adjudicated.

In addition, each complaint was coded against the clause of the code of practice that it was alleged to have broken. The major change in the code of conduct, introduced in January 1998 following the death of the Diana, Princess of Wales, meant that those complaints made after that time were adjudicated against a new code. However, the main thrust of the code did not change, only the way in which the commission was able to interpret it. So, for instance, there was a clause on privacy in both the old and new code, but the new code took a much stronger line preventing some invasions that would have been possible with the former.

The final outcome, as adjudicated by the PCC, was listed against one of the following categories:

- *upheld*;
- *upheld in part* (this usually means that the complaint fell under more than one element of the code and while one or more was upheld, others were not);
- *rejected* (occasionally listed as not upheld. The reason for this different use of wording is not explained by the PCC);
- *not pursued* (that is by the PCC – there are several instances where, having accepted a potential breach of the code, the commission refused to adjudicate);
- *resolved*.

It was decided to include a field called "well known", which would identify celebrities or well-known personalities, to see if the PCC was serving the ordinary person. The rich and famous, as is often pointed out, have a very different relationship with the media to ordinary people. They are also in a much better position to protect their rights through the courts or by more subtle means such as controlled access. It is a category identified by the PCC as significant and they have started identifying "those in the public eye" since 2001. The difficulty with identifying someone as well-known, for the purposes of analysing data on PCC outcomes, is that it is such a subjective judgement. In an attempt to bring consistency to the decisions it was decided to apply the following criteria:

Celebrities
- TV actors, performers and presenters who would be recognised by a reasonably wide section of the community;
- pop singers, musicians, producers, DJs and others who would be recognised by a reasonably wide section of the community;
- film actors, directors, writers and any others who would be recognised by a reasonably wide section of the community;
- celebrities from any artistic community who would be recognised by a reasonably wide section of the general community;
- those who are well known or notorious from any walk of life but particularly including entertainment, business, academe, trade unions, politics and charities;
- MPs are listed as well known regardless of how well-known they actually are;

- councillors are only listed as well-known if they would be recognised by some section of the general community (for instance, Lord Mayor of London, Ken Livingstone). However, for a small provincial paper, the general community might itself be quite small and so the councillor might be well known in those circumstances;
- royalty: where a complaint is made for a member of the royal family, it is usually made by the royal press office and so this is normally cited.

To ensure consistency of statistical display, the following rules were followed when identifying complainants:

- Where more than one person complained about the same story, a separate entry was made unless the complaint was clearly made jointly.
- Where complaints were made through a solicitor, the principal figure is used as the complainant, not the solicitors. It was normal for major celebrities such as Sean Connery or Elton John to complain using a solicitor.
- Any complaint involving more than one paper is listed as a separate complaint against each paper.

TOPPING THE COMPLAINTS LEAGUE

The two most significant complaint types are over accuracy and privacy. Accuracy tops the league both in terms of the number of complaints made and the number adjudicated. Some 60 to 70 per cent of complaints made concern accuracy. The PCC's annual reports for the first three years do not make it clear how many complaints have been made about accuracy so an average was calculated for complaints made about accuracy for years 1994-2000. Using this average percentage on the total number of complaints received for years 1991-1993 it was calculated that approximately 14,404 complaints were made about accuracy in the first ten years of PCC work (see Figure 2). The monthly reports of adjudications show that of these, only 422 (2.9 per cent) were adjudicated with 141 being upheld (33.4 per cent of those adjudicated, 1 per cent of the total) (see Figure 5).

Privacy is the second most complained of category with 12 to 14 per cent concerning privacy. Using the same method as above, it was calculated that approximately 3,127 complaints were made about privacy in the first ten years (see Figure 3). Of these, 220 (7 per cent of total complaints received) were adjudicated and 75 (34.21 per cent of those adjudicated, 2.4 per cent of the total) were upheld (see Figure 6).

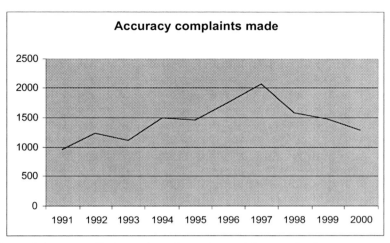

Figure 2 Accuracy: Estimated number of complaints made about accuracy

THE PCC'S PERFORMANCE

In the early years of this study, there was a rapid increase in both complaints and adjudications. Complaints continued to rise until 1996 after which they fell, a change the PCC identified as signalling that self-regulation was working. It is worth noting (although it is outside the scope of this study) that complaints for 2001 and 2002 showed an increase (see Figure 1). Adjudications also fell away sharply after an early rise to a peak in 1993. Again it is worth noting that despite an increase in complaints in 2001 and 2002, the number of adjudications continued to decrease (see Figure 4).

There has been a matching fall in the number of adjudicated complaints about accuracy (see Figure 7). Peaking at 69 in 1992, they have fallen steadily to 19 in 2000 with a low of 15 in 1999. Not only has the number of this type of complaint to be adjudicated fallen, but fewer adjudications have been upheld as a percentage (see Figure 8). The number upheld in 1991 was 52.2 percent. This fell in the following year to 35 per cent and continued to drop over subsequent years to 26 per cent (20 per cent in 1999). This means that not only has the PCC adjudicated fewer complaints about accuracy in real terms over a period during which complaints were generally on the increase, but that it has upheld fewer of these complaints year on year (see Figure 9).

The picture is not so clear with privacy. The percentage of total complaints concerning privacy have risen over the years until 1996 (see Figure 3) but have fallen steadily since then, although this seems to be

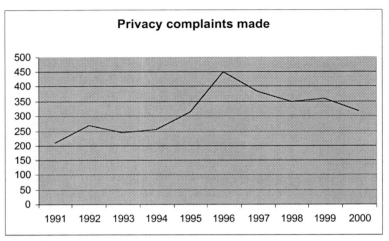

Figure 3 Privacy: Estimated number of complaints made about privacy.

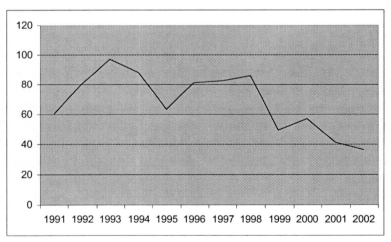

Figure 4 Total number of complaints adjudicated

because an increase in complaints about children and discrimination. The wide variation, year on year, of privacy complaints adjudicated make it almost impossible to detect any pattern (see Figures 6 and 10). However, the percentage of complaints made about privacy that were upheld (Figure 11) and the percentage of upheld complaints adjudicated about privacy (see Figure 12) have both reduced steadily.

COMPLAINTS FROM THE "WELL-KNOWN"

Most of the noteworthy cases involving privacy over the years have concerned celebrities. The PCC claims it does not favour celebrities:

> *...ordinary people continue to make up the vast majority of our complainants. Contrary to belief in some quarters, some 2,390 of the complaints we received in 2002 – or 91 per cent – were from ordinary men, women and children temporarily caught up in national or local newspaper attention.*
> *(http://www.pcc.org.uk/2002/statistics_review.html#table2: July 2003)*

This may be the case for complaints received, but it is not so when adjudicated cases are examined. The PCC uses the term "people in the public eye" but it is reasonable to suppose that this will be virtually indistinguishable for the term "well known" as explained above. The 2002 PCC annual report (http://www.pcc.org.uk/2002/statistics_review.html#table2: July 2003) shows that only 3 per cent of complaints came from "people in the public eye" (the same as in 2001) with 7 per cent being made by groups or organisations. It is impossible to compare the years used for this study as data on "people in the public eye" had not been recorded by the PCC before 2001. Using the criterion "well known" as detailed above, Figures 13 and 14 show the number of celebrity and "ordinary" complaints that were adjudicated in

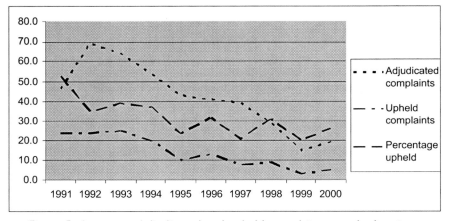

Figure 5 Accuracy: Adjudicated and upheld complaints matched against percentage upheld

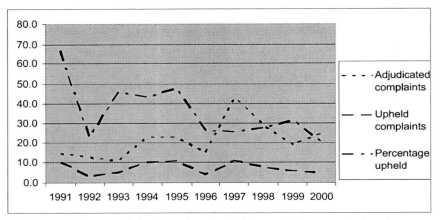

Figure 6 Privacy: Adjudicated and upheld complaints matched against
percentage upheld

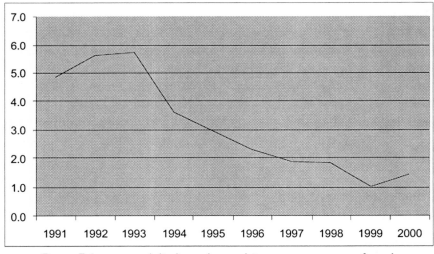

Figure 7 Accuracy: Adjudicated complaints as percentage of total
complaints received about accuracy

each year. In 1997, 4.6 percent of adjudications concerned "well known" people. This was the closest figure to the 3 per cent claimed by the PCC in 2002 but usually the number of adjudications concerning celebrities was much higher (see Figure 13 and 14).

It should be noted, however, that this is adjudications and not just complaints made, the category which the PCC is using as the basis of its

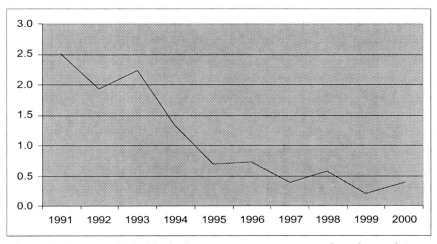

Figure 8 Accuracy: Upheld adjudications as a percentage of total complaints
received about accuracy

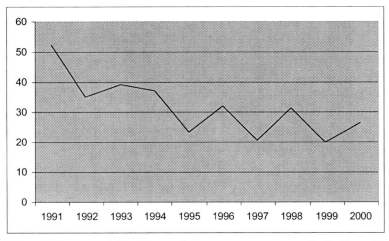

Figure 9 Accuracy: Upheld complaints as a percentage of adjudicated
complaints of accuracy

figures. Since many complaints from the "well known" are made through professional advisors (such as solicitors), it seems likely that a higher percentage of these complaints might be adjudicated as the advisors are more likely to be able to make best use of the system. It was found that the number of "well known" cases adjudicated on privacy were typically 9.3

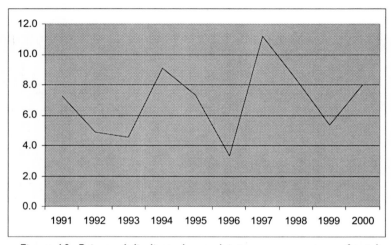

Figure 10 Privacy: Adjudicated complaints as a percentage of total
complaints received about privacy

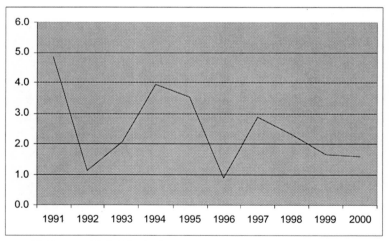

Figure 11 Privacy: Upheld adjudications as a percentage of total complaints
received about privacy

times higher than would be the case using the PCC's claimed 3 per cent
complaint rate and for accuracy they were 2.8 times higher.

More of the "well known" cases were upheld. Whilst this was not
significant in the case of accuracy with 33.8 percent of "well known"
complaints upheld on average compared with 30.6 percent of complaints

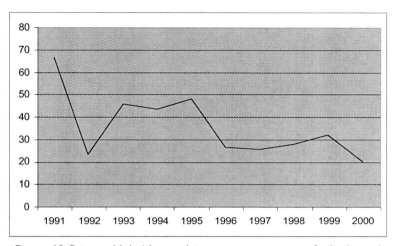

Figure 12 Privacy: Upheld complaints as a percentage of adjudicated complaints of privacy

from others, the difference was much more marked when it came to privacy. Here only 29.7 percent of "ordinary" cases were upheld compared with 47.4 percent for "well-known" (see Figure 15). This means that almost half of all "well-known" complaints about privacy were upheld compared with less than a third of non-celebrity complaints.

It is difficult to see any reason why this should be, particularly as many celebrities, certainly recently, seem to prefer approaching the courts if they think there is a strong case for invasion of privacy. It may be that celebrities are more used to appearing in the media and are less likely to complain for minor infringements of privacy compared with a non-celebrity and therefore the breaches of their privacy, when they do complain, tend to be a more obvious breach of the code.

PRESS INTRUSION

Although well-known people may only complain about obvious breaches, for many ordinary people, invasion by the media is often so appalling that seeking a remedy through the PCC also seems an unlikely option, especially as the only remedy on offer is the publication of an adjudication that risks either being virtually meaningless or repeating the original invasion. It would appear that most ordinary people would prefer that the invasion of privacy (and often the incident that had caused it) had not happened at all and are, therefore, not prepared to go to the trouble of complaining. "The

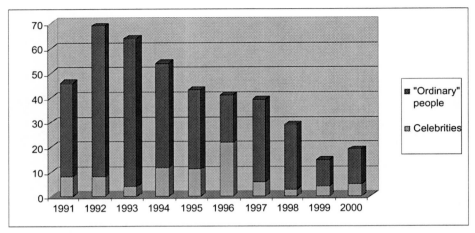

Figure 13 Accuracy: Total adjudicated complaints broken down by celebrity

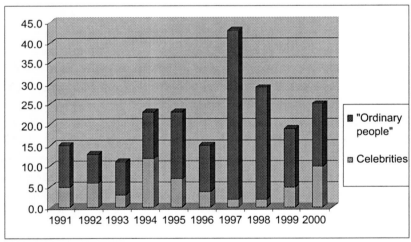

Figure 14 Privacy: Total adjudicated complaints broken down by celebrity

whole process would not be worth the upset," commented one person dragged into the news after the murder of her sister (House of Commons culture media and sport committee 2003 vol III: ev 203).

Rosemary McKenna MP, of the culture, media and sport select committee, described the attitude of many complainants: "These people do not want redress for themselves, but what they want to do is make sure it

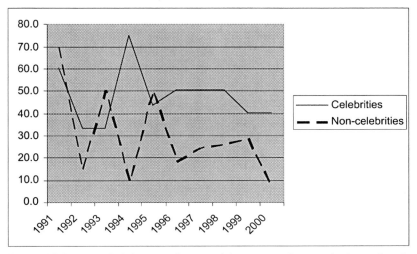

Figure 15 Privacy: Celebrity and non-celebrity complaints adjudicated and upheld as a percentage of complaints adjudicated

does not happen in the future, that ordinary families caught up in a tragedy do not end up in this situation" (ibid. Vol II ev 68). Some complainants to the PCC are satisfied with the process and find that the conciliation service offered is helpful. The PCC itself claims that 62 per cent of complainants felt their complaint had been dealt with satisfactorily or very satisfactorily in a survey of 492 complainants carried out in the first half of 2003 (http://www.pcc.org.uk/press/detail.asp?id=110 September 2003).

Some examples of satisfied complainants appear in evidence to the culture media and sport select committee report (Vol III ap80, ev131; ap83, ev132; Ap88, ev135; Ap90, ev136; Ap92, ev137; ap112, ev153; Ap114, Ev154). However, it is clear from most of these that the PCC has only acted as an intermediary to ensure a belated apology or the publication of a letter, something the newspaper could have offered immediately a complaint was first made: "I was favourably impressed with the way the commission handled my complaint. The *Telegraph* was persuaded to publish a letter setting the record straight." The writer went on to doubt that his letter "caught nearly so many eyes" as the original piece (ibid. ap80, ev 131). In another example, the writer said: "I contacted the commission at that time, and they were incredibly sympathetic and helpful, securing a written apology (after several attempts!) from the editor..." (ibid: app90, ev136).

Many complainants, while finding the PCC staff helpful and sympathetic, still feel that the PCC's idea of self-regulation did not deal with their complaints and much of the evidence sent to the select committee contains sentiments such as: "the Press Complaints Office was a waste of time..." (House of Commons select committee 2003: app 89, ev 135); "The PCC needs to be given more teeth..." (ibid: ap91, ev 137); "The complaint was upheld, although it did not prevent a further mention in another newspaper at a later date." (ibid: ap94, ev137); "The PCC is a toothless tiger" (ibid: ap97, ev 140).

CONCLUSION

The PCC has claimed that it has "changed the entire culture of British newspapers and magazines" by "raising standards through its adjudications and decisions" (PCC annual report 2000: 2). It also claims that complainants are generally satisfied with its services:

> *The PCC regularly monitors customer satisfaction levels. In the first three months of this year, overall satisfaction among complainants reached nearly 70 per cent - despite the fact that the complaints of many of those surveyed had not prospered. The PCC is determined to build still further on that (http://www.pcc.org.uk/press/detail.asp?id=104 Sept 2003).*

While many complainants do find the PCC a fast and efficient service, as it claims, acting with sympathy and sensitivity, this does not mean that they feel they are getting the response to their complaints that they would wish. The responses sent to the select committee suggest that they may well feel satisfied with the PCC's response, but they are not getting the result they seek. Most complaints are over accuracy, yet it is clear that many editors are still not prepared to print apologies, corrections or reader's letters unless forced to by the PCC. This may be the reason why the number of complaints about accuracy that were adjudicated and those that were upheld have fallen dramatically over the ten-year period of the study: editors are still ignoring complaints until the PCC becomes involved. If this is the case, then it might be some justification for the PCC's claim to be helping complainants to resolve their complaints:

> *Our main aim with any complaint which raises a possible breach of the Code of Practice is always to resolve it as quickly as possible.*

Because of our success in this, the Commission had to adjudicate on only 49 complaints in 1999 - the lowest ever number. That is a sign not of the weakness of self regulation - but its strength. All those which were critical of a newspaper were published in full and with due prominence by the publication concerned (PCC 1999: 1).

However, this claim to help with resolution is at variance with the PCCs claim to be "raising standards through its adjudications and decisions" (PCC annual report 2000: 2). Pressing editors to print apologies or corrections that should have been printed willingly weeks before is not changing "the entire culture of British newspapers and magazines".

Only the adjudication of complaints can make it clear to all editors what their obligations are under the code of practice. With only 707 complaints adjudicated from 22,988 complaints, there is little guidance available from the gathered considerations to be offered to editors in terms of advice for raising standards. The PCC must decide whether it is there to help complainants gain apologies or letters of correction, or whether its role is to give strong guidance to editors and raise the standards of press behaviour. It can only do that by adjudicating the majority of complaints obliging editors to offer apologies or letters of correction at a much earlier stage.

The PCC also claims that its services are for ordinary people and celebrities do not get special treatment. However, there is a much better adjudication rate for those "in the public eye" particularly for complaints about privacy. Privacy is the second most complained of breach of the code of practice and is the one that probably causes the most anger and distress. It is often linked with inaccuracy so that a newspaper report might well invade privacy and be inaccurate at the same time. Whilst adjudications on privacy and the number upheld have also fallen over the period of the study, the change is nothing like as marked as that for accuracy.

Those who are well known might have more attention paid to their complaints, but the small (and reducing) number of adjudications made mean that no-one who complains to the PCC about privacy gets what they really want: an end to what they see as sensational stories unreasonably and unnecessarily invading people's privacy. Since the PCC's only "punishment" is publication of an adjudication, this is likely to constitute a further intrusion, even if done anonymously; ironically, those who have had their privacy invaded and have objected to it, must see the intrusion repeated as part of the "punishment".

REFERENCES

Committee on Privacy (1972) *The Report on the Committee on Privacy*, London, HMSO
Department of Culture Media and Sport (2003) *The Government's Response to the Fifth Report of the Culture, Media and Sport Select Committee on 'Privacy and Media Intrusion'* (HC 458) Session 2002-2003 London: HMSO
Press Complaints Commission *PCC Reports* 1991-2001, London, HMSO
Press Complaints Commission Quarterly reports Nos 1-53, London, PCC
Frost, Chris (2000) *Media Ethics and Self-Regulation*, London, Pearson
Leonard, T (2003) "A press watchdog must have teeth to be credible", *Daily Telegraph*, 28 February
O'Malley, Tom and Soley, Clive (2000) *Regulating the Press*, London, Pluto
Robertson, Geoffrey (1983) *People Against the Press*, London, Quartet
Shannon, Richard (2002) *A Press Free and Responsible*, London, John Murray
House of Commons culture, media and sport committee (2003) *Privacy and Media Intrusion*: Fifth Report of session 2002-2003, London, HMSO

WEBSITES

www.presscouncils.org
www.pcc.org.uk

Chris Frost is Head of Journalism at Liverpool John Moores University, Liverpool, UK. He is the author of *Media Ethics and Self-regulation* (Longman 2000), *Reporting for Journalists* (Routledge 2001) and *Designing For Newspapers and Magazines* (Routledge 2003). He is also a member of the National Union of Journalists National Executive Committee, chair of the NUJ's Ethics Council and a former President of the NUJ. Contact details: Department of Journalism, Liverpool John Moores University, Dean Walters Building, St James Road, Liverpool L1 7BR. 0151 231 5029; 07976 296777; email: c.p.frost@livjm.ac.uk.

When rights collide: free speech, corporations and moral rights

Dean Ritz

Corporations use their claimed right to free speech for significant effect upon the world. This chapter examines what happens when that claim, as embodied in US legal doctrine, collides with the rights of natural persons. US case law that both protects commercial speech and prohibits governmentally coerced speech is reviewed briefly. I then examine how these two doctrines were conflated by the US Supreme Court to create opportunities for competing claims to free speech rights by natural persons and by corporations. I use the case of International Dairy Foods Association v. Amestoy to illustrate one such collision. A desired normative outcome for that case and the conflict it represents is proposed and two relevant theories are investigated. The main conclusion is that it is unethical for individuals – singly, or through associations – to grant legal rights to corporations. Rather, natural persons, through their representative governments, should grant legal protections and powers to corporations only as conditional privileges.

Keywords: commercial speech, corporate entity theory, moral rights, negative free speech, communication ethics

INTRODUCTION

Corporate power substantially shapes US public policy on issues from transportation, energy, taxes and military action, to education, the environment and healthcare. The acquisition of legal rights by the corporation made their influence on public affairs both feasible and formidable. From the perspective of wealthy industrialists this was a necessary progression, tracking wealth from its association with individuals through the mid-19th century to its subsequent reconstitution in corporations, specifically, limited liability corporations. This progression made it necessary that those rights which served to protect and project the wealth of individuals should then be awarded to corporations. In the US, the Supreme Court made the award and with it the legal basis for the collision of rights between natural persons and corporations.[1] US courts now consider corporate rights to be equally legitimate to those associated with natural persons; just as the court appears blind to a person's race or gender in recognising their legal rights, it is also blind to whether the person is natural or artificial, that is, a human being or a corporation.

DISTINGUISHING LEGAL AND MORAL RIGHTS

It is important to distinguish between legal and moral rights and their relationships to a nation's constitution. In his essay *Taking Rights Seriously*, philosopher Ronald Dworkin considers some of the rights declared in the US constitution to be moral rights. He notes the right of free speech, embodied in the constitution's First Amendment, for illustration.[2] Legal rights, to contrast, are established by law and these may or may not overlap with moral rights. Moral rights, moreover, exist outside the law and are characterised as those rights which people have against, and thus independent of, any government.[3] It does not matter how inconvenient moral rights are to other people or to a government; they remain sacrosanct.[4] Another important characteristic of moral rights is the popular consensus that attaches them to natural persons. The universal recognition of human dignity finds expression in this attachment. There is no parallel consensus for corporations, no expression of human dignity in seeing these rights as associated with the corporate form, and there are good reasons why we do not – and should not – find such a parallel consensus.

Lastly, governments are slow to recognise moral rights as legal ones.[5] But once recognised it is illegitimate for a government to revoke them even if its citizens appear to voluntarily demand this.[6] Some moral rights are essential prerequisites for self-governance. Again, free speech provides the example. The rights that make democracy legitimate cannot be revoked without destroying democracy – another reason for the sanctity that should be accorded moral rights. To insure democracy it is crucial that in collisions between moral rights and those that are merely legal ones, it is the merely legal ones that are subject to change. Taking rights seriously means honouring the inalienable and irrevocable properties of moral rights.

The foundation for conflicting claims to free speech rights

Some foundation must be laid before getting to the example of a collision of moral rights claims by natural persons and corporations, including the US Supreme Court's rationale firmly establishing First Amendment protection for commercial speech, and their rationale prohibiting governmentally coerced speech. Lastly, I briefly cover how these two doctrines were conflated by the US Supreme Court to create opportunities for these collisions, making possible such cases as International Dairy Foods Association v. Amestoy ("International Dairy").[7]

US legal doctrine currently relies upon the rights of those who hear commercial speech in order to justify its protection. The case of particular interest, Virginia Pharmacy Board v. Virginia Consumer Council,[8] deals with a challenge to a state law prohibiting pharmacists from advertising the prices they or their competitors charge for prescription medications. The Virginia Pharmacy court decided that First Amendment protections do extend to purely commercial speech, resting its rationale for such protections primarily upon the free speech rights of the information recipients, and to a much lesser degree on the rights of the speaker or on the content of the communication.[9] The Virginia Pharmacy decision firmly established commercial speech as being of value in the "marketplace of ideas", indeed that the purpose for protecting purely commercial speech is to assist populating that marketplace because recipients have a right to receive that information.[10]

Dissenting Justice Rehnquist criticised the majority decision. Of particular interest is his claim that a person's desire to know does not alone justify that the communication be protected by the First Amendment.[11] For him, the classification of both the content of the speech and the nature of the speaker influences the recognition of protected speech, particularly and uncontrovertibly, and that the First Amendment serves to protect political speech and natural persons speaking and hearing that speech.

The doctrines associated with governmentally coerced speech provides an interesting contrast with free speech doctrine. The two circumstances of particular interest are, firstly, when the government compels a person to express speech that violates their conscience, and secondly, when property is commandeered to provide for the speech of non-property owners. Regarding the former, the US legal doctrine restricts the government from compelling a person to make an expression that violates their conscience; e.g. forcing a person to salute the flag.[12] Simply, the court has held that the state is not allowed to coerce a person to express prescribed speech that violates their conscience.

Regarding the latter is the case of Wooley v. Maynard[13] where a husband and wife were repeatedly arrested for obscuring the motto "Live Free or Die" that appeared on the noncommercial automobile license plates in their state of residence. As Mr. Maynard explained: "I refuse to be coerced by the state into advertising a slogan which I find morally, ethically, religiously and politically abhorrent".[14] The court found in favour of Mr Maynard, ruling that the state of New Hampshire unconstitutionally violated his conscience when they commandeered his property for the purpose of expressing state-sanctioned speech. It is not merely Mr. Maynard's abhorrence of the speech that is at issue, it is also the use of his property to "speak". The Wooley court declared that the government may not "constitutionally require an individual to participate in the dissemination of an ideological message by displaying it on his private property in a manner and for the express purpose that it be observed and read by the public",[15] adding that the "right to speak and the right to refrain from speaking are complementary components of the broader concept of 'individual freedom of mind'".[16]

This case took the recognised limitations against governmentally coerced speech from the direct forced expression by individual persons themselves (e.g. saluting the flag) and extended them to include the property controlled by individuals. This extension of the coerced speech doctrine created an opening whereby corporations could make similar claims about coerced speech because, though corporations do not exist within a natural body that expressly "speaks", are themselves property the government may demand be used to "speak" on the behalf of a third party. The Supreme Court subsequently delivered to property – in the corporate form – protections from governmentally coerced speech that their owners find objectionable. This is the case of Pacific Gas & Electric Co. v. Public Utilities Commission.[17]

Briefly, the circumstances of Pacific Gas & Electric involve a California Public Utility Commission order to the Pacific Gas & Electric Company – a publicly regulated utility monopoly – to grant access to its utility billing envelopes for use by Public Utility Commission-sanctioned third parties. In Pacific Gas & Electric, the Court decided in favor of the utility corporation because it believed that the mandated access would have a chilling effect on the free speech rights of the corporation. For example, the third-party could express views that were contrary to the interests of the corporation and the corporation would then be under pressure to respond when they would prefer to be silent on the matter. "This pressure to respond 'is particularly apparent when the owner has taken a position opposed to the view being expressed on his property'".[18]

The Pacific Gas & Electric court first relied upon Virginia Pharmacy to affirm that purely commercial speech receives some First Amendment protections in order to better populate the marketplace of ideas. It then cited Wooley to conclude that First Amendment protections extend to the use of one's property when the property owner finds the coerced speech to be objectionable. This decision, paradoxically, limits the marketplace of ideas. This paradox suggests that the rationale confirming First Amendment protections for commercial speech, as set out in Virginia Pharmacy, was ignored, and that only the doctrine – sanitised of its foundations – was applied. Pacific Gas & Electric conflates the two doctrines, concluding that a corporation can have its artificial "conscience" violated; it mistakenly extends to corporations what Justice Rehnquist calls a "negative free speech" right.[19] Pacific Gas & Electric sets the stage for International Dairy Foods, the case that illustrates a collision of moral rights.

A COLLISION OF RIGHTS

Both parties in International Dairy made claims upon the First Amendment right to free speech found in the US constitution. On one hand there is the claim of negative free speech rights by the International Dairy Foods corporation (and other appellants). On the other hand there is the claim by natural persons to be well informed on both commercial as well as political matters.

The case revolves around a 1994 Vermont state statute requiring that "[i]f rBST has been used in the production of milk or a milk product for retail sale in this state, the retail milk or milk product shall be labeled as such."[20] The appellants argued the statute violated their corporate claimed First Amendment rights of negative free speech, forcing them to use their property (i.e. their product packaging) to make a statement contrary to their views.[21] The Second Circuit Court of Appeals agreed the statute violated the appellants' negative free speech rights.

The court of appeals listed a sequence of extant Supreme Court doctrines allegedly supporting their conclusion (and introduced above): commercial speech receives First Amendment protections; protected types of speech include facts as well as opinions;[22] "[t]he right not to speak inheres in political and commercial speech alike";[23] and corporate as well as human speakers possess negative free speech rights. Traversing this line of reasoning the court agreed with appellants that the statue "indisputably requires them to speak when they would rather not"[24] and thus violates their First Amendment rights.

International Dairy decided that dairy producers are under no compulsion to reveal its use while natural persons do not have the right to know where rBST is used. This dispute cannot be resolved through the marketplace as consumers who are denied access to information cannot possibly make decisions based on that decisive yet absent knowledge. Nor are voluntary negative-use claims an option, as the Monsanto Company (the sole producer of rBST for the US market) has successfully engaged in legal actions effectively silencing dairy product manufacturers that make them.[25]

The paradox introduced in Pacific Gas & Electric is fully visible in International Dairy and recognised by the dissenting judge who argued that the required disclosure statement demanded of milk producers was not judgemental and thus not speech that one could find as violating their conscience. Rather, it was factual information – exactly the kind that citizens have a right to request, and the government has the ability to procure an answer.[26]

THE DESIRED NORMATIVE ARRANGEMENT
At the heart of this case are not issues of trade nor of health and safety (human and bovine); rather the collision of rights between corporations and natural persons and whose interests shall triumph. By framing this as a collision I assume the interests of natural persons are opposed to the interests of corporations (and their owners and managers). Admittedly, these interests are not always at odds. But such occasions of agreement merely provide a necessary but insufficient condition for even considering the extension of moral rights to corporations. Rather, we are concerned with occasions of disagreement. The normative question is this: what resolution should we natural persons desire when these rights collide?

At this point it is useful to note that corporations have been the recipients of many US constitutional rights. All of them were awarded by the judicial elaboration of the US Supreme Court – not through the constitutional amendment process nor through the actions of elected representatives extending these rights through repealable statutes. Some of these elaborations are legitimate, particularly those concerning property rights.[27] But most are not, mistakenly taking the rights we commonly acknowledge as desirable for natural persons and bestowing them to the property natural persons possess. A very partial list includes status as legal persons, Fourteenth Amendment equal protection of the laws, First

Amendment protection for corporate political speech and commercial speech, and Fourth Amendment protection from unreasonable searches for corporate documents.[28]

Because political speech enjoys greater US constitutional protections than commercial speech corporations, not surprisingly, often seek these greater protections by claiming commercial speech is actually political speech. An example of this is documented in the 2002 decision by the Supreme Court of California, Kasky v. Nike, Inc.[29] There the Supreme Court of California overturned a lower court's decision that Nike Inc. had engaged in political speech when it made fraudulent claims in corporate communication about the labour practices and working conditions where its products were made. Bluntly, Nike claimed that it was allowed to lie because it was advancing the public debate on an issue of public concern and thus engaged in political speech. However, the court properly considered it as commercial information made by a commercial entity to achieve commercial ends and thus Nike Inc. could be pursued by the state of California for violations of its state consumer fraud laws.[30]

One more corporate speech example is worth noting. The Monsanto Company recently engaged in activities of disinformation in an area of great public concern. Either directly or through its public relations firms, the company has operated a covert public relations campaign that invents Internet personalities – fictitious persons who disclaim association with the company – to participate in Internet discussions groups regarding genetically engineered food, advance positions supportive of the company and attack the company's critics.[31]

These examples reflect efforts by corporations to influence public policy, ostensibly the domain of natural persons and their governments. Beneath all this is the question of who should be allowed to participate in the establishment of public policy. In a democracy we expect public policy to be set by its members, whom we normally consider to be the citizens.

Citizenship, at least in the US, remains reserved exclusively for natural persons. Yet democracy, at a minimum, should distribute rather than consolidate power, recognising the inherent value that those who must submit to laws should somehow be empowered to establish them; seek ways to prevent concentrations of private power from overwhelming public power, preserving the demos of democracy and preventing concentrations of private power from infringing upon the rights and liberties of the most vulnerable members of society specifically in ways which the government is forbidden to do.[32]

Economic power deserves special attention. It is a power for coercion. It is rational that a government seeking to protect democracy would seek to limit the power of wealth and theoretically that can be done without restricting the possession of wealth, distinguishing between those rights and liberties accorded a person and those accorded their money. Corporations are "mechanisms by means of which a number of persons unite for the purpose of assembling a fund of capital with which to carry on some business enterprises".[33] They are, by definition, a concentration of wealth. Being creations of the state and created specifically to engage in activities to exercise economic power, the corporate form is a proper object of democratic concern and state control.

In light of this, and assuming that a democratic government should work to achieve the democratic ideals defined above, these conflicts of moral rights between natural persons and corporations normatively should resolve with the rights accorded to natural persons as pre-eminent over the rights – if any – accorded to corporate persons. Further, it is argued that the best normative arrangement would require governments to grant legal powers and protections to corporate entities only as privileges and not as rights. The difference is that a right may be inalienable and irrevocable but privileges persist only at the pleasure of the grantor. The democratic ideal, outlined above, suggests that rights – particularly moral rights – be reserved exclusively for natural persons.

RESOLVING THE CONFLICT THROUGH SECONDARY MORAL AGENCY

In her book, *Persons, Rights, and Corporations*, Patricia Werhane proposes that corporations be classified as "secondary moral agents", and therefore objects of blame and praise to be held responsible for their actions and with claim to secondary moral rights.[34] This proposal is built from a "theory of secondary action" as applied to the corporate form.[35]

Secondary actions arise from a delegation of responsibility. Say I delegate a general responsibility to another person and this person then determines and executes specific actions in fulfilment of this responsibility. I am the primary agent for the act of delegation and they are the secondary agent performing secondary actions. Similarly, Werhane sees corporate actions as secondary actions. Shareholders delegate to corporate boards general responsibilities, providing only general instructions (described in corporate charters and by shareholder initiatives). Thus, corporate founders and shareholders are primary agents of the delegation and the corporate board and managers are secondary agents carrying out "collective secondary actions".[36]

There is some distance, however, from determining that corporate employees commit collective secondary actions to the point where moral agency may be ascribed to the corporate form. Moral agency requires the intentional application of reason. At first glance, ascribing moral agency to the corporate form, that is, "ascrib[ing] to such artificial entities an 'intellect' or 'mind' for freedom of conscience purposes is to confuse metaphor with reality".[37] A corporation is not a living physical entity as is a natural person; however, its actions do take place in a physical world and this suggests the corporate form is due recognition as an ontological individual. These actions are determined by other persons (e.g. corporate managers) in compliance with general instructions from its shareholders communicated through the board of directors.

Werhane acknowledges "the 'actions' of a corporation [as] not literally actions of a physical entity, but rather, 'actions' that are represented and carried out through persons" acting with intentionality and reason in the fulfilment of their corporate duties.[38] She calls the arrangement "methodological collectivism".[39] Thus, she argues, a corporation meets the requirements of moral agency: it is an ontological individual who through methodological collectivism acts with reason and intentionality. But because corporations "lack the autonomy necessary to perform primary actions" they cannot be primary moral agents, only secondary ones.[40]

Werhane alludes to a number of consequential effects of her theory. For example, corporations could no longer claim to be neutral or silent with regard to moral demands and corporate managers in particular would not be excused from secondary moral responsibility. After all, moral rights cannot be detached from moral responsibilities. More importantly, Werhane notes that while secondary moral agency is sufficient to justify moral claim to rights, these should be considered "secondary moral rights"; natural persons, on the other hand, have "primary moral rights" arising from their primary moral agency, and thus conflicting claims of rights between corporations and natural persons must always recognise the superior claims of natural persons.[41]

Regarding International Dairy, the court saw this as a conflict of equal claim to the same right. When faced with such a situation US courts first preferentially act to protect rights, but if no such protection is required the court may then seek to advance them. The court did follow that recipe in this case, protecting corporate free speech rights and thus not advancing human free speech rights. Ascribing the inferior status of secondary moral rights to corporations should have resulted in a judicial conclusion advancing the rights of natural persons rather than protecting the secondary rights claimed by corporations.

Classifying corporate rights as secondary has two broad practical effects. The first is that corporations may exercise their rights but only when such exercise does not infringe upon human rights. Second, it would legalise the promotion of human rights at the expense of the rights claimed by corporations. And while this arrangement would be of tremendous assistance to those seeking to exercise human rights as a means for protecting humans from corporate harms, secondary moral agency still extends to corporations constitutional protections from government infringement for purposes other than the protection of the rights of natural persons. So while this theory provides for the normative outcome desired with regard to International Dairy it would not justify a law which, for example, outlawed corporations from "speaking" (i.e. spending money) upon political referenda; such a law would unconstitutionally infringe upon corporate free speech rights because it lacks a collision with the rights of natural persons. Werhane's assertion of the corporation as an ontological individual largely and unfortunately maintains the political power of corporations and thus fails to support the second part of the desired normative arrangement.

RESOLVING THE CONFLICT THROUGH ARTIFICIAL ENTITY THEORY

The "artificial entity theory" of the corporate form provides a significant contrast to Werhane's ideas for secondary moral agency and satisfies both the first and second parts of the normative outcome desired with regard to International Dairy. Here it is useful to recall some additional early history of the corporate form. The earliest recorded corporations were peace and craft guilds.[42] Peace guilds provided for mutual protection. They later evolved into the idea of municipal corporations. Membership in a peace guild was determined by geographic proximity, that is, residency within a delineated territory. Both peace and craft guilds exercised some authority over their members, including the ability to levy taxes or other responsibilities upon its members. But their most important feature was in providing for the practical needs of societies, particularly state recognition both to hold property and to incur obligations in common.[43] These associations were artificial entities, creatures of the state. As creatures of the state an association's powers were only those directly conferred upon it by the state. This arrangement thus withholds moral rights for corporations[44] and justifies the granting to them of privileges – not rights – particularly those privileges that enable their primary purpose of holding property and obligations in common for an association of persons.

This contrasts with "natural entity theory" which is a theory asserting that a corporation possesses a corporate personality. There are two bases for this concept of corporate personality. The first views the corporation as an entity independent of its owners (i.e. shareholders), a basis compatible with Werhane's ideas of methodological collectivism, ontological individualism and the grant of secondary moral rights. In retrospect we may now see that Werhane built her theory of secondary moral agency upon a foundation of natural entity theory. She saw the corporation as a secondary moral agent of the shareholders, granted both moral rights and moral responsibilities. The second basis establishes corporate personality by viewing it as closely associated with its owners.

This does not separate the rights accorded a person with the rights accorded their property. It was this conception that appears to have been used to rationalise the first significant and enabling grant of US constitutional rights to the corporate form.[45] The right in question was the equal protection of the laws as enumerated in the constitution's Fourteenth Amendment.[46] Legal historian Morton J. Horwitz writes that "the central argument was that the Fourteenth Amendment protects the property rights not of some abstract corporate entity but rather of the individual [human] shareholders".[47] So to deny these rights of a corporation necessarily meant to deny them of its human shareholders. To prevent such "injustice" it was necessary to see corporations as included within the definition of "persons" for the equal protection clause of the Fourteenth Amendment (thereby preventing states from treating corporate property differently from the personal property of its shareholders). This established corporate personality and enabled the rights accorded to natural persons to permeate the corporate veil and link to the corporate form. A legal fiction created by the law now possessed rights against the law but without a physical body and without the capacities necessary for moral reasoning.[48]

Once we accept that moral rights for natural persons exist outside the law, we may be tempted to inquire as to their origin. In fact, it does not matter if they come from God or reason. All that matters is that these rights exist even without governments or other institutions. They must, for otherwise, as Dworkin has observed, natural persons would have no moral rights at all. Thus if we have moral rights, then these are rights against both the government and against associations of persons in whatever form they take – including the corporate form. Even Thomas Hobbes, a philosopher with a dismal view of human nature, argues that natural persons possess some natural rights.[49]

Granting rights to an association of persons is equivalent to putting them into potential conflict with the rights of individual natural persons. This may be acceptable for non-moral rights. Indeed, the social contract whereby societies are formalised involves this loss of some non-moral rights and the vesting of special rights in a sovereign in exchange for other tangible benefits of social cooperation. But, as noted above, taking rights seriously means that moral rights not only should not – but cannot – be given away. If, as is claimed, it is immoral to allow a government to infringe upon moral rights, then reasoning by analogy, it is just as immoral to have a corporation infringe upon them. Thus the grant of moral rights to corporations is immoral and thus unethical.

This second approach of artificial entity theory supports both parts of the desired normative arrangement: first, that the rights of natural persons are pre-eminent over any powers or protections granted to the corporate form; and second, that the powers and protections granted to the corporate form be classified as privileges, not as rights at all.

CONCLUSION

The most important implication for communication ethics is that corporate speech could be made subject to legal standards for ethical communication practices that are more ethically ideal than now implemented. For example, a content-neutral approach to corporate speech would be to limit their use of wealth to a certain ratio of that which the public is able and willing to spend "speaking" on a matter. Such changes are not restrictions of the rights of natural persons to speak freely but rather distinguish the rights accorded natural persons from the privileges granted to their property (corporations and corporate wealth being mere property). The point is the loudest voices regarding matters of public concern should be the natural persons in their capacity as self-governing human beings. These voices include those natural persons directing the wealth of corporations, but vocalised only in their civic capacity – not their business capacity and certainly not wielding the corporations they direct as weapons upon the body politic.

Rather than asking corporations to raise voluntarily their ethical communication standards – not to lie so much, not to use their wealth to influence public policy – ethical communication practices could instead receive legal force equal to those granted to ethical accounting practices now placed upon corporations under the rule of law. The moral right of free speech is an essential ingredient for democracy. The return of this moral right for exclusive use by natural persons is not just important to those who wish to advance ethics in communications, it is important for advancing global justice.

NOTES

1   There exists a rich history on the foundation for this "necessary progression", particularly the tensions between business interests and state governments, and the tension within state governments to either tame or expand private economic power; see Horwitz, Morton J. (1977) *The Transformation of American Law 1780-1860*, Cambridge MA, Harvard University Press; and Horwitz, Morton J. (1992) *The Transformation of American Law 1870-1960: The Crisis of Legal Orthodoxy*, New York NY, Oxford University Press

2   The relevant portion of the First Amendment reads: "Congress shall make no law [...] abridging the freedom of speech, or of the press [...]". Its legal interpretation remains in flux, under seemingly constant refinement by US courts

3   Dworkin p 184

4   For example, a society that takes seriously the right to free speech assumes that some of its members will have to hear speech that they find offensive: "[...] we are often 'captives' outside the sanctuary of the home and subject to objectionable speech" (Cohen v. California (1971) 403 US 15, p. 21)

5   The 1948 adoption by the United Nations of a "Universal Declaration of Human Rights" is one starting place for investigating specific assertions of moral rights and the consequent effort to legalise them

6   Dworkin p 191

7   International Dairy Foods Association v. Amestoy, 92 F.3d 67 (2d. Cir 1996)

8   Virginia Pharmacy Board v. Virginia Consumer Council, 425 U.S. 748 (1976)

9   There is no inherent free speech right to engage in the activities of deliberately inaccurate "factual" information, or commercial speech that is misleading, attempts to deceive, or promotes an illegal product or enterprise

10   The Court later consolidated and elaborated in Central Hudson Gas v. Public Service Commission, 447 U.S. 557 (1980) on the question of when the government may constitutionally infringe upon commercial speech

11   "It is undoubtedly arguable that many people in the country regard the choice of shampoo as just as important as who may be elected to [...] political office, but that does not automatically bring information about competing shampoos within the protection of the First Amendment" (Virginia Pharmacy p 787)

12   West Virginia State Board of Educations v. Barnette (1943) 319 US 624

13   Wooley v. Maynard (1977) 430 US 705

14 Wooley p 713
15 Wooley p 713
16 Wooley p 714
17 Pacific Gas & Electric Co. v. Public Utilities Commission (1986) 475 US 1
18 Pacific Gas & Electric 15-16
19 Pacific Gas & Electric p 26 (Justice Rehnquist, dissenting)
20 International Dairy p 69 quoting Vt. Stat. Ann. tit. 66, § 2754(c). Recombinant Bovine Somatotropin ("rBST") is a synthetic growth hormone approved in 1993 by the US Food and Drug Administration for use in dairy cows producing milk for human consumption (International Dairy p 69)
21 International Dairy p 71
22 This already is implied by Virginia Pharmacy, as the speech in question was that of prescription drug prices – purely factual information
23 International Dairy p 71
24 International Dairy p 72
25 Aboulafia, David (1998) "Pushing rBST : How the Law and the Political Process Were Used to Sell Recombinant Bovine Somatotropin to America", *Pace University Law Review*, Summer, Vol. 15 pp 617-618. Monsanto argues that claims of negative-use suggest that milk from rBST treated cows is somehow dangerous
26 International Dairy p. 80 (Justice Leval, dissenting)
27 "Property rights" refer to the rights that people have in their possession of property. They are not the rights that are accorded *to* property
28 The examples cited in this sentence are taken from Mayer, Carl J. (1990) "Personalizing the Impersonal: Corporations and the Bill of Rights", *The Hastings Law Journal*, Vol. 41 No. 13 p 580, pp 664-667. This list is quite extensive, and each item on the list deserves analysis similar to that given by this article to corporate speech rights. The best compact history of this may be found in Mayer and in the very recently published "Model *Amici Curiae* Brief to Eliminate Corporate Rights", by Richard L. Grossman, *et al*, available online at http://www.poclad.org
29 Kasky v. Nike, Inc. (2002) 45 P.3d 243 (Supreme Court of California)
30 For updated details on this case see http://www.reclaimdemocracy.org
31 Monbiot, George (2002) "The Covert Biotech War: The Battle to Put a Corporate Gm Padlock on Our Foodchain Is Being Fought on the Net", the *Guardian,* 19 November
32 This is critically different from the current implementation of American democracy. For example, US laws prohibiting racial discrimination and segregation in public accommodations (e.g. hotels and restaurants) have to be justified on economic – not moral – grounds, i.e., racial discrimination unlawfully interferes with interstate commerce
33 Dodd p 367
34 Werhane, Patricia H. (1985) *Persons, Rights, and Corporations*, Englewood Cliffs CO, Prentice-Hall, p 58
35 Werhane pp 52-56
36 Werhane p 55
37 Pacific Gas & Elec. Co. v. Public Utilities Commission, (1986) 475 US 1, p 33 (Justice Rehnquist, dissenting)

38 Werhane pp 50-51
39 Werhane p 51
40 Werhane p 57
41 What Werhane describes regarding the delegation of responsibilities largely is already covered in the agency law of business as determined by the laws of US states. Agency law, however, does not grapple with the issue of corporate moral agency and thus is silent on the issue of secondary versus primary rights
42 Williston, Samuel (1888) "The History of the Law of Business Corporations before 1800", *Harvard Law Review*, Vol. 2 No. 3 p 108
43 Williston p 107
44 Mayer p 582
45 We shall never know with certainty the rationale behind this momentous change in US constitutional doctrine, as it was made without the provision of written opinion, and without even the argument of counsel; see Horwitz (1992) pp 66-67
46 The relevant portion of the Amendment reads: "[...]nor deny to any person within its jurisdiction the equal protection of the laws"
47 Horwitz (1992) p 69. At the time of this decision all states still prohibited corporations from owning stock in other corporations, making it easier to connect corporations to the human rights of its direct owners
48 Corporations, given "life", have now turned against their creator. Some writers on this subject analogize this to Mary Shelly's Frankenstein; see Gabaldon, Theresa A. (1992) "The Lemonade Stand: Feminist and Other Reflections on the Limited Liability of Corporate Shareholders", *Vanderbilt Law Review* Vol. 45 pp 1390-1394. However such analogies are apt only to the extent that the creation turns against its creator and clearly possesses primary moral agency through the intentional application of reason to determine his actions
49 "The Right of Nature, which Writers commonly call *Jus Naturale*, is the Liberty of each man hath, to use his own power, as he will himselfe, for the preservation of his own Nature; that is to say, of his own life [...]" (Hobbes, Thomas (1997) *Leviathan*, New York NY, Norton and Co., p 72)

Dean Ritz is Master of Arts in Philosophy candidate, University of Montana, Missoula (United States). Most recently he was the author of "When Silence is not Golden: Negative Free Speech and Human Rights for Corporations", *New College of California Law Review*, Vol. 4 No. 1; and anthology editor for the book *Defying Corporations, Defining Democracy: A Book of History and Strategy,* Croton-on-Hudson NY, The Apex Press (2001). Currently co-producer of the Montana Public Radio show "Ethically Speaking" http://www.ethicallyspeaking.org. Contact: Dean Ritz / LA101, Department of Philosophy, The University of Montana, Missoula, MT 59812; voice: 1-406-721-1927; fax: 1-253-295-6670; email: dean@ethicallyspeaking.org

The media and moral literacy

Clifford Christians

In contrast to humans as rational or biological beings, this essay defines them as cultural beings constituted in language — with the media seen as agents of acculturation. Since cultural patterns are inherently normative, humans inescapably have moral agency. Our social existence is conjoined linguistically, and because the lingual is not neutral but value-laden, social bonds are moral claims. Therefore, given that our public life is not merely functional, but knit together by social values, the various technologies of public communication should engender moral literacy. Rather than oriented to internal professional standards, media practitioners ought to work out of the general morality.

Keywords: moral literacy, moral agency, culture, common morality, *animale symbolicum*, moral imagination

The global mass media are agents of acculturation: not neutral purveyors of information, but creators and shapers of culture. From this perspective, media technologies are not tools or products *per se* but cultural practices. Technology is a distinct cultural enterprise in which humans form and transform natural reality aided by tools and processes for practical ends. The contemporary media are cultural institutions. The communications enterprise is technological in character, requiring our analysis to go beyond messages and take hold of the medium in which the content is structured.

Communication technologies represent the outer edge of the technological system as a whole, where the meaning of human existence is negotiated publicly. While exhibiting the structural elements of all technical artifacts, the media's particular identity as a technology inheres in their function as bearers of symbols. Information technologies thus incarnate the properties of technology and serve as the agent for interpreting the very phenomenon they embody. Jacques Ellul calls our communication systems the "innermost, and most elusive, manifestation" of human technological activity (1978: 216, cf. 1964). All artifacts communicate meaning in an important sense but media instruments carry that role exclusively. Thus, as the media sketch out our world for us, monitor war and peace, influence our decisions and shape our self-identity, they do so with a technological cadence. The global media do not exchange neutral messages, but subtly weave industrialised societies into the warp-and-woof of an efficiency-dominated culture (Ellul 1965).

The technical artifice, out of which media technologies are born and which they perpetuate, is no longer a separate domain. Civilizations across history have produced technological products, but a qualitative change underway for the last century has now taken on its own identity. Industrial societies tend to idolise the genius behind machines at present and uncritically allow their technical power to infect not just engineering and business, but also government, education, the Church and international relations. Transnational information is a necessity for a modern planet. But as media systems expand in size and transmission is speeded up, cultures rooted in human distinctiveness are being undermined. The rapid movement of economic and cultural capital across national boundaries absorbs the particular into a global marketplace by the placeless language of technology and mobile financial systems. In the process of fabricating expert mechanical systems, the world is sanitised of the human dimension. Efficiency and human culture are a contradiction in terms.

The media are best understood as agents of acculturation because humans are fundamentally cultural beings. As creators, distributors, and users of culture, people live in a world of their own making. Rather than unidimensional definitions of the human species as *homo faber, homo economicus,* or *animale rationale,* the cultural character of our humanness illuminates both our dialogic composition as a species and the media-human relation.

HUMANS AS CULTURAL BEINGS

Humans are the one living species constituted by language. In mainstream epistemology since Locke and Descartes, the self is a "first-person-singular…disengaged from embodied agency and social embedding" (Taylor 1995: 59). In this view, human agents use language to engage the world outside or their fears and desires within. Meaning is explained in terms of the way things are depicted. The subject is first of all an "inner space — a mind, to use the old terminology, or a mechanism capable of processing representations". The I is the "centre of monological consciousness" (ibid: 60).

This view of the individuated subject separated from the representational domain has made deep inroads into the social sciences but "stands in the way of a richer and more adequate understanding of what the human sense of self is really like" (ibid: 60). Rather than seeing human agents as the locus of representations, our understanding itself is embodied. In traditional epistemology, all acts are monologic, though actions may be coordinated with others. However, when the lingual interpretation of ourselves and our experience constitutes who we are, human action is dialogic. Our experience is then understood largely in terms of rhythm with other nonindividuated actors. Humans are dialogic agents within a language community. Sociocultural systems precede their occupants and endure after them.

When the lingual is seen as the defining character of human beings, language refers in its broadest sense to the full range of symbolic forms. Since language expresses and constitutes us in our different dimensions and relations, no boundaries exist between the "symbolic-expressive creations of man: [prose], poetry, music, art, dance" and so forth (Taylor 1985: 233). Language's centre of gravity is best captured in the dynamic notion "symbol", the lingual does not primarily manifest a self but a world.

The symbolic motif established definitive form in an intellectual trajectory from Ferdinand de Saussure's *Course in General Linguistics* (1916) to Ernst Cassirer's four-volume *Philosophy of Symbolic Forms* (1953/1957/1996). For Cassirer, symbolisation is not merely the hallmark of human cognition, but defines us anthropologically.[1] He identified our unique capacity to generate symbolic structures as a radical alternative both to the *animale rationale* of classical Greece and Descartes' modernity and to the biological being of evolutionary naturalism. Arguing that the issues are fundamentally anthropological rather than epistemological *per se*, Cassirer's creative being is carved out against a reductionism to *intellectus* on one hand, and a naturalistic neurophysiology and biochemistry on the other.

In Cassirer's terms, humans have no static nature in itself, only history. We know ourselves through our symbolic cultural expressions. No inherent principle defines our metaphysical essence, nor is any inborn faculty or instinct ascertained by empirical observation. Rather than a philosophy of the human that is centred on overt manifestations of behaviour, the symbolic structure of human activities enables us to understand them as an organic whole. The main constituents of human work are language, myth, religion, art, science and history. And symbol is the bond that holds these human creations together.[2]

As compared with other animals, humans exist in a dimension of reality of their own making. They do not live in a merely physical universe nor confront reality face to face. The symbolic function enables human beings to create language and culture, and thus open up a new dimension of reality not accessible to other species. Humans have enveloped themselves in linguistic forms, artistic images, and religious rites, and cannot see nor know anything except through their own symbolic artifice. In Bruce Gronbeck's (2002) terms, classic Western dualism understands the social world as "both fundamentally animal and humanly cultured" whereas Cassirer and his legacy do not separate "the underlying animal from the overdwelling human".

The relationship of language to reality is much more complex than common sense assumes. Words do not merely transmit preexisting ideas and mirror real-world entities directly; but neither is language a random compilation of symbols. Language is not a transparent window on the world, but rather a map of it. "In order to find our way with a map we have to understand its own distinct codes, conventions, signs and symbols. A map organises, selects and renders coherent the innumerable sense impressions we might experience on the ground" (Hartley 1982: 15, see: 75-86). Language recapitulates reality just as a map does. Both maps and language collapse various elements together, enhance the importance of others and ignore some dimensions entirely.

As we reduce spatial luxuriance by maps, we impose organisation in all areas to serve human purposes. In the same formal sense that the alphabet organises the complex world of sound into a finite code, humans use lingual forms to endow their existence with order. We cannot look through language to determine what really occurred but live at those points where meaning is created in language. Language does not merely reflect reality from the outside; recomposing events into a narrative ensures that humans can comprehend reality at all.

Animale symbolicum contradicts at its roots the stimulus-response model in which stimuli are presumed to impact inert receptacles. Cassirer (1944) collapsed the hoary differences among human symbolic systems, placing music, art, philosophical essays, mathematics, religious language, and Bacon's scientific method on a level playing floor. James Carey (1989) described communication as a symbolic process the "ritual view". Rituals are ceremonies or sacraments through which we define meaning and purpose; they are events of celebration such as weddings and birthdays, and not merely exchanges of information.

The symbolic realm is intrinsic to the human species. From this perspective, communication is the symbolic process expressing human creativity and grounding cultural formation. Humans alone of living creatures possess the creative mind, the irrevocable ability to interpret and reconstruct. Realities called cultures are inherited and built from symbols that shape our action, identity, thoughts, and sentiment. Communication, therefore, is the creative process of building and reaffirming through symbols and culture signifies the constructions that result. Culture is the womb in which symbols are born and communication is the connective tissue in culture building. Symbol is the basic unit that carries meaning, thus anchoring the communicative capacity. The latter, in turn, is central to our humanity and humans are culture builders. Communication is the catalytic agent in cultural formation and its most explicit expressions are symbolic creations (communications phenomena) such as the dramatic arts, discourse, literature, and electronic entertainment.[3]

Words derive their meaning from the interpretive, historical context humans themselves supply. Language is the matrix of humanity; it is not privately nurtured and then made problematic when it enters the public sphere, as John Locke presumed (1894: book III). Defining us as cultural beings takes back our language and makes it inescapably communal, the public agent through which human identity is realised. The social and personal dimensions of language are woven into a unified whole.

Through the symbolic modality we experience epiphanal moments suspended outside our person, normative manifestations of compelling force though not grounded *a priori*. Thomas Nagel contends in his *View From Nowhere*, that as cultural beings we form an overriding conception of the world with us in it (1986: 4). We are contained within history and do not create ourselves from scratch. *Ergo*, humans consider it worthwhile to bring their values and beliefs "under the influence of an impersonal standpoint" even without proof that this more permanent vista is not illusory (ibid: 5). An independent reality, experienced phenomenologically, is from nowhere in particular, but we think it "natural to regard life and the world in this way" (ibid: 7). To seek its origin is philosophically uninteresting. Thus in describing our concrete situation, we appeal to the impersonal: "the truth is," "my dignity has been violated," "justice demands," "innocent victims," and so forth.

When defining humans as cultural beings, culture is understood as a created reality which establishes a meaningful cosmos; it is not just a derivative of social forces. In Paulo Freire's terms, it is our ontological vocation as creative subjects to act upon the world while being critical of it and transforming it to suit our purposes. Freire (1970) presumes an explicit anthropology, conceiving of humans as not only constructing the world but through symbols separating from it in their consciousness. Humans are able to adopt postures ranging from nearly undifferentiated spontaneous response, to a critical attitude which entails a conscious process of intervention, even objectifying themselves through existential experience. As with the cultural perspective generally, Freire sweeps epistemology into his anthropology. He declares that we understand reality when we get inside the self-in-relation. He presumes a symbolic paradigm with the radically human as the meaning-center.

MORAL AGENCY

Our self-understanding as cultural beings discriminates higher from lesser values. "To be a full human agent...is to exist in a space defined by distinctions of worth" (Taylor 1985: 3). In Charles Taylor's terms, we see ourselves against a background of "strong evaluation" where we characterise some practices or ideas as more worthy than others (Bowers 2002: 37-42). We make judgements about the quality of life. Some of these judgements are "given more authoritatively by the culture" than chosen by personal deliberation, but all are "incorporated into our self-understanding in some degree and fashion" (Taylor 1985: 3). Our humanness, understood culturally, means that we "exist inescapably in a space of ethical questions". We situate ourselves "relative to some goods, or standards of excellence, or obligations, that we cannot just repudiate". Our sense of who we are entails identifying "what are truly important issues, standards, goods, or demands" and making an assessment of where we "stand relative to these and/or measure up to them" (Taylor 1995: 58; cf. Taylor 1989: ch. 2).

Defining humans as cultural beings moves discourse from its Enlightenment home in cognition to an interpretive axis in values, beliefs, norms, the human spirit, that is, in culture. If the interpretive domain is lingual, then human bonds are not through reason nor action, but *hermeneia*.[4] The commonplace, "we're with you in spirit," is actually a powerful truth — that our species uniqueness is born along the stream of consciousness. I reasonate cross-culturally through my spirit with the moral imagination of others.[5] Our common humanity is not inscribed, first of all, in politics nor economics, nor in overcoming national boundaries by transportation or data. Our mutual humanness is actually an ethical commitment rooted in the moral domain all humans share.

If cultures are clusters of symbols that orient life and provide it significance, then cultural patterns are inherently normative. They constitute the human kingdom by organising reality and by indicating what we ought to do and avoid. Assuming that culture is the container of our symbolic capacity, the constituent parts of such containers are a society's values. As ordering relations, values direct the ends of societal practice and provide implicit standards for selecting courses of action. Our concern then is to articulate the ends communication should serve and the motives it should manifest. In this sense, communication's culture-forming task, normatively understood, is articulating the moral order.

For Robert Wuthnow, the moral order is a set of cultural elements with an identifiable symbolic structure. Wuthnow defines moral codes as cultural constructions that articulate "the nature of commitment to a particular course of behavior" (1987: 66). The nature of personal obligations and public responsibility continues to be addressed by philosophers under the rubric "moral standards," and as "moral development" by leading theorists (Carol Gilligan, 1982, for instance). Culturalists in sociology contribute fundamentally to this domain also by identifying the symbolic patterns humans create along the boundaries between moral objects and actual behaviour, the self and their roles, the intentional and the inevitable (Wuthnow op cit: 71-75). In Wuthnow's view, the content of these codes varies dramatically from fundamentalist religion to the market system, but explicit symbolic forms negotiating the boundaries "can be examined, not as a set of beliefs locked away in someone's head, but as a relatively observable set of cultural constructions" (ibid: 95). These constructs are the moral code which plays a role in human life comparable to that of instinct in the lower organisms. Therefore, in mass-mediated cultures aligned toward normlessness and illusive centers of textuality, the appropriate role for mass communication technologies is opening windows on the moral order.

A commitment to moral agency cannot escape the central antinomy in cultural theory, that is, the status of the notion of value. On the one hand, values appear as spontaneous activity, creatively or oppressively ordering our understanding of the human. On the other, values appear to have essential status, as mechanisms of orientation that are discovered and not constructed. Paul Ricoeur insists correctly that this problem of cultural life is an antinomy in the sense that both sides independently can be justified as self-evident.

Ricoeur (1986) attempts through a transcendental semiology to resolve the contradiction on a higher level of generality, but that project has proved inadequate. This leaves — at least for our purposes here — the values-as-discovered alternative. Foundationalist options are inconsistent with humans as cultural beings, representing as they do "idealist...speech situations...in which, unfortunately, no power circulates" (Hall 1989: 48). The understanding of cultural beings in this essay, however, represents a radically different approach to the values-as-discovered motif than does philosophical prescriptivism. History and culture are considered to be value-saturated phenomena (cf. Christians et al 1993: ch. 6). Transcendental criteria are shifted from a metaphysical plane to the horizon of everyday life and being, but transcendental norms they remain nonetheless. On this view, cultures are sets of symbols that organise the human kingdom and are, therefore, *ipso facto* evaluative. A culture's continued existence depends on identifying and defending its normative base. As Basil Mitchell (1980) maintains, the cultural ethos can be decisive without being exclusive. A determinate moral order is not dissolved in cultural phenomena.

SOCIETIES AS MORAL ENTITIES

With standards recognised as inherent in the concept of symbolic environments, we can begin putting content into the normative, asking what authentic social existence involves. Communities are knit together linguistically and because the lingual is not neutral but value-laden our social bonds are moral claims. Without allegiance to a web of ordering relations, society becomes, as a matter of fact, inconceivable. Words are concrete forms of life, whose meaning derives from an interpretive context that humans themselves supply. We negotiate the human order through language, but social entities are moral structures and not merely lingual orders.

The biological and moral grow up together. Children ascertain that, in general, "certain things belong to certain people" and as such they are "learning a partly moral fact...important to the structure of society" (Adams 1993: 93). They learn tolerance, for example — at least that physical assault is forbidden, though perhaps not sophisticated versions of tolerating various opinions. Sissela Bok (1995) calls these minimalist values, that is, a limited set of fundamental moral commitments that are necessary for collective survival. Minimalist moral values provide a basis for political dialogue and negotiation, but do not call for agreement as to their source or exceptionless character (ibid: 18-19, 53-59). The minimalist values "most easily recognised across societal boundaries" are the "positive duties of care and reciprocity; constraints on violence, deceit, and betrayal; and norms for procedures and standards of justice" (ibid: 41). Without a broad acceptance of such common values, or what appears to be a natural affinity for them, a viable social order is impossible. Without a framework broadly owned and roughly understood, resolution of practical issues and constructive theorising on particular matters is inconceivable.

As Robert Adams observes: "Every society must, and therefore will, have a shared morality; but…a shared ethical theory is not required for a common morality….No comprehensive ethical theory…is likely to meet with general agreement in any modern society that permits free inquiry" (1993: 93). The killing of human beings may be generally condemned, while disagreements rage at the same time over capital punishment, euthanasia, and justified warfare. All things being equal, societies are predisposed against lying while debating exceptions and theorising the nature and parameters of deception. The status of property is a complicated problem in social theory, while our ordinary moral obligations about other people's property are undisputed in everyday affairs.

Moral duty is nurtured by the demands of social linkage and not produced by theory. However, though the core of a society's common morality is pre-theoretical agreement, ethical theory is not useless or marginal in shaping the common good. Societies speak with divided voices and often in error. "What counts as common morality, indeed, is not only imprecise but variable…and a difficult practical problem" (ibid: 96). Ethical theory is primarily an effort to articulate moral obligations, within the fallible and irresolute voices of everyday life. Among disagreements and uncertainty, we look for criteria and wisdom in settling disputes and clarifying confusions. Although metaethics has been largely abstract and fragmented, normative theories of an interactive sort invigorate our common moral discourse. Even so, generally accepted theories are not necessary for common goods to prosper. The common good is not "the complete morality of every participant…but a set of agreements among people who typically hold other, less widely shared ethical beliefs" (ibid: 99).

Our references to moral matters involve the community. A self exists only within "webs of interlocution," and all self-interpretation implicitly or explicitly "acknowledges the necessarily social origin of any and all of their conceptions of the good and so of themselves" (Mulhall and Swift 1996: 112). Moral frameworks are as fundamental for orienting us in social space as the need to "establish our bearings in physical space" (ibid: 113; cf. Taylor 1989: 36).

> *Developing, maintaining, and articulating [our moral intuitions and reactions] is not something humans could easily or even conceivably dispense with.... We can no more imagine a human life that fails to address the matter of its bearings in moral space than we can imagine one in which developing a sense of up and down, right and left is regarded as an optional human task....Moral orientation is inescapable because the questions to which the framework provides answers are themselves inescapable (Mulhall and Swift op cit: 106-108).*

Alasdair MacIntyre (1988) may be correct in thinking that societies ought to share some moral goods — such as a conception of justice — that are developed theoretically enough to enable us to resolve conflicts through reasoned agreement rather than brute force. But instead of expecting more theoretical coherence than history warrants, Reinhold Niebuhr (1953) inspires us to work through inevitable social conflicts while maintaining "an untheoretical jumble of agreements" that provide a basic mutuality (Adams 1993: 107). Through a common morality of this sort we can approximate consensus on issues and settle disputes within democratic institutions.

MORAL LITERACY

Since our public life is not merely functional, but knit together by social values, moral literacy ought to be privileged as the media's mission. From this perspective, the media are challenged to participate in a community's process of moral evaluation. The possibility exists in principle. Taylor, for example, emphasises that moral judgements are capable of rational elucidation. Moral intuitions may appear to be instinctual, but "agents manifesting them are often capable of explaining just what it is about human beings that merits" reaction or involvement; "in other words, we articulate our intuitions by developing a particular ontology of the human" (Mulhall and Swift op cit: 103). The communal character of our moral interpretations enables the public media to come to grips with the common good.

Thus, the various technologies of public communication ought to engender moral literacy. If societies are moral orders, and not merely lingual structures, communications in the social arena ought to stimulate the moral imagination. This language often appears in a sanitised sense: for instanced: "Do these programmes have any redeeming social value?" To be a symbolically mature art form, television, for instance, ought to enable us to traverse the moral landscape. In this regard, investigative reporting has been deficient and news reporting ought to rectify it.

The hard-hitting stories, the investigative stories, lack a morally sensitive vocabulary. They don't talk about moral issues in moral terms. They go to great lengths to do what, in a morally technical language, might be called "objectifying morality" by taking moral claims and making them appear to be empirical claims (Glasser 1992: 44). The media ordinarily engage in language practices that legitimise existing structures of power. But moral literacy requires alternative discourses and subversive texts that struggle against consensus. On those invigorating occasions when the moral contours of the taken-for-granted world are illuminated, the news media enhance our social dialogue. From this perspective, journalism is obligated to appeal to listeners and readers about human values. Such inclusion furthers a community's ongoing process of moral evaluation by helping it penetrate through the political and economic surface to the moral dynamics underneath. Rather than merely providing readers and audiences with information, the press's aim is morally literate citizens.

In the mainstream advocacy model of public relations, organisations seek to dominate and control. The relational model, however, works in harmony with the audience, is committed to symmetrical interdependence, and promotes mutual understanding (see Gregory 2003: 9-12). From this perspective, the practice of public relations has a responsibility for the public good beyond its own self-interest. In contrast to partisan values and one-way propaganda, persuasive communication rooted in mutual values honors the audience's right to accurate information and participation in decisions that affect them. While increased visibility or profitability are immediate ends, listeners and viewers need "the freedom to make a voluntary choice" (Baker and Martinson 2001: 153). Rooted in respect for the public, professional persuasive communications must meet the same standard of truthfulness in the news and of authenticity in entertainment (ibid: 158-160). When there is "parity between the persuader and persuadee in terms of information, understanding and insight" (ibid: 165), then moral literacy comes into its own.[6]

Public life cannot be facilitated in technical terms only, but the moral dimension of issues needs to be represented in appropriately moral discourse. When journalists investigate government policies that are vacuous or unjust, they ought to do so in terms of common values that have broad acceptance in the community as a whole. Our widely shared moral intuitions —respect for the dignity of others, for instance — are developed through discourse within a community. In this sense media professionals participate in the citizens' process of moral articulation. Therefore, public texts must enable us "to discover truths about ourselves;" narratives ought to "bring a moral compass into readers' lives" by accounting for things that matter to them (Denzin 1997: 284; cf. 2003 ch. 5). Communities are woven together by narratives that invigorate their common understanding of good and evil, happiness and reward, the meaning of life and death. Recovering and refashioning moral discourse help to amplify our deepest humanness and provide the soil in which democracy can flourish.

Wherever one observes reenactments of purposeful history and justice, one sees the results of moral literacy. News can be considered redemptive when it serves as an instrument not of accommodation but of critique and social change. Despite unrelenting pressure from media commercialism, public broadcasting often resonates with a redemptive accent and stirs the human conscience. We all know stations and reporters who have refused infotainment and sought to awaken the civic conscience. Major league awards are still won by professionals in journalism who distinguish themselves for public service. Editorials have raised our consciousness of anti-semitism, and heightened our moral awareness of racism and gender discrimination. In the debate over the Iraqi invasion, the moral issues in terms of just war theory and pacifism emerged at various times in news and commentary. Affirmative action, environmental protection, health policy, global warming, gun control, incarceration, arms trade, and welfare reform raise moral conflicts that journalists have helped the public negotiate. Over time and across the media, one observes a redemptive glow on occasion in which the news, commentary, and documentaries have facilitated moral discernment by their insight into humankind as a distinctive species and by their affirmation of purposeful history.

Race in the 21st century United States remains a preeminent issue. In entertainment television overwhelmingly viewers see "media images of blacks on welfare, of black violence in local news, and of crude behavior — open sexuality and insolence....The habits of local news, for example, the rituals in covering urban crime, facilitate the construction of menacing imagery" (Entman and Rojecki 2000: 21). However, research demonstrates that the media committed to moral literacy can tip the balance away from suspicion and animosity, and enhance racial understanding among those most open to it (cf. Keeble 2001: ch. 6). Along these lines we redeem news and persuasion as agents of cultural formation. Building on their unique aesthetic capacities, they are empowered toward moral literacy by appealing to our conscience.

CONCLUSION

If we understand humans as cultural beings, we are not inclined to construct an apparatus of professional ethics. We work instead within the general morality. Rather than developing rules for experts, our preoccupation is the moral dimension of everyday life. Professionals committed to moral literacy do not establish codes of ethics for themselves, but reflect the same social and moral space as the citizens they report. How the moral order works itself out in community formation is the issue, not, first of all, what media practitioners by their own standards consider virtuous. The moral domain is understood to be intrinsic to human beings, not a system of rules, norms, and ideals external to society and culture.

Media practitioners are not constituted as ethical selves antecedently but moral discernment unfolds dialectically between reporter and citizen. Rather than searching for neutral principles to which all parties can appeal, professional guidelines rooted in the general morality rest on a complex view of moral judgements. They are seen as a composite that integrates everyday experience, beliefs about the good, and feelings of approval and shame into an organic whole. This is a philosophical approach that situates the moral domain within the general purposes of life that people share contextually in their personal and social relations. Ideally, it engenders a new normative core for responsible reporting.

The ultimate standard for media professionals is not role-specific ethical principles but the general morality. The mass media are institutions of power while decisions and policies can be self-serving, and practitioners defensive when criticised. Competition and careerism often cloud the application of professional codes or ethical guidelines. Journalists may have an understanding with sources that all information will be treated confidentially, for example, and then change their mind when they come under severe pressure and conclude that the public has a right to know this privileged material. Whereas we agree in the general morality that we ought to keep our promises, in this case canons of professional practice allow self-defined exceptions for the journalist as expert.

A preoccupation with privilege and authority cuts the media loose from the very public they are meant to serve. For journalism, objectivity rooted in the prestige of science has fueled the status of specialised expertise in the mainstream press. On the other hand, the concept of humans as cultural beings presumes that facts and values are intermixed rather than dichotomous. Given the moral dimension intrinsic to the social order, interpreting its various configurations sufficiently means elaborating the moral component. To resonate intelligently with people's values means that media workers know the general morality which they share with the public at large. Rather than developing internal standards oriented to professional privilege, the challenge for media practitioners is the moral life as a whole: no harm to innocents, truth-telling, reparations for wrong actions, beneficence, gratitude, honouring contracts, human dignity. Moral literacy understands moral behavior in interactive terms, with reporters, advertising executives, script writers and producers and public relations practitioners operating in the same arena as citizens themselves.

NOTES

1   Cassirer's Philosophy of Symbolic Forms was the label he used in describing his work. His monograph summarising this work he titled *An Essay on Man* (1944). Cassirer saw modern philosophy as a progressive formulation of neo-Kantian thinking. But his neo-Kantianism considers the noumenal world as a limiting concept, rather than, as did Kant, an existent, though unknowable realm. Reality is for Cassirer a "construct of the mind" rather than another domain. The phenomenal world is the arena of ideas. Neo-Kantianism in Cassirer is anti-metaphysical; it is typically called "phenomenalistic idealism" as opposed to Kant's metaphysical idealism.

2   Symbolism as a special endowment of the human species, to the exclusion of other organic beings and their sign-language is a fundamental question that is not resolved in Cassirer and of paramount importance today. His basic task in the Philosophy of Symbolic Forms is to trace the evolution of cultural symbols from early history to modern times, where he focuses on the origin and role of language in homosapiens. He does not deal with the metaphysical aspects of the issue, while arguing that there is no conclusive proof that any animal has ever made the decisive step to propositional language, that is, advancing from direct or indirect responses to propositions.

3   As with Jacob Burckhardt (1943), this essay appropriates a semiotic definition, which stands in contrast to anthropology where culture refers to entire civilizations as complex wholes, and in contrast to common parlance where culture is identified as refined manners. Most definitions of culture are expansive, encompassing under the term virtually all social activity. Culture thus involves technologies, customs, arts, sciences, products, habits, political and social organisations that characterise a people. The semiotic definition distinguishes culture from political and social structures, from direct efforts to understand nature (such as chemistry, physics, astronomy), and from

religious institutions. Culture thus becomes essentially human communicative activities, and refers primarily to the products of language and the arts.

4   *Hermeneia* (interpretation, the interpretive process or domain) and its cognates appear in such familiar ancients as Plutarch, Xenophon, Euripedes, Longinus, Epircurus, and Lucretius. Plato develops the concept as the art of interpretation in his *Seventh Letter*. Aristotle in the *Nicomachean Ethics* locates it in the moral domain as distinct from theoretical knowledge (*episteme*), and defines *hermeneia* as self-knowledge governing moral action. Aristotle's understanding is used here. What he identifies in the classical period is considered in this essay as a condition of our humanness.

5   Out of an African philosophical perspective, Kwasi Wiredu (1996) develops the implications for ethics from the thesis that the human species lives by language. He observes that all languages are similar in their phonemic complexity and all languages serve not merely foundational roles but cultural formation. Through language people everywhere arbitrate their values and establish their identities. Through the commonness we share as lingual beings, we can believe that there are cross-cultural universals at the same time as we live in particular communities.

6   For elaboration of how humans-as-cultural-beings applies to public relations, see Wilkins and Christians (2001).

REFERENCES

Adams, Robert M. (1993) "Religious Ethics in a Pluralistic Society", *Prospects for a Common Morality*, Outka, G. and Reeder, J.P. (eds), Princeton NJ, Princeton University Press, pp 93-113

Baker, Sherry, and Martinson, David L. (2001) "The TARES Test: Five Principles for Ethical Persuasion", *Journal of Mass Media Ethics*, 16 (2-3) pp 148-175

Bok, Sissela (1995) *Common Values,* London and Columbia, University of Missouri Press

Bowers, Peggy (2002) "Charles Taylor's Practical Reason", *Moral Engagement in Public Life: Theorists for Contemporary Ethics*, Bracci, S. and Christians, C. (eds.), New York, Peter Lang pp. 35-52

Burckhardt, Jacob C. (1943) *Force and Freedom: Reflections on History*, New York, Pantheon

Carey, James W. (1989) *Communication as Culture: Essays on Media and Society*, Boston, Unwin Hyman

Cassirer, Ernst (1944) *An Essay on Man: An Introduction to the Philosophy of Human Culture,* New Haven, CT, Yale University Press

Cassirer, Ernst (1953-57, 1996) *Philosophy of Symbolic Forms,* trans. R. Manheim and J.M. Krois, Vols. 1-4, New Haven, CT, Yale University Press (orig. 1923-1929)

Christians, Clifford, Ferre, John, and Fackler, Mark (1993) *Good News: Social Ethics and the Press,* New York, Oxford University Press

Denzin, Norman (1997) *Interpretive Ethnography: Interpretive Practices for the 21st Century*, Thousand Oaks, CA, Sage

Denzin, Norman (2003) *Performance Ethnography: Critical Pedagogy and the Politics of Culture*, Thousand Oaks, CA, Sage

de Saussure, Ferdinand (1959) *Course in General Linguistics,* trans. W. Baskin, New York, Harper and Row (orig. 1916)

Ellul, Jacques (1964) *The Technological Society,* trans. J. Wilkinson, New York, Vintage

Ellul, Jacques (1965) *Propaganda: The Formation of Men's Attitudes,* trans. K. Keller, New York, Alfred A. Knopf

Ellul, Jacques (1978) "Symbolic Function, Technology and Society", *Journal of Social and Biological Structure,* October pp 207-218

Entman, Robert M. and Rojecki, Andrew (2000) *The Black Image in the White Mind: Media and Race in America,* Chicago, University of Chicago Press

Freire, Paulo (1970) *Pedagogy of the Oppressed*, New York, Seabury Press

Gilligan, Carol (1982) *In a Different Voice: Psychological Theory and Women's Development*, Cambridge, MA, Harvard University Press

Glasser, Theodore L. (1992) "Squaring with the Reader: A Seminar on Journalism", *Kettering Review*, Winter, 44

Gregory, Anne (2003, February) "Public Relations and the Age of Spin," discussion paper, Institute for Communication Ethics Conference, London

Gronbeck, Bruce (2002) Email to mediaecology, 2/23/02

Hall, Stuart (1989) "Ideology and Communication Theory", *Rethinking Communication. Vol 1: Paradigm Issues,* Dervin, Brenda, et al. (eds), Newbury Park, CA, Sage pp 40 - 52

Hartley, John (1982) *Understanding News*, London, Methuen

Keeble, Richard (2001) *Ethics for Journalists*, London, Routledge

Locke, John (1894) *An Essay Concerning Human Understanding.* Oxford, Clarendon Press. (orig. 1690)

MacIntyre, Alasdair (1988) *Whose Justice? Which Rationality?* Notre Dame, IN, University of Notre Dame Press

Mitchell, Basil (1980) *Morality: Religious and Secular*, Oxford, Clarendon Press

Mulhall, Stephen and Swift, Adam (1996) *Liberals and Communitarians,* 2nd ed., Oxford, Blackwell

Nagel, Thomas (1986) *The View from Nowhere*, New York, Oxford University Press

Niebuhr, Reinhold (1953) *Christian Realism and Political Problems*, New York, Charles Scribner's Sons

Ricouer, Paul (1967) "The Antinomy of Human Reality and the Problem of Philosophical Anthroplogy", *Readings in Existential Phenomenology,* Lawrence, N. and O'Connor, D. (eds), Englewood Cliffs, NJ, Prentice-Hall pp. 390-401

Ricouer, Paul (1973) "Ethics and Culture: Habermas and Gadamer in Dialogue", *Philosophy Today*, 17 pp 153-165

Ricouer, Paul (1986) *Fallible Man*, trans. C. A. Kelbley, 2nd ed, New York, Fordham University Press

Taylor, Charles (1985) *Human Agency and Language*: Philosophical Papers, vol. 1, Cambridge, Cambridge University Press

Taylor, Charles (1989) *Sources of the Self: The Making of the Modern Identity,* Cambridge, MA, Harvard University Press

Taylor, Charles (1995) "The Dialogical Self", *Rethinking Knowledge: Reflections Across the Disciplines,* Goodman, Robert and Fisher, Walter (eds), Albany, State University of New York Press pp 57-66

Wiredu, Kwasi (1996) *Cultural Universals and Particulars: An African Perspective,*

Bloomington, Indiana University Press
Wilkins, Lee and Christians, Clifford (2001) "Philosophy Meets the Social Sciences: The Nature of Humanity in the Public Arena", *Journal of Mass Media Ethics*, 16 (2-3) pp 99-120
Wuthnow, Robert (1987) *Meaning and Moral Order: Explorations in Cultural Analysis*, Berkeley, University of California Press

Clifford Christians is Professor of Media Studies, Journalism and Research at the Institute of Communications at the University of Illinois-Urbana, Champaign. He received his PhD. in Social Communication and served as director 1987-2001. He is co-author of *Responsibility in Mass Communication* (3rd. ed., 1980), *Good News: Social Ethics and the Press* (Oxford, 1993), and *Media Ethics: Cases and Moral Reasoning* (6th ed., 2001). He is co-editor of *Jacques Ellul: Interpretive Essays* (1981), *Communication Ethics and Universal Values* (1997), and *Moral Engagement in Public Life: Theorists for Contemporary Ethics* (2002). He is editor of *The Ellul Forum* and former editor of *Critical Studies in Mass Communication*. He has been a visiting scholar in philosophical ethics at Princeton University, in social ethics at the University of Chicago, and a PEW fellow in ethics at Christ Church-Oxford University. On the faculty of the University of Illinois since 1974, he has won five teaching awards. He has lectured or given academic papers in 25 countries, and is listed in *Outstanding Scholars of the 21st Century (Ethics)*, *Who's Who in America*, and *International Who's Who in Education*.

Ethical work practices, communication and organisational commitment
Ethics as the ordinary embodiment of organisational identity

Paul R. Jackson

Companies seek to protect themselves against harmful consequences of unethical behaviour through implementing ethical codes of conduct despite weak evidence that such codes are effective. For such codes to have any impact they need to be enacted within the day-to-day routine of the organisation, as part of the psychological contract between the organisation and its employees. This chapter explores the link between managers' everyday ethical work practices and the commitment that employees give to their organisation, and emphasises the importance of open and honest management communication strategies. Data from a survey of 640 employees at a UK steel plant were used to test relationships between role conflict (contradictions among work role demands), role ambiguity (lack of clarity about what is expected of workers and how their performance is judged) and autonomy on the one hand and employees' organisational commitment on the other. Strong relationships were found between them, and these were strongly mediated by whether managers were believed to be acting fairly. Fairness, in turn, was a strong predictor of trust in management. On the other hand, lack of clarity about what managers expect of workers and how they judge performance can lead to conflicts. The findings show a strong chain of inference from managers' decision-making processes to perceived fairness to trust to organisational commitment. If managers want employees to commit themselves to their employer, they must act and communicate ethically and earn their trust.

Keywords: ethical communication, trust, organisational commitment, fairness, psychological contract

This chapter explores some of the linkages between ordinary work practices within organisations and their consequences for employees and, indirectly, therefore for the organisation itself. Implicit in the point of view presented here is an instrumental view of the relationship between organisations and their employee stakeholders as argued convincingly by Jones (1995). He says: "Firms that contract (through their managers) with their stakeholders on the basis of mutual trust and cooperation will have a competitive advantage over firms that do not" (p. 422). Evidence in support of the general proposition that unethical and illegal behaviour harms companies comes from numerous examples in the business press. For example, Schwartz (2001) cites the fraud which led to the collapse of Barings Bank, racial discrimination at Texaco, and the poisonous leak that killed thousands living around the Union Carbide chemical plant at Bhopal.

One of the commonest ways in which companies seek to protect themselves against such risks is through the implementation of ethical codes of conduct in which the importance of ethical communication strategies is stressed. These codes are now widely prevalent, at least in large companies; but the evidence for their effectiveness in influencing the actions and decisions of employees is equivocal at best. Schwartz reviewed 19 studies, and found a tenuous link between the presence of an ethical code within an organisation and the ethical behaviour of employees. Less than half (8 out of 19) of the studies found that ethical codes were effective; two studies found a weak relationship; while almost half (9 out of 19) found no significant relationship between the presence of codes and employee behaviour. Clearly then, the presence of an ethical code alone cannot guarantee ethical behaviour from employees. However finely crafted and widely publicised, words in a document may not reflect business practices. For codes to be effective, in the words of Fritz et al. (1999: 290), they must be "articulated by the organisation in its day-to-day routine activities".

Most approaches to thinking about ethical work practices and their consequences have started from the idea of a contract between organisations and their stakeholders (e.g. Donaldson and Preston 1995; Jones op cit). Central to a contract is a set of commitments and obligations on both sides, and such contracts may be either specified in writing as the basis for an agreement between two or more parties, or be informal and unwritten. These informal contracts have been conceptualised as *psychological contracts* (Rousseau 1995) and consist of "the beliefs employees hold regarding the terms of the informal exchange agreement between themselves and their organisations" (Turnley and Feldman 1999: 897). So-called violations of the psychological contract occur when employees see imbalances in the exchange relationship, particularly when they see themselves receiving less than they were promised. In such circumstances, it has been argued (e.g. Rousseau op cit) that employees will act to restore equity, either by reducing what they give or seeking to increase what they get.

A well-known taxonomy for these actions distinguishes two dimensions of active versus passive responses and positive versus negative responses (see Farrell 1983; Hirschman 1970) which combine to give four types of response. The responses are: *exit*, which involves leaving the organisation altogether, and *neglect*, which involves reduced effort relative to the requirements of the work role, or increased absenteeism and lateness; *loyalty,* engaging in activities outside the immediate role, such as positively defending the organisation to outsiders, and *voice*, taking the initiative with more senior management to improve conditions. Turnley and Feldman (op cit) found strong evidence of a relationship between perceived psychological contract violation and all four types of behaviours. Strongest effects were found for exit and loyalty, and the authors suggest that these responses are relatively safer because attempts to leave or decreased loyalty can be invisible to other employees while voice and neglect are likely to be much more visible to supervisors and co-workers. This study, then, provides evidence that unethical behaviour on the part of managers, in terms of unmet promises to employees, results in employee actions which can harm the company.

One of the responses outlined by Farrell (op cit) is a reduction in employee loyalty to the company and van Dyne et al. (1984) have examined a similar set of ideas from a different perspective, that of the extent to which employees are willing to engage in behaviours which go beyond the immediate requirements of their work roles, *organisational citizenship*. They found evidence for the role of a number of antecedents of organisational citizenship behaviours. Among these was the presence of a two-way covenantal relationship, which they see as a special kind of relational psychological contract "based on commitment to the welfare of both parties to the exchange and is also based on values" (ibid: 769). Two important features of the covenantal relationship are that they are reciprocal (involving support of employees by the organisation, as well as commitment to the organisation by employees) and that they involve an internalisation of organisational values. Covenantal relationship was assessed by combining together a measure of the management's support for employees and a measure of the employees' commitment to the organisation. In a large-scale study, they found a strong relationship between the presence of a covenantal relationship and employees' organisational citizenship behaviours.

THE CONCEPT OF THE ETHICAL WORK CLIMATE

The concept of ethical work climate summarises the shared assumptions within organisations about how things are done. A number of studies have used the Victor and Cullen (1988) Ethical Climate Questionnaire to assess typical modes of organisational ethical decision-making. This assesses: benevolence towards others, compliance with legal and professional standards and with company rules and procedures, and regard for individuals' egoistic interests as well as for their own moral and ethical beliefs. Using this scale, Barnett and Schubert (2002) found a correlation between ethical work climate and the presence of covenantal relationships. Fritz et al. (op cit) also examined aspects of ethical work climate and found that organisational commitment was predicted most strongly by managerial adherence to organisational standards. Finally, Valentine and Barnett (2002) showed that perceptions of corporate ethical values and the organisation's ethical environment were strongly correlated with employee organisational commitment.

As well as direct relationships between ethical work climate and employee actions, there is also evidence that the climate of an organisation provides a powerful context within which employees decide whether to act on the basis of their personal beliefs. Barnett and Vaicys (2000) looked at the link between individuals' own ethical beliefs and intention to act on them, as a function of the ethical climate of the organisation. They found a stronger link between the two when respondents perceived their organisation as having a low climate of social responsibility (i.e. a consideration of the consequences of actions for others outside the organisation). In other words, the effect of a strong social responsibility climate is to lead individuals to base their behaviour on those values rather than on their individual beliefs – in such circumstances, individuals who themselves do not see morally questionable behaviour as unethical are less likely to act on their beliefs.

Taken together, the literature reviewed above provides strong evidence in support of some aspects of Jones' proposition (op cit) that ethical organisational practices have beneficial consequences. The study presented here contributes further to that literature by its central focus on trust in management – and the ethical communication of that trust. A model is tested which considers both *antecedents* of trust in job characteristics and role enactments and also *consequences* of trust as employee commitment to the organisation. The analysis reported below uses data gathered as part of a larger programme of research on organisational interventions to promote good work design, funded by the UK Health and Safety Executive (Jackson and Parker 2001; Parker et al. 1998).

EMPIRICAL STUDY – METHOD

The research site – Hi-Steel
Hi-Steel was a mini-mill set up in 1972 as the European subsidiary of a North American company. The plant was the main employer in the region around the plant (50 per cent of homes are dependent on the company). It was easy for the company to recruit and retain staff, turnover was low, and pay levels were high relative to the local labour market. Hi-Steel had adopted a high-involvement form of work design for employees, based on a number of elements. Drastic delayering meant that seven job grades were reduced to three technician grades and job demarcations were removed. Work designs were enriched and teamworking was developed, such that shopfloor workers had much greater responsibility, with high work demands but also a high degree of autonomy.

Single staff status for all was introduced: an annualised payment system and no extra pay for overtime; no clocking of hours worked; private health insurance for employees and their families, full salary for the first six months of sickness; an improved injury compensation package; and the introduction of a staff assistance programme. A gain-share system had been implemented some years earlier, within which payments were not linked to individual performance but rather to the performance of the company as a whole. There was also an annual appraisal for all staff, using clear and transparent criteria rigidly applied to all staff, regardless of individual responsibility.

In many ways, therefore, the work practices adopted by senior management communicated a message of trust in the workforce and commitment to them, consistent with the concept of covenantal relationship described above. The survey set out to examine some of these work design features, and also to assess the fairness of management decision making processes. Together, these indicate how management's ethical values are enacted through their day-to-day practices.

Measures
Procedural fairness was measured by six items. Example items are: "Decisions are based on accurate information" and "Decisions are

consistent, based on standard procedures" (reverse scored). The coefficient alpha index of scale reliability was 0.85.

Distributive fairness was measured by four items based on the scale of Price and Mueller (1986), reflecting the allocation of rewards to individuals relative to their inputs and to the rewards of others. The items were: "I am fairly rewarded by the company given the responsibilities", "Compared to others, I am well rewarded for the amount of effort I put into my job", "Compared to others, I am fairly rewarded for the work I have done well" and "Compared to the past, I am fairly rewarded for what I do". The coefficient alpha index of scale reliability was 0.87.

Five items were used to assess the extent of employees' *trust in management*. The items were: "Managers have an open and honest style", "Management always act on decisions they make", "I can be open with management about my thoughts and feelings", "Managers deal with mistakes in a non-threatening manner", and "By their actions, management show they believe people are the company's most valuable asset". The coefficient alpha index of scale reliability was 0.84.

Team leader support was assessed through five items reflecting a supportive supervisory style. Respondents were asked whether their team leader: "is friendly and approachable", "puts suggestions made by the team into operation", "makes sure I get the help I need to work effectively", "offers new ideas for solving job-related problems" and "encourages people to exchange opinions and ideas". The coefficient alpha index of scale reliability was 0.85.

Employee *job control* was measured by combining together scores on the two task control scales devised by Jackson et al. (1993). The timing control scale (six items) measures the extent to which employees have discretion over when they perform work tasks: work scheduling, the timing of starting and stopping tasks. The method control scale (four items) measures the extent to which employees can control the methods they use in carrying out their work. The coefficient alpha index of scale reliability was 0.89.

Role conflict was measured by a 10-item scale from Rizzo et al. (1970) which covered the extent to which employees were faced with dealing with contradictory work demands. The conflicts included: having to break company rules in order to complete a work assignment, conflicts between instructions from different people, and conflicts between different work criteria (for example quality and meeting work targets). The coefficient alpha index of scale reliability was 0.88.

Role clarity was measured by an eight-item scale by Sawyer (1992) which asked employees how clear they were about work goals (work objectives, duties and responsibilities), working procedures, and performance criteria. Responses were recorded on a 6-point scale from *very unclear* (1) to *very clear* (6). The coefficient alpha index of scale reliability was 0.86.

Organisational commitment was assessed using the 9-item scale developed by Cook and Wall (1980). This scale includes items assessing primarily the strength of employees' affective ties to the organisation. Example items are: "I am proud to be able to tell people who it is I work for" and "I would not recommend a close friend to join Hi-Steel" (reverse scored). The coefficient alpha index of scale reliability was 0.86.

Survey procedure

The survey instrument for this company was developed by a project management group consisting of members of the university research team, with 15 members drawn from all levels of the organisation and a variety of functional areas (including direct production, maintenance, and office and administrative support). Questionnaires were administered by independent researchers to groups of employees, and consent to take part in the survey was obtained after the research team explained the purpose of the survey. Employees were given time off during their normal working day to complete the questionnaires in a room away from their production area. Before the employees completed the questionnaires, they were briefed in groups of between 10 and 20 people about the background to the relationship between the researchers and the company, the development and the content of the questionnaire and the intended use of the results. Confidentiality was assured and completed questionnaires were removed from the study site for processing. Feedback was provided on the main findings of the survey to all employees who took part. The sample for this study consisted of the 642 employees from all levels who took part in the survey (response rate of 72%).

RESULTS

The origins of employee commitment to Hi-Steel: the importance of accurate information

Procedural fairness – Hi-Steel was seen to base its decisions on accurate information, to give feedback on the implementation of decisions and to clarify decisions where necessary.

Distributive fairness – there was a clear link between effort and rewards at Hi-Steel. For example, 44% at Hi-Steel reported that rewards were distributed fairly given people's responsibilities *quite a bit* or *a great deal*. Having said that, there were down-sides to the rigidly applied performance management system. For example, one of the performance criteria on which individuals were rated was accidents, even if the person was not to blame. The policy was defended by a senior manager in these terms: "It was hard luck if an employee was innocently involved in a works accident, or he could not attend work because he rushed his wife into hospital to have a baby. As it was a new system, the definition had to be precise and assessment absolutely consistent to all."

The benefits for employees of the HR strategy in terms of pay and job security were clear (see Jackson and Parker op cit; Parker et al. op cit). However, there were costs associated with the process whereby Hi-Steel implemented their high-involvement strategy. They used a coercive "top-down" management style, where threat was a prominent part of the change process. As a result of this way of working, employees reported very low levels of trust in management. Only 22% of respondents agreed that managers have an open and honest style, and even fewer (19%) agreed that managers at Hi-Steel deal with mistakes in a non-threatening manner.

Role conflict at Hi-Steel seems to be quite high, with potential for dangerous consequences. More than half of employees (52%) said they sometimes had to break a rule in order to carry out an assignment, and 62% said they sometimes had to trade-off the demands for quality against other demands. There also seems to be a high level of conflicting demands from different people: 48% said their team leader or supervisor sent them conflicting messages about what is important; and 76% said they sometimes had to do things which were likely to be accepted by one person and not by others. These responses to individual questions were backed up by comments written by respondents at the end of the questionnaires.

The impact of these practices seems on employees' *commitment to the company* seems clear. Less than half of respondents (49%) agreed they were proud to tell people who they worked for, compared with a range of equivalent responses from 33% to 85% from other companies – reported in Parker et al. (op cit); and 43% said they had sometimes felt like leaving their job for good.

Regression analysis

The model of antecedents and consequences of trust was tested by a series of five multiple regression analyses taking each dependent variable in turn. Summary results are shown for each regression analysis in Table 1, and

Table I. Results of multiple regression analyses, standardised regression weights (n = 462)

	Procedural fairness	Distributive fairness	Trust in management	Team leader supportiveness	Organisational commitment
Job control	.17 **	.10 *	.15 **	.01	.22 **
Role conflict	-.29 **	-.10 *	-.15 **	-.04	-.02
Role clarity	.32 **	.22 **	.03	.10	.07
Procedural fairness	-	-	.49 **	.37 **	.00
Distributive fairness	-	-	.13 **	.15 **	.11 **
Trust in management	-	-	-	-	.46 **
Team leader supportiveness	-	-	-	-	.08

$* p < .05; ** p < .01.$

Table 2 shows how the correlations between organisational commitment and each predictor variable in the model are partitioned into direct and indirect effects.

Looking at antecedents first of all, job control and role conflict and clarity are all significant predictors of both *procedural* and *distributive fairness*. Employees with greater autonomy in the conduct of their work report higher levels of fairness in the process of decision making and in the ways in which rewards are allocated. Greater procedural and distributive fairness are also associated with lower role conflict and greater clarity in role requirements.

Turning to the predictors of *trust in management* (column 3 of Table 1), four out of the five predictors in the model framework are significant. Trust in management is higher among workers with greater autonomy in their jobs; contradictory role requirements reduce trust in management; and higher levels of both procedural and distributive fairness are associated with higher trust in management. While role clarity is not a significant direct predictor of trust in management, the extent of ambiguity in work roles does have an important indirect impact on trust (see Table 2b), especially through procedural fairness. Workers faced with ambiguous role requirements, where they are not clear about what is expected of them or how their performance will be judged, see the process of decision making as unfair and

Table 2. Direct and indirect effects of predictors

a) organisational commitment

	Direct effect	Total indirect effects
Job control	.22 **	.41 **
Role conflict	-.02	-.16 **
Role clarity	.07	.14 **
Procedural fairness	.00	.25 **
Distributive fairness	.11 **	.07
Trust in management	.46 **	-
Team leader supportiveness	.08	-

b) trust in management

	Direct effect	Total indirect effects
Job control	.15 **	.10
Role conflict	-.15**	-.16 **
Role clarity	.03	.18 **

c) team leader support

	Direct effect	Total indirect effects
Job control	.01	.08 *
Role conflict	-.04	-.12 **
Role clarity	.10	.15 **

* p < .05; ** p < .01.

this in turn reduces their trust in management.

Team leader support was included in the model as a plausible mediator of senior management decision making: team leaders, supervisors and middle managers are typically the ones with direct contact with lower level workers and are the channel for transmitting management decisions. The findings in column four of Table 1 are rather puzzling at first sight in that the only significant predictors of perceived support are the two fairness measures. However, Table 2c shows that job control and the two indices of role characteristics are important predictors, but that their effects are indirect rather than direct. Job autonomy, role conflict and role clarity influence both procedural and distributive fairness, as described above, and both fairness measures in turn predict team leader support. The major impact of job and role requirements on team leader support is thus mediated by perceptions of fairness in how decisions are made and in the distribution of rewards based on those decisions.

The major predictor of employee *commitment to the organisation* is the extent of their trust in management, and the other significant predictors are job control and distributive fairness. Higher commitment to the organisation is reported by employees who trust their management, have greater autonomy in their work, and believe that rewards for performance are distributed equitably. Table 2a shows that the other predictors in the model are also important, but their effects are indirect rather than direct. High levels of role conflict reduce perceptions of fairness (especially procedural fairness), erode trust in management, and thereby reduce organisational commitment. Ambiguity in work roles (low levels of role clarity) has a similar indirect effect on organisational commitment.

CONCLUSIONS

The findings of this study are important in a number of ways. Employee commitment has been shown to depend on a number of factors, the most important of which is the extent to which employees trust their management. Of course, the distribution of economic rewards (measured by distributive fairness) is also important in a company where employee pay depends both on their own efforts and on their contribution to the profitability of the company as a whole (through the gainshare scheme).

The study also shows a number of important ways in which management trust can be fostered or eroded. The biggest factor in promoting trust is whether employees see managers acting in a fair way through their decision making processes and how they communicate those decisions. Senior management said that they recognised the importance of open and transparent procedures and criteria for decision making and applying them fairly. However, employees in many areas of the company told us that whatever management say, their actions belied their espoused commitment to fairness and openness. Their actions often just did not match up to their talk, and this is reflected perhaps most clearly in the effects of role conflict on trust and commitment indirectly through fairness.

Senior managers articulated very clearly how they wanted the company to be, reflecting a rhetoric of trust, mutual commitment and high expectations. However, the imperatives of business priorities seemed to lead them often to ask workers to compromise company values to achieve urgent work targets. Many workers reported that they were sometimes asked to do things that were against their better judgement or were given contradictory instructions by different people.

Lack of clear communication and ambiguity in work role requirements is also a powerful factor in eroding trust in management and commitment in the organisation, and its impact is indirect rather than direct. Ambiguity in what is required of employees and in how their performance will be judged breeds a sense of unfairness in how things are done and how decisions are made. This perceived unfairness in turn impacts on trust and commitment.

The role of job autonomy is an interesting one, in that the relationship to trust and commitment is likely to a dual one. First of all, workers with more autonomy have more options to define their proximal work environment and thereby have greater influence over the enactment of business decisions. It is likely therefore that they can be influential actors in the construction of fairness, rather than simply passive recipients of the actions of others. Autonomy has another implication though, in that it represents management "giving away" their power, at least in part. As such, empowerment of workers by granting them greater autonomy is an indictor of management trust in employees – one part of the covenantal relationship discussed by Turnley and Feldman (op cit) and van Dyne et al. (op cit).

There are, of course, multiple determinants of employees' commitment to their employing organisation and this study has considered only some of them. What we find though is that there are powerful consequences of management failure to adopt decision making practices which are consistent with their espoused values. Ethical work practices embodying respect for the welfare of employee stakeholders are not an optional, "nice" element of the conduct of business. Rather, the ways in which day-to-day business is conducted reflect the enacted identity of the organisation with powerful consequences for the willingness of employees to commit to it. Companies need employees to be committed to them, and one way to achieve this commitment is through behaving ethically. This study has teased out some of the antecedents and consequences of such ethical practice – and highlighted the importance of open, transparent communication processes.

REFERENCES

Barnett, Tim and Schubert, Elizabeth (2002) "Perceptions of the ethical work climate and covenantal relationships", *Journal of Business Ethics* 36 pp 279-290

Barnett, Tim and Vaicys, Cheryl (2000) "The moderating effect of individuals' perceptions of ethical work climate on ethical judgments and behavioral intentions", *Journal of Business Ethics* 4 No 27 pp 351-362

Cook, John D. and Wall, Toby D. (1980) "New work attitude measures of trust, organisational commitment and personal need non-fulfilment", *Journal of Occupational Psychology* 53 pp 39-52

Donaldson, Thomas and Preston, Lee E. (1995) "The stakeholder theory of the corporation: Concepts, evidence and implications", *Academy of Management Journal* 20 pp 65-91

Farrell, Dan (1983) "Exit, voice, loyalty, and neglect as responses to job satisfaction: A multidimensional scaling study", *Academy of Management Journal* 26 pp 596-607

Fritz, J. M. Harden, Arnett, R. C. and Conkel, M. (1999) "Organisational ethical standards and organisational commitment", *Journal of Business Ethics* 20 pp 289-299

Hirschman, Albert O. (1970) *Exit, voice and loyalty: Responses to decline in firms, organizations, and states*, Cambridge, MA, Harvard University Press

Jackson, Paul R. and Parker, Sharon K. (2001) *Change in manufacturing: How to manage stress-related risks*, London, HSE Publications

Jackson, Paul R, Wall, Toby D, Martin, Robin, and Davids, Keith (1993) "New measures of job control, cognitive demand and production responsibility", *Journal of Applied Psychology* 78 pp 753-762

Jones, Thomas M. (1995) "Instrumental stakeholder theory: A synthesis of ethics and economics", *Academy of Management Review* 2 No 20 pp 404-437

Parker, S. K, Jackson, P. R, Sprigg, C. A. and Whybrow, A. C. (1998) *Organisational interventions to reduce the impact of poor work design*, London, HSE Publications

Price, James L. and Mueller, Charles W. (1986) *Handbook of organisational measurement*, Marchfield, MA, Pittman

Rizzo, John, House, Robert J. and Lirtzman, Sidney I. (1970) "Role conflict and ambiguity in complex organisations", *Administrative Science Quarterly* 15 pp 150-163

Rousseau, Denise M. (1995) *Psychological contracts in organisations: Understanding written and unwritten agreements*, Thousand Oaks, California, Sage Publications

Sawyer, John E. (1992) "Goal and process clarity: Specification of multiple constructs of role ambiguity and a structural equation model of their antecedents and consequences", *Journal of Applied Psychology* 2 No 77 pp 130-142

Schwartz, Mark S. (2001) "The nature of the relationship between corporate codes of ethics and behaviour", *Journal of Business Ethics* 32 pp 247-262

Turnley, William H. and Feldman, Daniel C. (1999) "The impact of psychological contract violations on exit, voice, loyalty, and neglect", *Human Relations* 7 No 52 pp 895-922

Valentine, Sean and Barnett, Tim (2002) "Ethics codes and sales professionals' perceptions of their organisations' ethical values", *Journal of Business Ethics* 3 No 40 pp 191-200

van Dyne, Linn, Graham, Jill W. and Dienesch, Richard M. (1984) "Organisational citizenship behaviour: Construct redefinition, measurement, and validation", *Academy of Management Journal* 4 No 37 pp 785-802

Victor, Bart and Cullen, John B. (1988) "The organisational bases of ethical work climates", *Administrative Science Quarterly*, 1 No 33 pp 101-125

Paul Jackson is Professor of Corporate Communications at the Manchester Business School. He is a Fellow of the British Psychological Society in recognition of his contributions to research and professional practice in Work Psychology, with major research publications in the areas of the psychological effects of unemployment and the impact of work design on employee health. He has published more than 150 books and articles, and his most recent book is on stress among employees working in call centres (funded by the Health and Safety Executive). He is also Director of CAMaR, the Centre for Applied Management Research where he undertakes research on ethical decision making processes. Contact details: Professor Paul R Jackson, Manchester Business School, PO Box 88, Manchester M60 1QD, UK.Tel: +44 (0) 161 200 8795 Fax: +44 (0) 161 200 3505; email: Paul.R.Jackson@umist.ac.uk

Corporate social responsibility through communicational discipline: A theoretical enquiry

Bas van der Linden and Jan Jonker

Complexity, diversity and paradox characterise modern society. Organisations are supposed to add various values based on needs and expectations of stakeholders. Handling this leads to controversies in a society in which every stakeholder seems to be entitled to have legitimate demands. Communication with stakeholders representing society is therefore an important aspect of corporate social responsibility (CSR). Two questions will be addressed here. [1] With whom should the corporation communicate? [2] How should they communicate? The first is elaborated by performing a critical analysis of the stakeholder approach, a popular but often intuitively used theoretical concept. The second will be examined on the basis of Habermas's Theory of Communicative Action (TCA). This contribution leads to the conclusion that corporations have to place themselves under the provision of a "communicational discipline of responsibility" to be legitimate citizens in society.

Keywords: corporate social responsibility, communication, legitimacy, communicative action, stakeholder

INTRODUCTION

Corporations are increasingly supposed to add economic value as well as value to the environment and to society at large (Jonker 2000). This responsibility (whether or not self-imposed) is often referred to as "Corporate Social Responsibility" (CSR). Much effort has been invested to produce definitions of CSR, but it remains complex, arbitrary and fuzzy (Jonker 2003). According to Dubbink (2002: 17) four important components of a definition of CSR can be observed. [1] Corporations should comply with the law and norms of decency, [2] participate in the public debate in an upright manner, [3] try to avoid damage as much as possible, and [4] be favourably disposed towards claims of the public that are directly related to the behaviour of the corporation.

Although this general definition gives a decent impression of what is covered by the notion of CSR, it is impossible to develop a practical "translation" on its basis. How could a corporation comply with norms of decency if there is no fundamental agreement? How much damage is allowed in order to reach an efficient production? Where should one draw the line when being favourably disposed towards claims of the public? Even if a corporation has the intention to behave responsibly, it is still difficult to assess the needs and expectations of constituents in society. Given these circumstances, reciprocal communication with society is a prerequisite to determine the nature of expectations. This contribution aims to address the issue of communication between the corporation and society based on demands to behave socially responsible.

When exploring the problem of communication with society, two subjects should be examined. Since communication with society as a whole is impossible, concrete communicational partners that can articulate societal interests should be identified. For this purpose, Freeman's stakeholder approach (1984) is adopted after some alterations. When the term "stakeholder" is used to identify communicational partners, the criterion by which stakeholders are selected is quite relevant. Once stakeholders are identified the communication itself should be examined. The question is how the corporation should communicate with those stakeholders (Foster and Jonker 2003). Basis to elaborate a response is provided by choosing the Theory of Communicative Action (TCA) (Habermas 1981a and 1981b). This is an obvious choice since this theory attempts to describe the influence of economy and state-power on communication, both important issues in the CSR debate. The properties of a good dialogue, as well as the relation between communication and legitimacy are also treated in Habermas's theory. It will become clear that the TCA is not completely appropriate to apply to the problem of communicating about CSR. So, based on critiques, relevant concepts will be adjusted to use in this article.

WITH WHOM SHOULD THE CORPORATION COMMUNICATE?

In recent studies on CSR the term stakeholder is often used to describe individuals and groups whose interests should be taken into account by the corporation to be socially responsible. Here the stakeholder approach is used to tackle the problem of the vague notion "society" by means of a concrete "stakeholder map". It is literally impossible and quite impracticable to communicate with society as a whole. Identifying those stakeholders that articulate relevant, valid and workable societal interests can solve the problem. To do so Freeman's original stakeholder approach (op cit) will be briefly introduced. His approach will be examined to establish whether it can provide a valid representation of societal interests. As a result of this examination some alterations will be suggested.

At the time Freeman developed his approach it became increasingly clear that the stable picture of a corporation's environment in which only a limited number of stakeholders operated was no longer valid. Other constituencies like governmental organisations, pressure groups and media became important in influencing the corporation's operations. This development led to Freeman's classical definition: "A stakeholder is any group or individual who can affect or is affected by the achievement of the organisations objectives" (ibid: 46). The environment is described through a "stakeholder map" in which all stakeholders and their mutual relationships are depicted (ibid: chapter I). A benefit is that it shows that stakeholders can form coalitions and act with various "hats on". Good stakeholder management is to balance the interests of stakeholders and the corporation in such a manner that the interest of the corporation is served as good as possible (ibid: chapter III).

Freeman's stakeholder approach is above all a strategic management concept and "may not be understood as another call for social responsibility or business ethics" (ibid: 107). Freeman's focal point is the corporation and its interest; not necessarily CSR-related beforehand. At first sight Freeman's stakeholder definition can include anyone who has an interest in the corporation, "ratio" being that in the end stakeholders are selected on their ability to have an impact on the corporation. Stakeholders affected by the corporation are identified because they can affect the corporation in the future (ibid: 46). The reason to identify certain stakeholders is not a legitimate interest but the possible impact on the self-interest of the corporation. It is not necessarily true that only interests of stakeholders affecting the corporation are legitimate. Furthermore, the way in which the corporation would balance conflicting interests is not based on striving for legitimacy but on striving for profit. The extent to which the acting of the corporation is adjusted to the interests of the stakeholders is determined by the intention of the corporation to avoid future repercussions instead of the intention to be socially responsible.

To introduce Freeman's approach is to identify those communicational partners that can articulate a societal interest relevant to legitimise corporation's decisions. But if this approach cannot be applied satisfactorally in selecting societal partners some alterations are needed. According to Ulrich (2000) corporations should not only focus on economy and law in order to legitimate their acts, norms and intentions. They should also focus on the "general public": "… the regulative idea of the unlimited community of all moral persons who are willing to participate as reasonable citizens in the public deliberation on all matters of the *res publica,* i.e. the public affairs" (ibid: 50). Since corporations as well as all stakeholders, are parts of the general public, they should participate in the deliberation. They should not only legitimate themselves towards the general public represented by the stakeholders but also critically examine the legitimacy of needs and expectations. Responsibility becomes thus reciprocal since not all stakeholders have legitimate interests. Corporations should therefore actively engage in various public dialogues. In return stakeholders have the obligation to legitimate their interests towards the corporation (ibid: 52).

WHAT DEFINES A PROPER STAKEHOLDER?
Accepting these alterations leads to the question as to what defines a proper stakeholder. A corporation's communication should not only aim at legitimating the corporation's acts, norms and intentions to achieve social responsibility. It should also focus on the critical examination of the legitimacy of the interests of individuals and groups that pretend to be a stakeholder. Therefore, a stakeholder is a group or individual that has — or is claiming to have — a legitimate interest in the acts, norms or intentions of the organisation. This definition does not implicate the restriction of the identification of stakeholders by a perspective that is oriented towards organisational self-interest. The alternative does not imply that a corporation is not allowed to strive for maximising her self-interest; it only states that the quest for profitability may not influence the selection of stakeholders. In addition, it also adds issues regarding the reciprocity of responsibility. It emphasises the importance of communication to legitimate the corporation's behaviour and implies that stakeholders should legitimate their own interests.

The stakeholder approach fundamentally views society as an arena of (conflicting) interests. By making an inventory of all interests that are legitimate, the corporation can get an overview of what society is expecting in terms of its social responsibility. Conflicting interests not only occur between the corporation and its stakeholders but also between stakeholders themselves. Balancing these conflicts in a legitimate manner is what CSR is all about. Not all interests can be honoured simultaneously. Legitimately balancing conflicting interests can, thus, be seen as the fair distribution of chances. It can be achieved by negotiating the fairest compromise, trying to find win-win solutions or finding functional equivalents et cetera. Achieving a legitimate distribution of chances to realise intentions is dependent on mutual understanding of facts, norms and intentions. Developing shared views on the world and its relations is a prerequisite to assign intentions and acts to (trans-intentional) consequences thus distributing responsibility. Shared norms are necessary frames of reference for legitimating acts and intentions. Mutual understanding of intentions is a necessity since not all intentions can legitimate acts identically.

Communication contributes to the process of balancing interests by offering the ability to reach mutual understanding on norms to be applied and on whether these norms are any good at all. Communication also allows the expression and evaluation of intentions as well as deliberation about the common understanding of facts and its appliance. Communication, then, plays a key role in the process of identifying stakeholders and balancing their interests. To understand what this role exactly is and how it can contribute to the issue of realising CSR, the concept of communication is explored by means of Habermas's Theory of Communicative Action (TCA). Below relevant concepts are described as they were published in 1981. It will be argued that TCA cannot fully respond to the question how a corporation should communicate with its stakeholders to enable legitimate identification and balancing interests. A typology consisting of three types of communication based on Habermas's theory will turn out to provide a suitable elaboration.

HOW SHOULD A CORPORATION COMMUNICATE?

According to Habermas (1981a and 1981b) legitimacy is not only a matter of "scientific rationality". The classical view on rationality may be a useful concept when creating a theory of some kind of physical phenomenon. When trying to understand how legitimacy is constructed in "social reality" scientific rationality is not sufficient. In this reality the validity of knowledge does not only depend on its ability to explain an objective world. Central to social reality is that actors involved reach (inter-subjective) consensus about the validity of shared knowledge by means of speech acts. This "communicative rationality" (1981a: 525) supposes a focus on human relations between subjects instead of relations between single subjects and the outside objective world. Actions on the basis of communicative rationality are called "communicative action".

In Habermas's view, it is categorically distinct from "strategic action" based on instrumental (scientific) rationality. Individuals engaging in communicative action are co-ordinating their acts by achieving mutual understanding of "the world" as they perceive it, normative aspects of the situation and personal subject related intentions. Communicative action is, therefore, always the result of mutual understanding. As a consequence good reason or "rational motivation" stimulates actors. Strategic action on the contrary is not based on motivation by good reason but on "empirical motivation" (ibid: 65). Actors are motivated by means of sanctions and gratifications (e.g. force or money) and not directed towards achieving mutual understanding. An individual acts in an instrumental way due to which other actors are seen as means that should be influenced to achieve the individual's end (ibid: 384).

Good deliberation is a time-consuming process that cannot take place at any occasion. Besides achieving mutual understanding is only feasible when some non-controversial and shared understanding precedes it. This non-controversial understanding forms, according to Habermas, the "life world". This world contains shared definitions of reality to which actors can refer when they are trying to achieve mutual understanding concerning a specific situation (1981b: 187). In discussing the legitimacy of investing in a dictatorial governed country, for example, the corporation and stakeholders usually do not have to convince each other of the undesirability of violating human rights. This understanding creates the background to any (speech) act and contributes to the co-ordination of acts, achieving further mutual understanding about the present situation creating a basis for legitimacy. Understanding of the life world enables communication in order to legitimate acts, norms and intentions. Life world also decreases the societal demand for communication. But it is not the life world alone that reduces the demand for communication.

According to Habermas, co-ordination by means of the societal subsystems "economy" and "state administration" can also relieve the demand for communicative co-ordination (ibid: 393). Within these subsystems, acts are functionally integrated by means of the steering media "money" and "state-power". Functional integration is the steering medium-based co-ordination of the consequences of acts. To this purpose mutual understanding of norms, facts and intentions is unnecessary, according to Habermas. Acts and communication within subsystems do not have to be directed at mutual understanding; a goal-oriented (strategic) attitude is sufficient (ibid: 269). This view allows the economy for an efficient integrated exchange of goods and services and the state administration for an efficient realisation of the public purposes. Societal subsystems are linked with steering media "money" and "state-power" in society.

TAKING ACCOUNT OF MONEY

The steering medium "money" can be viewed as a generalised exchange medium that permits seller and buyer to exchange something without the need to be at the same place at the same time. Money represents an exchange value that can be effectuated any time (1981b: 396). The steering medium "state-power" is exclusively related to the state administration. The state in society has a monopoly regarding the use of force to influence individuals to behave in a specific manner. This makes it possible to integrate acts efficiently since achieving mutual understanding is not a prerequisite (ibid: 400). Steering media involve specific information that is also an incentive and can, therefore, motivate someone to accept a proposition.

Typically co-ordination by means of steering media is not dependent on achieving mutual understanding through language. Referring to the commonly understood world is, therefore, not necessary. According to Habermas this creates the possibility to separate the life world from subsystems (ibid: 273). As a consequence, systemically integrated action is not placed under the provision of legitimacy only provided through the life world and communicative action. Subsystems can develop their own "cluttered" dynamic which, in turn, cannot be controlled by the life world (ibid: 275). In Habermas's view, any societal pathologies can be understood when seeing them as the consequences of uncoupling subsystems and life world (ibid: 293).

The original concept of TCA is only useful to examine the problem of communication related to CSR after some modifications. Habermas aims at explaining which problems occur when certain fields of action are not entirely integrated by means of communicative action and life world. He aims at explaining what happens if certain fields of action are entirely systemic integrated. These two foci of the TCA do not allow a direct application with regard to CSR since the domain of action of CSR is more a matter of economic integration as well as communicative rationality. Here an attempt is made to clarify these issues relying on some of Habermas's critics. Broadly speaking there are two major critiques relevant here. The first concerns the distinction between communicative action and strategic action [1]. The second questions the distinction "social integration" and "systemic integration"[2].

[1] The (speech) acts of an actor can be oriented towards achieving mutual understanding or to realising the actor's ends. In the latter case, the other actor including his opinions is only seen as a mean to this end. Acts can thus be assigned to the category of communicative action or to the category of strategic action. They cannot have qualities of communicative action and of strategic action at the same time. Many authors reject this view because "people can achieve mutual understanding while realising private aims and people also can realise private aims while achieving mutual understanding" (Berger 1986: 266). If one looks upon the difference between communicative action and strategic action as a distinction between integrating intentions and integrating consequences of acts it becomes obvious that a clear distinction is not possible. An integration of intentions cannot be successful when actors do not take into account their own interests related to possible acts. Integration of consequences cannot lead to satisfactory solutions if actors do not take into account their own intentions. In social reality a categorical distinction seems not to exist (Joas 1986: 156-157). Any interaction is oriented towards mutual understanding as well as to realising self-interest.

Besides the impossibility of a categorical distinction in reality, it is also impossible to describe the difference between communicative action and strategic action when only the communication is taken into consideration. The truthfulness of a speech act can only be assessed on the basis of the self-expression of one-self. Habermas tried in vain to find "structural qualities of communication" that "objectively" can determine the truthfulness of self-expression (Kneer 1996: 53-57). In practice communicative and strategic action cannot be distinguished on the base of communication. The inner world of actors can never be known so objective determination of the kind of action that (really) takes place is impossible.

COMMUNICATIVE ACTION

This has consequences for this contribution. Theoretically, strategic action can lead to legitimacy problems while communicative action provides circumstances under which legitimacy is possible. Still it is impossible to describe a category of communication that guarantees legitimacy through communicative rationality since the self-expression of one's "inner world" can never be known. Furthermore, a clear distinction between communicative and strategic action does not seem to exist. Still the concept of communicative rationality remains useful. It explains how and what kind of mutual understanding should be achieved to realise legitimacy.

[2] The way in which Habermas distinguishes social and systemic integration is controversial. It is clear that a categorical distinction between these two seems impossible. Perhaps the co-ordination of acts can emphasise too much systemic integration or social integration. Critics (e.g. Honneth 1985; McCarthy 1986 or Martens 2003) have shown that systemic integration is always influenced by the life world. Functionally integrated acts, which are performed within a subsystem, always happen within a normative "framework". Therefore, systemic co-ordinated action always must take into account norms that are situated in the life world of the actors (Honneth op cit: 228). Systemic co-ordination cannot take place without the life world at all.

THE SHARED UNDERSTANDING OF ECONOMIC SYMBOLS

Taking a look at the formal division of functions and responsibilities within an organisation makes this clear. The formal structure of an organisation cannot be understood without the implicit routines, culture etc which belong to the life world of the employees (McCarthy op cit: 185). The possibility of economic co-ordination is always dependent on shared understanding of economic symbols, the unwritten rules of economic interaction and norms. "The economic subsystem presupposes a particular shared life world that is confirmed by successful or failed economic transactions and communications" (Martens op cit: 432). Apparently any action within a subsystem confirms, proposes or rejects mutual understanding on facts, norms or intentions inside the life world. Several other theories support this statement. According to Elias' figuration theory, Martens argues, people learn to take into account the functional structures that exist in society anytime they co-ordinate their acts with others. The life world is not shaped through speech acts, but rather through personalities influenced by a highly functionally integrated society (ibid: 422).

In Luhmann's view any social interaction consists of the functional co-ordination of the consequences of action that result from intentions of the actors involved. Therefore any "social co-existence" has a certain independence with respect to the individual (Luhmann 1986: op cit 43). As a result people have to take into account the independent existence of society making it inevitable that life world is co-shaped by systemic integration (Martens: 431).

Systemic integration cannot be detached from the life world since life world is a condition for systemic integration. Integration always produces life world and action constructs functional integration. So the problem of illegitimacy can not be understood by means of separating the two. Therefore, the question "how can systemic rationality contribute to the legitimacy of the corporation?" is relevant to CSR. After all, legitimate acts can only exist because they are connected with definitions of the objective, normative and subjective reality. The fact that people can have a "life world-view" on subsystems allows them to make the prerequisites under which systemic co-ordination can lead to legitimate results explicit. Co-ordination through means of a steering medium within a subsystem therefore leads — under certain circumstances and to a certain extent — to legitimacy.

If systemic integration and social integration contribute to legitimacy it leads to the question how a corporation should communicate with its stakeholders to realise a common ground for CSR. Answering it can determine the limitations of systemic co-ordination. So communication of various types that are related to social and economic integration and integration by means of state power should be described. One particular form of communication always accompanies co-ordination by means of the steering media money and state power. Communication mediated by a steering medium is an encoded form of communication that allows the deliberation of a specific aspect of action. Achieving legitimacy by means of communication mediated by a steering medium is only possible if the concerned actors have reached mutual understanding with respect to relevant issues. In situations in which the application of steering media lead to illegitimate results a communicative dialogue is appropriate. Therefore, in the next section we will describe the conditions for the legitimate application of the steering media. Communicative dialogue that allows for legitimacy in situations in which steering-media cannot lead to legitimate results, will be described as well.

TYPES OF COMMUNICATION

The stakeholder theory is a theory of conflicts of interest of the various parties involved. CSR is finding a legitimate solution for these conflicts with communication as an important mean to this end. TCA can be used to answer questions regarding the characteristics of this communication. TCA shows that if stakeholders do not share definitions of reality, communicative dialogue is necessary. In specific situations communication mediated by steering media is legitimate, but the application is restricted due to the provision of legitimacy. As a result the question when a corporation should have a communicative dialogue with its stakeholders is formulated negatively: it is necessary when money-mediated-communication or state-power-mediated-communication leads to illegitimate results. Below we will investigate what the conditions are under which money-mediated-communication is legitimate [1]. Second the prerequisites for a legitimate appliance of state-power will be explored [2]. Finally significant characteristics of a communicative dialogue will be described [3].

[1] When money-mediated-communication takes place it can be described as an "exchange". One actor proposes an "exchange proposal", the other actor accepts or rejects it. In this way actors can efficiently co-ordinate their acts without being dependent on a time-consuming dialogue. In society goods and services are frequently exchanged for money causing increase of complexity and decrease of surveyability (Habermas 1981b: 395-400). The corporation and stakeholders compare their possible actions only on the basis of economic profitability or cost-effectiveness in the case of money-mediated-communication. An actor can decide for itself whether the proposed action is in accordance with its norms and intentions. Whenever the corporation communicates with its stakeholders by mediation of money, all those concerned are presupposed to think, decide and act in a specific manner. The meaning of acts and things is reduced to purely economic expressed in terms of money. Other meanings disappear from the communication. Any other consideration except whether a good price is paid is systematically erased.

Money-mediated-communication can easily lead to illegitimacy. Acts exist that are profitable for corporations whereas these acts are also in conflict with norms or intentions of stakeholders. Also, certain acts exist that are not profitable and therefore unfeasible for corporations whereas stakeholders require the performance of these acts by the corporation. Considering this, it becomes clear that the relative importance of profitability or cost-effectiveness in relation to other norms and intentions is not the same to all actors. A situation can contain aspects that should not be described in terms of profitability at all. The "illegitimatising effect" of the money-medium consists of the fact that the shared life world of actors moves out of view. Therefore a "legitimising frame" of mutual understanding is necessary to achieve a legitimate use of the money-medium.

[2] Like money, state-power is also a steering-medium (ibid: 400-404). It has the capability to motivate actors to behave in a certain manner without

further deliberation. The ruler (a governmental body) provides permission or prohibition, the subordinate actor has to obey in order to prevent a reprisal. Although mutual understanding has not been achieved, legitimate state-power-mediated-communication is possible. To make this happen exercise of power should not only be covered by the latent use of physical force but should also contribute to the realisation of a public good. The institutional structure of a democracy provides a representation of all citizens within the process of determining public purposes and goods. Institutions secure that governmental organisations exercise state power in accordance with the public intent. Use of state power is legitimate since collective purposes correspond with the life world of civilians.

LIMITATIONS OF LAW AND POLICYMAKING

Institutions cannot always co-ordinate acts in a legitimate way due to limitations of law and policymaking (partly adopted from Steinmann and Scherer 2000: 160-162). An amount of time always lapses between the moment a certain societal problem appears and the moment when appropriate legislation has been made or is updated. Second, the degree of complexity of law is limited; not every detail of human co-existence can be organised by means of written rules. Third, the possibilities to enforce compliance with the law are also limited. The costs of supervising all actions in society are prohibitive. The majority of people must obey voluntarily. Fourth, countries exist in which laws and policies are not made in accordance with democratic principles. Legitimacy-problems of multinationals doing business in undemocratic governed countries provide vivid illustrations. Finally the circumstances under which law and policy have been developed can change. As a result a certain law is no longer applicable in situations for which it was meant.

In conclusion it can be stated that a legal act is not necessarily legitimate and that a legitimate act is not necessarily legal; law addresses not every act and these acts cannot be defined in terms of legality or illegality. To make sure that state-power-mediated-communication is legitimate in a certain situation, the following seems important. Corporation and stakeholders should check whether the applicable law indeed represents their norms and values. Second, the actual existence of applicable law for the particular situation should be determined. If necessary, corporation and stakeholders should have a communicative dialogue that goes beyond possible gaps in — or improprieties of — law to achieve mutual understanding on how to act in a legitimate manner given a specific situation.

[3] Although it is impossible to really determine communicative action, it is possible to describe a communicational stance that increases communicative rationality. Speech acts of the corporation and its stakeholders are implicitly connected to criticisable validity claims with respect to the three different "worlds": the objective, normative and subjective (Habermas 1981a: 35). A communicative dialogue permits the corporation as well as the stakeholders to criticise and defend validity claims that are relevant to the situation. In this way mutual understanding as the basis for legitimately balancing the interests of corporation and stakeholders can be achieved. The realisation of "symmetric communicational conditions" which ensures that all concerned actors can be heard is important here. Although corporations themselves might be slightly preoccupied with facts, an attitude to discuss norms and values with stakeholders and the willingness to authentically represent intentions can contribute to the realisation of symmetric communicational conditions.

CONCLUSIONS

Corporations are economic entities as they can be distinguished from others by a primary orientation on profitability. Profit is a necessary condition for the survival of any business. All acts of the firm are, therefore, assessed on their profitability. To perform the most profitable acts money-mediated-communication is often adequate and forms a vital part of the information. CSR adds the prerequisite of societal legitimacy to the profit-objective of the corporation. Therefore, the distribution of chances to realise intentions among all stakeholders that have a legitimate claim should not only be determined on the basis of the money-medium. The critical examination of claims to identify the legitimate stakeholders should not be founded solely on the degree in which the particular individual or group can influence the corporations profitability. This would hinder determining with whom the corporation should communicate to become social responsible. Not just those that can influence the corporation's profitability can have legitimate claims representing a societal interest.

What insight has been gained by investigating the communication between corporation and stakeholders in relation to CSR? Money-mediated-communication can only lead to legitimate results under the prerequisite of mutual understanding between the corporation and its stakeholders. Mutual understanding should especially been reached on the relative importance of economic efficiency and those aspects which should not be communicated in terms of economic efficiency. This way shared provisions are added to the life world. Before legitimising money-mediated-communication actors involved must have achieved mutual understanding on all relevant norms, intentions and facts. After all, money-mediated-communication can only lead to mutual understanding in terms of economic efficiency.

State-power-mediated-communication is also relevant to CSR. In principle, legislation and policy that underpin state-power-mediated-communication reflect the public opinion. Therefore, state-power-mediated-communication can lead to legitimate results in many cases. Corporations and stakeholders have to persuade themselves that applicable legislation exists and that a law, indeed, reflects the norms and values within their life world. In all situations in which state-power-mediated-communication is not controlled by a shared life world as well as in all situations in which money-mediated-communication cannot lead to legitimate result, a dialogue founded on communicative rationality is a prerequisite. A dialogue is also vital to all communication on the appropriateness and justness of norms, the truthfulness and legitimacy of intentions and the truth of facts. In the end corporations have to place themselves under the provision of the described "communicational discipline of responsibility" to be legitimate citizens in modern society.

REFERENCES

Berger J. (1986) "Die versprachlichung des Sakralen und die Entsprachlichung der Ökonomie", *Kommunikatives Handeln: Beitrage zu Jürgen Habermas Theorie des Kommunikativen Handelns*, Honneth, A. and Joas, H. (eds), Frankfurt am Main, Suhrkamp Verlag

Dubbink W. (2002) "Het kapitalisme als kwetsbare orde: De radicale implicaties van maatschappelijk verantwoord ondernemen", *Krisis: Tijdschrift voor empirische filosofie*, Amsterdam, Uitgeverij Boom, No 1 pp 14-38

Foster D. and Jonker J. (2003) "Third generation quality management: the role of stakeholders in integrating business into society", *Managerial Auditing Journal*, No 4 pp 323-328

Freeman R.E. (1984) *Strategic management: A stakeholder approach*, Boston, Pitman Habermas J. (1981a) *Theorie des kommunikativen Handelns: Handlungsrationalität und gesellschaftliche Rationalisierung (band I)*, Frankfurt am Main, Suhrkamp Verlag

Habermas J. (1981b) *Theorie des kommunikativen Handelns: Zur Kritik der funktionalistischen Vernunft (band II)*, Frankfurt am Main, Suhrkamp Verlag

Habermas J. (1986) "Entgegnung", *Kommunikatives Handeln: Beitrage zu Jürgen Habermas' Theorie des Kommunikativen Handelns*, Honneth, A. and Joas, H. (eds), Frankfurt am Main, Suhrkamp Verlag

Honneth A. (1985) *Kritiek der Macht: Reflexionsstufen einer kritischen Gesellschaftstheorie*,

Frankfurt am Main, Suhrkamp Verlag

Joas H. (1986) "Die unglückliche Ehe von Hermeneutiek und Funktionalismus", *Kommunikatives Handeln: Beitrage zu Jürgen Habermas' Theorie des Kommunikativen Handelns*, Honneth, A. and Joas, H. (eds), Frankfurt am Main, Suhrkamp Verlag

Jonker J. (2000) "Organisations as Responsible Contributors to Society: linking Quality, Sustainability and Accountability", *Total Quality Management*, Bradford, MCB, No 3 pp 741-746

Jonker J. (2003) "In Search of Society: Redefining Corporate Social Responsibility, Organisational Theory and Business Strategies", *Research in International Business and Finance*, Oxford, Elsevier Science, Vol 17 pp 423-441

Kneer G. (1996) *Rationalisierung, Disziplinierung und Differenzierung: Zum Zuzammenhang von Socialtheorie bei Jürgen Habermas, Michel Foucault und Niklas Luhmann*, Wiesbaden/Opladen, Westdeutcher Verlag

Luhmann, N. (1986) *Ökologische Kommunikation: Kann die moderne Gesellschaft sich auf ökologische Gefährdungen einstellen?*, Wiesbaden/Opladen, Westdeutcher Verlag

Martens W. (2003) "Wie transintentional ist das moderne Wirtschaftssystem?", *Die transintentionalität des Sozialen*, Greshoff, R., Kneer, G. and Schimank, U. (eds), Wiesbaden/Opladen, Westdeutcher Verlag

McCarthy T. (1986) "Komplexität und Demokratie: Die Versuchungen der Systemtheorie", *Kommunikatives Handeln: Beitrage zu Jürgen Habermas' Theorie des Kommunikativen Handelns*, Honneth, A. and Joas, H. (eds), Frankfurt am Main, Suhrkamp Verlag

Mitchell R.K., Agle, B.R. and Wood D.J. (1997) "Toward a theory of stakeholder identification and salience: Defining the principles of who and what really counts", *Academy of Management Journal*, New York, Briarcliff Manor, No 4 pp 853-886

Steinmann H. and Scherer A.G. (2000) "Corporate ethics and management theory", Koslowski P. (ed.), *Contemporary economic ethics and business ethics*, Berlin, Springer Verlag

Ulrich P. (2000) "Integrative economic ethics: Towards a conception of socio-economic rationality", Koslowski P. (ed.), *Contemporary economic ethics and business ethics*, Berlin, Springer Verlag

Bas van der Linden (MA) graduated from the Nijmegen School of Management (University of Nijmegen, Holland) with a theoretical thesis regarding the theory of Habermas in relation to CSR. This paper is an adapted version of his Masters thesis. Contact details: Nijmegen School of Management (NSM), University of Nijmegen (KUN), PO Box 9108 – 6500 HK Nijmegen, The Netherlands. Tel: 00.31.24.322.93.78; email: b.vanderlinden@aacee.nl

Jan Jonker is associate professor and research fellow at the Nijmegen School of Management (NSM) of the University of Nijmegen. His research interest lies on the crossroad of management and corporate social responsibility, particularly in relation to the development of business strategy. He is among the founding members of the Dutch National Research Network on CSR and actively participates in this network as a researcher. In 2003 he chaired the International Research Conference Managing on the Edge — which attracted 225 participants from 25 countries. Contact details: Nijmegen School of Management (NSM), University of Nijmegen (KUN), PO Box 9108 – 6500 HK Nijmegen, The Netherlands. Tel: 00.31.314.363.253; fax 00.31.314.325.180; email: J.Jonker@nsm.kun.nl

Journalists as interpreters: Gadamer and elements of a communication ethics in news practice

Donald Matheson

The task is to find an account of communication that erases neither the curious fact of otherness at its core nor the possibility of doing things with words.
John Durham Peters (1999: 21)

We can paraphrase communication ethics both as the ethics of the communication professions and as an ethics focused on communicative interaction. The two formulations are quite different, one tending to point us towards the deontological or utilitarian ethics which have dominated thinking on the professions, and the other towards an understanding of what it means to communicate well. This chapter takes the latter path, focusing in the first instance on journalism, although the argument is by no means restricted to it. It begins by posing three problems to which journalism ethics tends not to have confident answers, on the way to arguing for a more hermeneutical, interpretative ethics. Drawing firstly on the reflections of a number of journalists, and then, as a way of theorising these, on the philosophical writings of Hans-Georg Gadamer, it suggests we place the act of interpretation and the goal of understanding at the heart of our understanding of the ethical in journalism. The paper's aim is to bring into clearer focus within journalism studies some neglected aspects of how ethical journalism is practised.

Keywords: communicative ethics, media ethics, interpretative journalism, news, journalists, Gadamer

INTRODUCTION: RICHNESS IN DISTANCE

Critics who discuss the ethics of public language use often take dialogue as the ground for a communicative ethics, in opposition to the social distances and isolation blamed on mass society and its mass media. From the use of Buber's opposition of I–Thou versus I–It relations (e.g. Cissna and Anderson 2002) to Habermas's use of the pragmatics of talk to outline principles of ethical publicness (1992), to Christians' communitarian ethics (1997), a central ideal of communication is the sharing of minds through true dialogue. This paper follows an alternative thread, expressed in the epigraph from John Durham Peters' history of communication theory, which sees communicative richness also in distance and the scattering of messages in one-way communication. An ethics of communication, in Peters' view, need not resort always to ideals but can also look to the achievement of the everyday.

THREE PROBLEMS

Journalism is, of course, a communicative practice, describing society to itself and carving out public and other cultural spaces within which society can understand itself. Reporters and academics alike judge the practice by the extent to which it communicates successfully: informing the people, interpreting social change, critiquing government. Yet ethical codes and statements about journalism tend to have little purchase on what makes for good communication — good interpretation, good informing, good critique — and instead rely on liberal assumptions about the benefit of a free market of independent-minded reporters. Bill Rosenstiel and Tom Kovach, for example, give a succinct and articulate nine-point list of the "elements of journalism" which they regard as active principles among US newspeople. Their first four elements are:

1. Journalism's first obligation is to the truth.
2. Its first loyalty is to citizens.
3. Its essence is a discipline of verification.
4. Its practitioners must maintain an independence from those they cover. (Rosenstiel and Kovach 2001: 12)

The overwhelming responsibility placed on the reporter here is to find out what s/he believes the public should know or wants to know, to reflect the real without fear or favour to sources. Such statements, as James W. Carey has put it, turn a moral and political question of how journalists relate to others in society into a scientific and epistemological one of representing society accurately (Carey 1992: 76). Kovach and Rosenstiel's "discipline of verification", or as one strand of journalistic wisdom puts it, "If your mother says she loves you, check it out" (Fuller 1996: 4), imagines the complex and nuanced ways of knowing in society as reducible to factual data.

The journalist's fiduciary relation to the audience is expressed more as a responsibility to provide publics with those facts which will allow them to act as good citizens than as a relationship formed in communication. Similarly in the British context, the Press Complaints Commission's code of practice defines good reporting, within relatively loose constraints of privacy and decency, as the absence of inaccurate, distorted or misleading material (PCC). Whenever journalism is doing its important jobs of making sense of things, contextualising them and helping us understand them — whenever, indeed, we regard it as doing something other than objectively reflecting the world — such principles are of decidedly limited help in describing its ethical base.

This leads to a second problem. Ethical discourses of independence and distrust of sources might have had some purchase on journalistic practice during the eighteenth and nineteenth-century battles of the press for independence from political power and during the rise of empirical science as a model for knowing society, but are evidently on their own no longer adequate. There is general recognition that the most severe pressures upon western journalism are internal to its capitalist structure and cannot easily be walled off (Curran 1996), and there is similar recognition that science is not immune, in the questions it asks and the methods it employs, from politics (Christians 1997). If, as Jeremy Iggers argues, journalism ethics can be thought of as a self-interested discourse, which buttresses practitioners' interests against external pressures and is subject to the incoherencies and silences of any discourse (Iggers 1999: 15; Matheson 2003), then its silence on the ways it makes meaning seems to have outlived its usefulness. We live in a culture where it is becoming more common to recognise a multiplicity of truths and where universalist assumptions are breaking down into much more fragmented pictures of global social life.

In such a context, Kovach and Rosenstiel (and the dominant ethical discourses within journalism I am using them to represent) do not provide journalists with very complex ways of talking about their purpose within society or their struggles against co-optation by its more powerful groups. Statements in journalism textbooks such as "the primary purpose of news gathering or reporting [is] the truth" (Herbert 2000: 77) on their own provide little help for journalists who recognise a cultural base to truth claims. Similarly, we live in a global society dependent upon ever changing networks of relations, in which what is at stake is often the locking out of large numbers of people from influence and in which the news media play an active role (Castells 1996). In such a context, it is becoming clearer that distance and independence from sources can only be half the challenge for the journalist. S/he must also get close to power and recognise her/his implication in networks of meaning-making in order to talk adequately about how society is changing.

THE PROBLEM OF PROFESSIONALISM

These problems should not be posed simply as problems of practice. Indeed, the paper will argue below that there is a rich, countervailing strand of thinking and practice by journalists, who have to work through such challenges on a daily basis, which we can draw upon. Instead, I would suggest we frame the issues discussed above within a third, more methodological problem, one of the relationship between ethical discourse and practice. Journalists, when they are talking ethically, have few ways to discuss how they communicate with both sources and audiences. Following a number of critics, we can trace this problem partly to the dominance of professional theory among those who seek to give journalism a philosophical base.

Zelizer (1999) points out that journalism does not fit well into sociology's definitions of a profession. It does not have a well-defined client group to whom it is ethically responsible, as doctors or lawyers do. It does not have, at least in the Anglo-American tradition, registration procedures to define who is a journalist. It does not have codified rules of practice, and it does not have well-theorised sets of skills or universally accepted training in those skills. If it has principles, as Rosenstiel and Kovach and others can show, these are embedded in practice.

To study journalism as if it were self-evidently a profession, therefore, risks focusing on "only those dimensions of journalism emphasised by the frame through which we have chosen to view them" (Zelizer 1993: 219). When we study journalism as a cultural practice, as ways of knowing through newsgathering, newswriting and the stories and other forms of "wisdom" (Glasser and Ettema 1989) which inform practice, however, we begin to see a slightly different object. One aspect of this is its ethical base, as I hope to show below. As a methodological principle, then, this paper looks to journalists' own statements to begin to explore a richer ethics.

The following three sections explore three threads in journalism's exploration of ethics as something broader than the ethics of distrust and distance pointed at above. They have been chosen for the ways in which they explore the journalist's interpretative role as the basis of good journalism. Most are white, liberal men of considerable standing within British journalism, and an earlier oral version of this paper has been criticised for choosing a limited range of voices. This is indeed a limitation, in that it shuts out many alternative and radical perspectives, but it is also perhaps a strength. My aim has been to explore aspects of the mainstream culture of journalism, which is dominated by precisely such white, male voices. An interpretative ethos is not, the paper is keen to show, a characteristic just of the fringes of news practice.

THE BIAS AGAINST UNDERSTANDING AND 'INTERPRETATIVE JOURNALISM'

The term "interpretative journalism" is strongly associated within British news circles with John Birt and Peter Jay's very public accusation in 1975 and 1976 that the news contained a "bias against their audience's understanding of the society in which it lives" (Birt 1975). For these two senior television editors, contemporary TV news and features were much too narrow in their approach to complex political and economic events and, in particular, failed to provide context because of their emphasis on the purely factual. In a series of three articles in *The Times,* they argued that the news failed to help the public understand events:

> *The news, devoting two minutes on successive nights to the latest unemployment figures or the state of the stock market, with no time to put the story in context, gives the viewer no sense of how any of these problems relate to each other (Birt ibid).*

Their solution involved an "interpretative journalism", by specialists with a broader and more in-depth understanding than news reporters. They were criticised for advocating an elitist kind of public service news and for applying their thinking in "the most unwatchably tedious current affairs programme of all time", Weekend World (Wheen 2000). Such specialist correspondents are, however, a major legacy of Birt's time as Director-General of the BBC in the 1990s, and a major plank of the BBC's claim to excellence in news (although the editorial processes of BBC news are under question in the light of the 2004 Hutton Inquiry's heavy condemnation of them).

At the heart of the Birt-Jay argument is a rejection of the distinction between news and news analysis and an explicit statement that news requires interpretation for it to make sense. They proposed that this sense-making work should be consciously valued and put into dynamic relation with news material:

> *Intelligent — in the sense of understanding, not of intellectual — news means continuous news analysis. This requires many qualified — that is, knowledgeable and educated — journalists, sometimes working in teams and continuously blending inquiry and analysis, so that the needs of understanding direct the inquiry and the fruits of inquiry inform the analysis (Birt and Jay 1975).*

In this vision, facts do not lie, as Claud Cockburn caricatured journalists imagining them, like gold ore in the Yukon, waiting to be picked up (Cockburn 1981: 104). Indeed, Birt and Jay do not speak of facts but of fruits of inquiry, understanding and analysis. The idea of the seasoned, generalist reporter who knows instinctively what audiences want and need is also rejected, or rather, that reporter's knowledge is (in the ideal version described in their articles) turned into something more reflexive and therefore dynamic, being consciously revised and improved on.

The "bias against understanding" critique clearly takes place within the public service context of the BBC, in which the organisation takes on a role of making British society intelligible to itself by bringing it together through a particular set of public idioms — described by Scannell as its communicative ethos (Scannell 1992). Yet it is an explicit statement of a long thread in journalism of news as analysis, from the nineteenth-century *Times* correspondent to the *Financial Times* "value-added" journalism (Lambert 1998: x-xii) or Channel 4's in-depth 7pm news programme, which seeks to challenge mainstream news agendas. Their purposes might be different — the *Financial Times*, for example, seeking to differentiate itself in a crowded financial information market — but we can find many senior journalists invoking interpretation as the grounds of good journalism, at times, as Birt and Jay, as something of an ethical imperative.

THE SUBJECTIVE REPORTER

A distinction is traditionally made in this interpretative tradition between analysis and opinion, impartial reporting and bias. The BBC's Producers' Guidelines tell its reporters that they "may express a professional, journalistic judgement but not a personal opinion" (BBC: 37). Yet a number of journalists, particularly foreign correspondents and investigative reporters, have taken the position that quality journalism emerges out of a self-conscious subjectivity, extending the reflexivity discussed above beyond the limits of the reporters' role to the wider personhood of the reporter. These include but are by no means limited to famous names such as Martha Gellhorn, James Cameron and Joan Didion. In exploring such thinking, we can extend beyond romantic clichés of the haunted correspondent who cares too much, who gets too involved in events, to explore some of the strategies adopted by committed journalists in extreme situations of violence and of radically different cultures struggling to communicate those situations, and to explore their wider applicability.

Gellhorn found it not only senseless but also inhuman to attempt to withdraw some part of herself by attempting an objective account of the suffering of child victims of American bombing in Vietnam:

> *I don't know what [objectivity means]. We have only our own eyes and our own ears. You can't just look...and say there is no difference between right and wrong,...between just and unjust. I believe that is a definition of insanity... (1997 interview on ABC News, quoted in Huntting 2001).*

Cameron similarly argued that he could only engage meaningfully with the foreign events he covered by bringing something of himself to the coverage. He wrote:

> *It never occurred to me in some situations to be other than subjective. And as obviously as I could manage to be...A reporter whose technique was formed by no opinion lacked a very serious dimension (Cameron, quoted in Terkel 1997: 4).*

These reporters bring a personal commitment to attempt to form coherent ideas about the world, particularly at its most unjust. However, their subjectivity is further motivated, almost paradoxically, by a strong ethical sense of the inadequacy of that understanding and of the limitations imposed by time, news style and other constraints, as precursors to attempting to overcome those. If few reporters go as far as Didion in attesting that she could truthfully record only "how it felt to be me" in encountering people and events (Didion 1968: 134), a number foreground the human struggle to understand as much as Birt and Jay's fruits of analysis.

Such thinking need not be limited to extreme situations, allowing us to think further about journalistic strategies to bridge differences of understanding. The writer and critic Torunn Borge argues that such quality reportage — which she defines as reporting informed by depth of understand and an "unabashed subjectivity — has the power to involve us in what we thought did not concern us or what we thought we were not interested in (Borge 2001: 2). It communicates across the barriers we build around ourselves. Thus good journalism, in this way of thinking, arises not out of personal disinterest, but out of the opposite, an avowed commitment to understand events and to communicate that understanding. Its strength is perhaps in the openness — even vulnerability — of the text to the reader's assessment, something that allows us to begin to trust it as something that speaks to us.

As pragmatics has shown, trust is a fundamental condition of communicative interaction (see, for example, Allwood 1997). Cambridge philosopher Onora O'Neill speaks of an "assessable journalism" as an imperative to stem the ebbing of trust between news media and the public, in which journalists and editors include clear statements in their writing about their financial or political interests (O'Neill 2002). It is perhaps not so much journalists' pecuniary interests which need to be assessed, however, as their ethical engagement in communication, their commitment to fostering understanding of events by both themselves and their audiences. The journalists discussed above, in the self-aware subjectivity they bring to their work, are perhaps more deeply assessable in this regard. They place themselves at risk by showing their presence and the presence of their presuppositions in the text.

POWER WITH RESPONSIBILITY

Journalism has traditionally seen little value in recognition of its involvement in making the world meaningful. As journalists interviewed by Herbert Gans put it, they were responsible for the facts, not their implications (1980: 182). There is especially little to be gained from envisaging news events as constructed for journalists' benefit or with their collusion, and any recognition that interviews, press conferences, press visits and the like are, in Daniel Boorstin's (1971) words, "pseudo-events" must be repressed. There is, in fact, an explicit sanction on journalists or photographers staging events for their own purposes. To give just one example, Shoemaker and Reese (1996) quote an editor who suspended and publicly humiliated a photographer for staging a shot, full of pathos and contrast, of a firefighter splashing himself with water from a swimming pool while a house burned in the background:

> *The photograph challenges a crucial news-gathering conceit: that respectable journalism is a passive exercise in fact-gathering that conveys to the reader an unadulterated slice of reality (Lewis 1994: 11; quoted in Shoemaker and Reese 1996: 251).*

The argument turns on the nicety that events staged for the journalist by others are fundamentally different to events staged by the journalist her or himself. This position has come under challenge from a number of journalists, among them the BBC's Martin Bell and the independent television journalist Jake Lynch. Bell argues for a "journalism of attachment", in which journalists accept a responsibility to take moral stances alongside the suffering of civilians in war zones. He writes:

> *I see nothing object-like in the relationship between the reporter and the event, but rather a human and dynamic interaction between them (Bell 1998: 18).*

This statement is consonant with some of what was discussed in the preceding section, but makes explicit what is rarely made explicit elsewhere. The truth that emerges from the war correspondent's intervention in the war zone emerges from a relationship rather than from something independent of that journalist. Bell does not explore the implications of this position in any depth, and formulated these thoughts at the end of his career as a journalist, so that it is difficult to trace through in his own practice where this thinking might lead.

But such thinking has also emerged in the work of Johan Galtung and the peace journalism movement, and has been expanded into a much more systematic agenda for journalism. Jake Lynch provides journalists with sets of questions they might ask themselves to become aware of and hence begin to address the adverse impact they have on events when they give disproportionate coverage to those holding the guns and to the violent solutions they advocate. He calls on them to ask:

> *how far can we predict the likely consequences of particular*

*patterns of coverage, how far can we build that into the reporting
process — to make those judgements before and as we report, not
just afterwards? (Lynch 2002).*

He terms this an ethic of responsibility, which might sit alongside the
"ethic of conviction" of telling truth without fear or favour, and thereby
moderate truth-telling by an acknowledgement that journalists are active
participants in the interpretation of social action.

The ethic of responsibility is thus a negative one, in the sense that it asks
journalists to limit the ethic of conviction. However, when we examine the
practical suggestions for journalists that emerge from such thinking (e.g.
McGoldrick and Lynch 2001), we can find a more radical and more positive
position. In the questions that Lynch suggests journalists ask of events and
in the assumptions that he invites them to question, he sketches an ethos that
constructs understanding by consciously acknowledging the journalist's
preconceptions and opening them up to challenge by engaging with the
perspectives of those reported on. I will quote just two from their 17 points:

AVOID treating a conflict as if it's only going on in the place and time
that the violence is occurring.

INSTEAD try to trace the links and consequences for people in other
places now and in the future (McGoldrick and Lynch ibid: 8).

If the reporter sees an event as linked to a large number of social issues
and also as having wider consequences for attitudes to solving dispute, then
it is harder to treat violence as a solution to conflict, and easier to envisage
the "woolly" solutions of social or political reform or cultural
understanding as potential solutions.

AVOID letting parties define themselves by simply quoting their
leaders' restatement of familiar demands or positions.

INSTEAD enquire deeper into goals:
How are people on the ground affected by the conflict in everyday life?
(ibid.).

McGoldrick and Lynch invite journalists to seek to bring their
perspective closer to the perspectives of those they report on and to extend

beyond thinking of events as another instance of what the reporter already knows. Lynch cites an example of such thinking in a joke common in one BBC newsroom about how reports on the Israeli-Palestinian conflict might be shortened:

> *Arabs and Jews hate each others' guts. They always have, they always will. John Smith, BBC News in the Middle East" (Lynch op cit).*

To extend beyond the conservative, self-referential journalism which the joke draws on, McGoldrick and Lynch sketch a space where the co-construction of meaning between the reporter and the reported on is acknowledged. Rather than simply call the reporting clichéd, a strategy which would lead back to Orwell's call for greater purity of language use and greater faithfulness to the "real" (Cameron 1996: 325), they encourage journalists to constantly unpack and rebuild the conventions of conflict reporting. A distinct set of questions is able to arise. These are future-oriented, because they recognise the impact of the report upon what may happen; they provide more space for the meanings of those they report on to emerge outside of the demands for sound bites and oppositional statements; and they invite news audiences to imagine the position of understanding of those who are victims of conflict.

CONCLUSION: VIEWING REPORTING THROUGH GADAMER'S HERMENEUTICS

All three of these interpretative strategies developed by journalists point towards the practice as a set of hermeneutic acts and towards the need to shape those interpretative processes within ethical statements as well as within epistemological ones. They also point us towards ethics as an attitude, a basic interpretative stance towards the world, rather than as the universal principles of deontological traditions. They thus take us in the direction of a more phenomenological ethics, grounded in Heidegger's notion of how we exist in the world as socially-situated selves, what he terms "Dasein" (literally, "being there-ness"). I will draw in particular on the thinking of one of Heidegger's students, Hans-Georg Gadamer to try to begin to theorise such strategies.

Within this phenomenological conception, the notion of an ethos describes the intentionality of the journalist in interpreting the world and in engaging with others. Ethics, as the basic relation of social actors which motivates and underpins their criteria for good living, is defined in terms of how the socially situated person — in this case, the person in the newsroom — comes into being most fully as a journalist in the way she or he interprets. For Gadamer, in *Truth and Method* (1979), this is a fundamentally linguistic process. You place yourself, he proposes, in a moment of being through language, a "thereness" and a "nowness", a position in relation to the world and all the rest of language (ibid: 496). As the interpretative tradition within journalism also knows, we cannot perceive people or events without engaging in interpretation of them.

For Gadamer, moreover, each moment of being is not only a placement of the self in relation to the social but is specifically, in the spatial metaphor he favoured, a placement of yourself in relation to a "horizon" of what you already know and what you expect. Thus, crucially, as both the journalists of subjectivity and Lynch's journalism of responsibility discover in practice, Gadamer argues we can only make sense of things by coming to them with presuppositions and testing those against what we perceive. We ask questions of what we hear to understand it and, in doing so, bring to bear our existing hermeneutic horizons.

Gadamer uses the idea of the horizon to theorise how interpretation happens, but at the same time he sketches criteria for quality or successful interpretation, and allows us to draw out of the journalistic reflections above the beginnings of a communicative ethics of the news. We can pinpoint a number of ethical attitudes, as follows:

- *Openness*; given that we interpret in terms of a particular horizon of pre-judgements and expectations, quality interpretation must always push against that horizon. It depends on journalists holding themselves ready for their preconceptions to be proved wrong. We must hold ourselves ready to be "pulled up short", Gadamer writes, "so that the text may present itself to us in all its newness and thus be able to assert its own truth against our fore-meanings" (ibid: 238). This does not mean a journalist must accept a text, such as a press release, uncritically, or ask her/his audience to follow its preconceptions. On the contrary, recognising how the text makes sense in its own terms may well involve recognising the narrowness of its horizon. Thus, in Birt and Jay's constant interchange of analysis and inquiry, a key ethical base for the interpretation must be a critique of the analysis in terms of the many possible perspectives which inquiry opens up. Similarly, Gadamer's thinking calls for the constant provision of new, challenging material to audiences in order, as Andrew Edgar argues, to extend their interpretative horizons (Edgar 2000). The ethical reporter is open too to the audience, providing a text that is assessable (O'Neill op cit), even one that is vulnerable in its self-critical subjectivity.

- *Listening*; for Gadamer, it is a condition of understanding that we listen in such a way that we take seriously what we encounter, assuming that the text or person talking truly contains a meaning that is in some sense true to what it intends to say. An attitude of sincere consideration towards the other lies at the heart of a number of models of communication (Allwood op cit). Importantly for journalism ethics, it suggests that a hermeneutics of distrust, a "discipline of verification", risks failing to hear that which differs from our viewpoint, however much it makes the reporter confident about avoiding factual error, while an attitude of cynical distance to political debate will lead to weak interpretation.

- *Close distance*; listening entails what Gadamer calls a "close distance", a useful phrase to describe both interpretative reporting's blending of analysis and reporting as well as the tightrope journalism walks between understanding and being co-opted by the powerful interests it writes about. Gadamer argues that "true understanding", which he defines as understanding which reaches out beyond the interpreter's horizon, does not take on what the other means, but understands what the other "truly says to us". Understanding the other thereby depends on recognising that there will always be a gap between us. Thus, if any truth emerges, it emerges in that gap between people, in the communication that gives both parties space to be different and to disagree. As Paul Ricoeur puts it, we can find ourselves with a "double motivation: willingness to suspect, willingness to listen, vow of rigor, vow of obedience" (1970; cited in Robinson 1995: 12). The ethical reporter is not disinterested. Indeed, as Cameron and Gellhorn's reflections suggest, journalism's great strength is often its reaching out in subjective witnessing of what happens to others, but a reaching out which recognises some ultimate otherness which cannot be bridged without misrepresentation.

- *Self-knowledge*; a basic tenet of Gadamer's hermeneutics is that we must understand what our own horizons are in order to reach beyond them. For him, interpretation is predicated on prejudgement, and denial of our interpretative situation impedes understanding. He rejects, therefore, any attempt at objectivity, but urges us instead to understand

and make explicit the position from which we are seeing others. O'Neill's assessable journalism, and particularly the assessableness of the consciously subjective journalist, places such self-awareness at the heart of the reporting. Similarly, as Lynch shows, recognition of journalism's participant role in society and its conventional nature are basic to quality journalism.

These attitudes do not lead to an ethical code, for that would take us back to a deontological ethic. Their strength is that they describe some grounds on which to critically reflect upon journalists' news judgement. All journalism of course depends upon layers of explicit and implicit interpretative acts, and this paper should not be taken as suggesting that only certain journalists interpret well or in depth. Rather, it has sought to draw out of news culture and out of hermeneutic philosophy some sense of what we might mean by "well" or "in depth". If we can begin to describe a communicative ethos — an attitude towards the world which prioritises understanding — in aspects of news practice, we can begin to help provide develop tools with which to build on such practice.

Thus, the paper has not sought to critique journalism as much as critique a journalism ethics which misses such features. If journalism frequently falls back upon defences of the impartial account and the self-evident fact, it is perhaps not because reporters have failed to work through the complex ethics of their interpretative work, or because they are impossibly naïve, but because they have few ways of talking about that work, and therefore as well few ways to value the collective interpretive work that they and audiences are engaged in. The journalists discussed above and many of their like-minded colleagues are certainly valued within the journalism profession, held up as having integrity or stature. Yet the strategies they deploy, of engaging in reflexive reporting, of acknowledging their subjective participation in reporting news events, of committing themselves to overcoming their limitations and of communicating such attitudes in news reports are not merely character traits, but an ethical attitude.

REFERENCES

Allwood, Jens (1997) "Notes on Dialog and Co-operation", *Collaboration, Cooperation and Conflict in Dialogue Systems*, Jokinen K, Sadek D. and Traum D. (eds) pp 9-11 Proceedings of the IJCAL-97 workshop Collaboration, Cooperation and Conflict in Dialogue Systems, Nagoya, August 1997. Available online at: www.ling.

gu.se/~jens/publications/index.html

Bell, Martin (1998) "The Journalism of Attachment", *Media Ethics*, Kieran, Matthew (ed.), London, Routledge pp 15-22

Birt, John and Jay, Peter (1975) *The Times*

Birt, John (1975) *The Times*

Boorstin, Daniel J. (1971) "From News-Gathering to News-Making: A Flood of Pseudo-Events", *The Process and Effects of Mass Communication*, Schramm, Wilbur and Roberts, Donald F. (eds), Urbana, IL. University of Illinois Press pp 116-150. Revised edn. First publ. 1961 in *The Image: A Guide to Pseudo-Events in America*

Borge, Torunn (2001) "Foreword", *Profession: Journalist*. Available online at: http://www.uiowa.edu/~iwp/SAMPLES/SAMPLESfall2001/Borge_Ed1.pdf

British Broadcasting Corporation (BBC) (n.d.) Producers' Guidelines. Available online at: http://www.bbc.co.uk/info/policies/producer_guides/

Cameron, Deborah (1996) "Style Policy and Style Politics: A Neglected Aspect of the Language of the News", *Media, Culture and Society* 18 pp 315-33

Carey, James W. (1992; orig 1989) *Communication as Culture: Essays on Media and Society*, London, Routledge

Castells, Manuel (1996) *The Rise of the Network Society*, Oxford, Blackwell.

Christians, Clifford (1997) "The Ethics of Being in a Communicative Context", *Communication Ethics and Universal Values*, Christians, Clifford and Traber, Michael (eds) London, Sage pp 3-23

Cissna, Kenneth N. and Anderson, Rob (2002) *Moments of Meeting: Buber, Rogers, and the Potential for Public Dialogue*, Albany, State University of New York Press

Cockburn, Claud (1981) *Cockburn Sums Up: An Autobiography*, London, Quartet

Curran, James (1996) "The New Revisionism in Mass Communications Research: A Reappraisal", *Cultural Studies and Communication*, Curran, James, Morley, David and Walkerdine, Valerie (eds) London, Arnold pp 256-78. First publ *European Journal of Communication* 5: 2/3 pp135-64

Didion, Joan (1968) "On Keeping a Notebook", *Slouching towards Bethlehem*, New York, Delta pp 131-41

Edgar, Andrew (2000) "The 'Fourth Estate' and Moral Responsibilities", *Ethics and Media Culture: Practices and Representations*, Berry, David (ed), Oxford, Focal Press pp 73-88

Fuller, Jack (1996) *News Values: Ideas for an Information Age*, Chicago, University of Chicago Press

Gadamer, Hans-Georg (1979; orig 1965) *Truth and Method* (trans. by Glen-Doepel, William), London, Sheed and Ward

Gans, Herbert (1980) *Deciding What's News: A Study of CBS Evening News, NBC Nightly News, Newsweek and Time*, London, Constable

Glasser, Theodore L. and Ettema, James S. (1989) "Common Sense and the Education of Young Journalists", *Journalism Educator* 44: 2 pp 18-25; 75

Habermas, Jürgen (1992) *Moral Consciousness and Communicative Action* (trans. by Lenhardt, Christian and Weber Nicholsen, Shierry), Oxford, Polity Press

Herbert, John (2000) *Journalism in the Digital Age: Theory and Practice for Broadcast, Print and On-line Media*, London, Focal Press

Huntting, Nancy (2001) "The Fight in Every Woman between Selfishness and Generosity;

Part 4: Honesty about Regret". Presented at Aesthetic Realism Seminar, New York, Dec. 2001. Available online at: http://www.nancyhuntting.net/Gellhorn-sem3.html

Iggers, Jeremy (1999) *Good News, Bad News: Journalism Ethics and the Public Interest*, Oxford, Westview Press

Lambert, Richard (1998) "Introduction", Dawkins, William and Inman, Colin (eds), *Inside the FT: The Art of FT Journalism*, London: FT Republishing pp ix-xiii

Lewis, M (1994) "Lights! Camera! News!" *New Republic*, February 28 pp 11-12

Lynch, Jake (2002) "Ethics of Reporting the World". Reporters and Reported lecture series, Cardiff University, Spring. Available online at: http://www.cf.ac.uk/jomec/reporters2002/lynchmain.html

McGoldrick, Annabel and Lynch Jake (2001) "What Is Peace Journalism?" *Activate*, Winter pp 6-9

Matheson, Donald (2003) "Scowling at Their Notebooks: How British Journalists Understand Their Writing", *Journalism* 4: 2 pp 165-83

O'Neill, Onora (2002) "Licence to Deceive" Lecture 5 of *BBC Reith Lectures 2002: A Question of Trust*. First broadcast BBC Radio 4, May 1, 8pm. Available online at: http://www.bbc.co.uk/radio4/reith2002/lecture5_text.shtml

Peters, John Durham (1999) *Speaking into the Air: A History of the Idea of Communication*, Chicago, University of Chicago Press

Press Complaints Commission (1999) "Code of Practice". Available online at: www.pcc.org.uk/cop/cop.asp

Ricoeur, Paul (1970) *Freud and Philosophy: An Essay on Interpretation*, Newhaven, Yale University Press

Robinson. G.D. (1995) "Paul Ricoeur and the Hermeneutics of Suspicion: A Brief Overview and Critique", *Premise* 2:8, 12. Available online at: http://capo.org/premise/95/sep/p950812.html

Rosenstiel, Ton and Kovach, Bill (2001) *The Elements of Journalism: What Newspeople Should Know and the Public Should Expect*, New York, Crown

Scannell, Paddy (1992) "Public Service Broadcasting and Modern Public Life", *Culture and Power: A Media, Culture and Society Reader*, Scannell, Paddy, Schlesinger, Philip and Sparks, Colin (eds), London, Sage pp 317-48

Shoemaker, Pamela J. and Reese, Stephen D. (1996) *Mediating the Message: Theories of Influences on Mass Media Content*, White Plains, Longman

Terkel, Studs (1997) "Studs Terkel Talks His Own History", *QS News*, Fall 1997, 1, pp 4-5

Wheen, Francis (2000) "Return of the BertJay", the *Guardian*, July 12

Zelizer, Barbie (1993) "Journalists as Interpretive Communities". *Critical Studies in Mass Communication*, 10 (2) pp 219-37

Zelizer, Barbie (1999) "Making the Neighborhood Work: the Improbabilities of Public Journalism", Glasser, Theodore L. (ed) *The Idea of Public Journalism*, New York, Guilford Press pp 152-72

Donald Matheson lectures in journalism and mass communication at the School of Political Science and Communication, University of Canterbury, New Zealand. He has worked at Cardiff University and Strathclyde University in the

UK where he studied for a PhD on the discourse analysis of newswriting practices. He has also worked as a journalist in the New Zealand press. Research on newswriting includes "Weblogs and the Epistemology of the News: Some Trends in Online Journalism", *New Media and Society* (forthcoming); "Scowling at Their Notebooks: The Management of Writing within British Journalism's Reflexive Identity", *Journalism*, 2003, "The Birth of News Discourse: Changes in News Language in British Newspapers, 1880-1930", *Media, Culture and Society*, 2000. Contact details: Dr Donald Matheson, School of Political Science and Communication, University of Canterbury, Private Bag 4800, Christchurch, New Zealand. +64 3 366 7001; email: donald.matheson@canterbury.ac.nz.

An earlier version of this chapter was presented at the Institute of Communication Ethics inaugural conference, City University, London, 28 February 2003

Ethical messages: R. H. Tawney confronts the information age

Alistair Duff and Rob Melville

This chapter sets ethical thinker R.H. Tawney in context as a dissident son of the British establishment. We explore the roots of his politics in philosophical idealism and religious socialism, before translating his famous critiques of acquisitiveness and inequality for the information age. Our main thesis is that Tawney's work supplies the resources for an important critical perspective on the information age. The chapter also emphasises Tawney's relevance for contemporary journalism practice, drawing comparisons with the contemporary school of public journalism in the USA. Tawney aimed to make a practical difference to society and employed academic writing and journalism as his tools.

Keywords: Tawney, Information Age, ethics, journalism practice, religious socialism

INTRODUCTION

R. H. Tawney (1880-1962) was one of those British rarities, a politically-committed academic. As a theorist and strategist he made a major contribution to the liberal left which in his day included the Labour Party, several of whose election manifestos he helped to write. At a memorial service in his honour at the House of Commons he was referred to by Hugh Gaitskell, the then Labour leader, as "*the* Democratic Socialist philosopher *par excellence*" (cited in Tawney 1964a: 211). He has also been described by a leading American political philosopher as "the most important socialist moralist of the 20th century" (Walzer 1981: 487).

Our intention here is to review Tawney's ideas within the context of the current information society debate (Duff 2000, 2003; Webster 2004). Does Tawney's work speak meaningfully to an emergent post-industrial order? Can his formerly influential critique of inequality and his prescriptions for social justice be reinterpreted in terms of modern socio-technical categories such as the politics of information or the political economy of communication? What would Tawney be saying today were he still writing the newspaper columns and editorials to which he devoted so much of his spare time? What, in short, are Tawney's ethical messages for the 21st century?

THE ETHICAL BASIS OF THE LIBERAL LEFT

"To estimate men simply by their place in a social order is to sanction the sacrifice of man to that order. It is only when we realise that each individual soul is related to a power above other men that we are able to regard each as an end in itself. In other words the idea of 'humanity' stultifies itself. The social order is judged and condemned by a power transcending it" (Tawney 1972 [1913]: 67-68).

Firstly, we will aim to identify the ethical underpinning of Tawney's politics, or what Tony Benn—in many ways Tawney's most faithful disciple in modern Britain—once called "the moral basis of the radical left" (Benn 1990). Tawney occupied the crucial period of modernity, in terms of both technological innovation and political ideology. Born into the upper middle class, his life became an uncompromising crusade against the shallow values and false consciousness of Edwardian England. It is not certain when he began to form the radical political beliefs that belied his conventional upbringing. We know, however, that Tawney attended Rugby School and that social moralism of a Christian stamp is a time-honoured Rugby tradition, established by the great reforming headmaster of the 19th century, Thomas Arnold. While not a socialist, Arnold was an outspoken opponent of the wage-slavery of early industrialism (Stanley 1844: 348).

Later, as an undergraduate at Balliol College, Oxford, Tawney would have heard Edward Caird, master of college and a distinguished Idealist philosopher, proposing that "a religion is nothing which does not create out of itself a new politics, a new social and even economical order of life" (Caird 1888: 6). It was Caird who charged his students to go and find out why England had poverty alongside riches and do something about it (Terrill 1973: 25). Equally significantly for the development of Tawney's thought, at Oxford he came into contact with a vibrant tradition of Christian socialism. Originating in an organised movement between 1848 and 1854, Christian socialism was an important strand of British left-wing thought throughout the 20th century (Cort 1988; Greenleaf 1983). For Christian socialists, even Marxists were "not revolutionary enough" since all they seemed to want was a *volte-face* in the class distribution of resources, the restoration of the booty, rather than a spiritual emancipation from enslavement to physical wealth (Tawney 1972 [1913]: 69).

Tawney drew a fundamental distinction between "acquisitive" and "functional" societies. Acquisitive societies are those whose "whole tendency and interest and preoccupation is to promote the acquisition of wealth" (Tawney 1920: 17). The tendency is symptomatic of "industrialism", a bloated individualism which exaggerates the rights of the individual in much the same way that imperialism is a perversion of patriotism (ibid: 27). Against the acquisitive society Tawney posited a more socially responsive doctrine of rights involving an organic link between individual and community (ibid: 17). In practical terms, the cure for acquisitiveness is public ownership of industry, a prescription which returns us to more familiar socialist categories. In *The Acquisitive Society* (1982 [1921]), Tawney argued against blanket state nationalisation. In worthy Fabian style, he suggested that socialisation must be "gradual" (Tawney 1982 [1921]: 123; Cole 1961), although his hit list of industries for immediate political surgery was extensive including arms, mines, railways, canals and alcoholic drinks.

However, Tawney was always clear that public ownership or control was only a means to an end, only half the story of social justice. The other half was egalitarianism, the main theme of perhaps his most influential work of political philosophy, *Equality* (Tawney 1964b [1931]). His belief in socio-economic equality sprang from an intuitive response to the violent contrasts in circumstance—the poverty alongside riches—he saw around him in the acquisitive society of industrial England, and to what, borrowing Matthew (Thomas's son) Arnold's phrase, he interpreted as an underlying "religion of inequality" (ibid: 33). At one level, Tawney articulated socio-economic equality as a logical extension of political democracy, a standard move in the liberal socialist tradition. However, egalitarianism for Tawney went far beyond legal or democratic categories to express an organic, even spiritual, relation. As he put it, "because men and men, social institutions—property rights, and the organisation of industry, and the system of public health and education—should be planned, as far as is possible, to emphasize and strengthen, not the class differences which divide, but the common humanity which unites, them" (ibid: 49).

Social justice requires not just the opening of the social heights to outstanding individuals but also a general narrowing of the space between valley and peak because only a large measure of equality of circumstance (or what today is usually called equality of outcome) could embed "the fact of human fellowship" (ibid: 113). When viewed in such a light, class divisions are anathema, shallow man-made appearances militating against a transcendental order. It is egalitarianism not only as economic justice, nor merely as ethical idealism, but as metaphysics. From Tawney's perspective, were politics only about restoration of the booty to the poor, the sickness of the acquisitive society would not have been cured but only spread. This Christian-inspired vision of brotherhood is at the heart of Tawney's position: it is indeed socialism as fellowship (Terrill 1973; Ormrod 1990). Therein lies, it will be argued below, Tawney's main positive legacy for the development of an ethical information society.

A TRANSLATION OF TAWNEY FOR THE INFORMATION AGE

There can be no doubt that at a straightforward level Tawney fully appreciated the political importance of information and knowledge. This is evident throughout his writings, for example in a proposal for what would quickly today be dubbed FOI (freedom of information) as part of his influential argument for free secondary schooling in the UK (Tawney 1923: 13). Tawney recognised as well as any radical that "ignorance and docility go hand in hand" (ibid: 33). Moreover, he envisaged higher education occupying an elevated epistemological position as "a centre of moral authority" in society, its job to teach the "infinite difference between what is false and what is true" (Tawney 1972 [1912]: 43). In such ways, information has its rightful place in a progressive democratic polity. However, nowhere in the Tawney canon does information emerge from such roles to become a major category in its own right. On the contrary, Tawney went out of his way to resist a line of thinking, prevalent even in his own day (especially among Fabians), according to which information is all that is needed to solve the problems of society. "More knowledge we certainly need," he wrote, "but what we need still more is the disposition to act on the knowledge which we possess" (ibid: 30).

A pioneering economic historian by profession, Tawney was diligent in the discovery of facts, but he believed that policymakers must strive to apply normative principles to their empirical data. So he would today have been found asking searching questions of the much-lauded information explosion and the political claims often associated with it. He would have enquired about the *social function* of all this information production and the *moral purposes* that it might serve. He would have seen it as his task to remind us that the social problem is a problem not of quantities but of proportions, not of the amount of information but of the moral status of the information society. And he would have utterly repudiated the pervasive "cult" of information (Roszak 1994).

A Tawney perspective also enables us to ask some pertinent normative questions about the central plank of empirical post-industrialism, the claim that the economies of advanced nations have progressed from secondary to tertiary and quaternary occupations, from goods to services and information (Bell 1999 [1973]): 121-164). What exactly is the function of the proliferating information worker segment of the economy? What social purposes do information workers fulfil? Can their putatively high status be morally justified? Such hard questions are seldom properly considered on the transformative wing of the information society. Yet they are good questions for much that currently goes on in the information economy, especially in the information services and media of communication sectors, appears to be redundant from a social-moral point of view. It is difficult to escape the feeling that direct email advertisers, Internet gambling outfits, or the less salubrious satellite television channels, to pick on three prominent, if arbitrary, examples, are essentially parasitic on the body politic. And Tawney would have gravely doubted the viability of an economy modelled on so-called teleworkers. He would have made it his business, as trade unions are beginning to do today, to investigate the scope for exploitation and alienation of this scattered labour force, particularly its numerically predominant non-professional elements.

A dubious claim that has been made on behalf of the information society is that it is deeply corrosive of social inequality, that it even signifies the imminent doom of hierarchy. Given that Tawney's crusade was principally against the disease of social inequality, we can be confident that he would have paid close attention to such speculations. How would he have reacted? No doubt, he would have welcomed any actual levelling effects of the Internet. Yet Tawney, one can be sure, would have been deeply sceptical about the contemporary and futurological rhetoric of equality—and rightly so. Basically, he would rejected any technology-based aspiration towards a society similar to that offered by socialists without the need for political action. For a deontological moralist like Tawney, the problem of an acquisitive society could never be cured by alchemy, either mystical or technical, but only by "sustained and strenuous efforts" (Tawney 1964a

[1952]: 170). There are no short cuts to the good society.

Furthermore, there is much in the content of Tawney's doctrine of equality that should be appropriated by those serious about problematising and then tackling information inequalities. As a rule, the recent literature on the digital divide is woefully superficial, although there are exceptions (e.g. Wyatt *et al.* 2000). What it almost always omits is a whole-hearted doctrine of relational justice, and specifically an admission that social justice is as much bad news for the excessively rich as good news for the poor. What the digital divide policy literature needs today is a deep draught of Tawney's strongly normative political philosophy, of his principled distaste for violent inequalities and what they do to human fellowship and of recognition that real democracy inevitably entails the overthrow of social privilege. Though a gentleman and a scholar, Tawney felt that he had to tell the unvarnished truth: socialism is the only road to a decent society.

THE MESSAGE FOR CONTEMPORARY JOURNALISM PRACTICE

Finally, we aim to bring into focus the activist dimension of Tawney and specifically consider how his journalism can guide us today. It was clear from the start that he used his journalism like his lectern to advance his social philosophy. Tawney's journalism spanned a period of 55 years; he began in 1907 with the *Westminster Gazette* and was still writing reviews for the *Manchester Guardian* in the mid-1950s when he was 75. According to his biographer Ross Terrill, he had "hesitat[ed] between journalism and teaching. Like others at Balliol in his time... Tawney felt the urge the college gave men to write, to address a public on the issues of the day" (Terrill 1973: 38). That he chose education over journalism as a career probably arose out of his belief that "education is a path to emancipation for every man" (ibid: 23). It might also have arisen out of his belief in fellowship and a desire for direct contact with his chosen milieu, namely the English working class (in the form of Workers' Education Association classes he gave until the outbreak of World War One). Nevertheless, it was a loss to the journalism profession. As Pauline Webb, the BBC broadcaster, noted in her R H. Tawney Memorial Lecture: "We should encourage young people of integrity and commitment to ideals of social justice to go into the profession of journalism" (Webb 1990: 120).

Today Tawney's books are undoubtedly his best legacy but his journalism was also influential "because he made responses to challenges widely felt" (Terrill op cit: 10). His was an opinionated journalism whose aim was "to create an integrated society of shared values" (Wright 1987:

138). There was nothing "objective" about his views: this was very much the journalism of attachment closely associated today with the former BBC journalist Martin Bell (Sanders 2003: 43). Here was an independent Christian voice who could choose his publications, especially from 1920 onwards when he secured tenure at the London School of Economics. Editors, including the great C. P. Scott of the *Manchester Guardian*, courted him for his strong opinions on the social questions of the day, seeing him as an authentic voice of the liberal left. This was a man of vision who knew the difference between right and wrong and who was determined to make a difference by bringing about a new order based upon social justice.

Tawney retained a Victorian liberal optimism grounded in the belief that reason could make things better through teaching and writing and in this there are parallels to the 1990s and the public journalism of Jay Rosen and Davis Merritt in the United States. He would have agreed with Merritt that "journalism has a role beyond telling the news, beyond the mere provision of information" and "beyond only describing what is going wrong to also imagining what going right would be like" (Merritt 1998: 140). This is classic Tawney territory, where a critical and informed analysis of the present is combined with a vision of the future to encourage readers to shape their own destinies. Unlike Rosen and Merritt, however, whose critics claimed they had no coherent political programme to bring about significant and lasting progress, Tawney had a fully-fledged social philosophy and a political party to boot, namely the Labour Party.

Like contemporary left-wing critics, Tawney would have ascribed the ethical ills of modern journalism to advanced capitalism and specifically to the avarice of individual press barons pursuing their own private ends—those whom George Orwell described as the "immediate enemies of truthfulness" (Orwell 1997 [1946]: 161). Tawney knew that vicious market competition for readership is often at the expense of ethical journalism. His position is best reflected in the outlook of ex-MP and member of the Labour left, Tony Benn, who, in his own Tawney Memorial Lecture, noted that the mass media "increasingly acts as a propaganda machine rather than an information service" (Benn 1990: 103). Benn attacks the power of market competition and the pursuit of profit at the expense of fellowship and morality:

"We are taught to worship money and power at the expense of community. The hours of TV broadcasting time and pages of newspaper coverage dealing with money matters have elevated them into a religion that has obscured and overlaid the moral values taught over centuries by

Christians and socialists who represent traditions of human concern" (ibid: 105).

This is surely the voice of Tawney translated to the present day, a voice questioning the human value of much of the information we receive. The problem that remains is how to make Benn and Tawney's democratic socialist values more appealing in a pluralistic and hedonistic post-industrial world, one in which commitment and belief are accorded little value; where the independent voice is increasingly lost amidst agendas of spin and propaganda and celebrity appeal; where print journalism has lost its dominant and authoritative accent to soundbites and moving images. As Amy Brand, a staff writer on the *New Republic,* plaintively observes in the current film Shattered Glass, based on the fabrications practised by fellow journalist Stephen Glass in 1998: "They don't want policy pieces anymore, they want quirky characters, bizarre events, colour..."

REFERENCES
Bell, D. (1999) [1973] *The Coming of Post-Industrial Society: A Venture in Social Forecasting*, New York, Basic Books
Benn, T. (1990) "The Moral Basis of the Radical Left: The Best Hope for the Future of British Politics", Ormrod, D. (ed) *Fellowship, Freedom and Equality: Lectures in Memory of R. H. Tawney*, London, Christian Socialist Movement pp 103-109
Bromley, M. and O'Malley, T. (eds) (1997) *A Journalism Reader*, London, Routledge
Caird, E. (1888) *The Moral Aspect of the Economical Problem: Presidential Address to the Ethical Society*, London, Swan Sonnenschein, Lowrey and Co
Cole, M. (1961) *The Story of Fabian Socialism*, Stanford, CA, Stanford University Press
Cort, J. C. (1988) *Christian Socialism: An Informal History*, Maryknoll, New York, Orbis Books
Duff, A. S. (2000) *Information Society Studies*, London, Routledge
Duff, A. S. (2003) "The Great Information Society Debate", *Review of Communication* 3 (3) pp 220-224
Greenleaf, W. H. (1983) *The British Political Tradition, Vol. 2: The Ideological Heritage*, London, Methuen
Merritt, D. (1998) *Public Journalism and Public Life: Why Telling the News Is Not Enough*, (2nd edition) Lawrence Erlbaum Associates
Ormrod, D. (ed.) (1990) *Fellowship, Freedom and Equality: Lectures in Memory of R. H. Tawney*, London, Christian Socialist Movement
Orwell, G (1997) [1946] "The Prevention of Literature", Bromley, M and O'Malley, T (eds), *A Journalism Reader*, London, Routledge pp 159-164
Roszak, T. (1994) *The Cult of Information: A Neo-Luddite Treatise on High Tech, Artificial Intelligence, and the True Art of Thinking*, (2nd edition) Berkeley, CA, University of California Press
Sanders, K. (2003) *Ethics and Journalism*, London, Sage
Stanley, A. P. (1844) *Life and Correspondence of Thomas Arnold*, D. D., London, Ward,

Lock and Co

Tawney, R. H. (1920) *The Sickness of an Acquisitive Society*, London, the Fabian Society

Tawney, R. H. (ed.) (1923) *Secondary Education For All: A Policy For Labour*, London, the Labour Party; George Allen and Unwin

Tawney, R. H. (1964a) [1952] "British Socialism Today", *The Radical Tradition: Twelve Essays on Politics, Education and Literature*, Hinden R. (ed), London, George Allen and Unwin pp 168-180

Tawney, R. H. (1964b) [1931] *Equality*, (4th edition) London, George Allen and Unwin

Tawney, R. H. (1972) [1912-1914] *R. H. Tawney's Commonplace Book, Winter*, J.M. and Joslin D.M. (eds), Cambridge, Cambridge University Press

Tawney, R. H. (1982) [1921] *The Acquisitive Society*, Brighton, Wheatsheaf Books.

Terrill, R. (1973) *R. H. Tawney and His Times: Socialism as Fellowship*, Cambridge, MA, Harvard University Press

Walzer, M. (1981) "From R.H. Tawney's Commonplace Book", *Dissent* 28 (4) pp 487-490

Webb, P. (1990) "The Media and Social Morality", Ormrod, D (ed) *Fellowship, Freedom and Equality: Lectures in Memory of R. H. Tawney*, London, Christian Socialist Movement pp 110-120

Webster, F. (ed.) *The Information Society Reader*, London, Routledge

Wright, A. (1987) *R. H. Tawney*, Manchester, Manchester University Press

Wyatt, S., Henwood, F., Miller, N., and Senker, P. (eds) (2000) *Technology and In/equality: Questioning the Information Society*, London, Routledge

Alistair Duff specialises in information policy in the School of Communication Arts, Napier University. His background is a combination of political philosophy and information studies. He worked in professional research and library positions for several years before becoming a lecturer in information management. He has published papers in journals of information and communications, as well as a book, *Information Society Studies* (Routledge 2000). Contact details: School of Communication Arts, Napier University, Craighouse Campus, Craighouse Road, Edinburgh EH10 5DT; a.duff@napier.ac.uk; tel: 0131 455 6163/6150; fax: 0131 455 6193.

Rob Melville lectures in journalism and media ethics in the School of Communication Arts, Napier University. A former journalist, he has taught in higher education for the past 20 years. Over the past four years he has served on the national executive of the Association of Journalism Education (AJE) and has been an active member of the European Journalism Training Association for 10 years. He writes regularly on journalism education and training. Contact details: School of Communication Arts, Napier University, Craighouse Campus, Craighouse Road, Edinburgh EH10 5DT; r.melville@napier.ac.uk; tel: 0131 455 6150.

Journalism online: Ethics as usual?

Ari Heinonen

This chapter examines possible changes in the ethical attitudes of journalists in the context of the increasingly new media-dominated communication environment. Using thematic in-depth interviews, 20 print and broadcast journalists in Finland were surveyed. The study revealed that journalists tended to consider ethical issues constant across old and new media. Most interestingly, it was possible to identify emerging ethical issues which could lead to a redefinition of proper journalistic conduct within the new media environment.

Keywords: journalism, professional ethics, online journalism, new media, changing communication, Finland

ETHICS AS PROPER PROFESSIONAL CONDUCT

This paper examines how journalists as a profession are accommodating to the changing communications environment in the Information Age focusing on the norms and values that journalists consider important for their occupation. Journalistic ethics is understood in terms of guidelines for good professional practice. All professional ethics, including that of journalism, can also be fruitfully approached from a philosophical perspective. Cooper (1989) and Christians (1989), for instance, have pointed out that discussion about professional ethics has important dimensions leading to questions of epistemology, ontology and universal truth. However, as White (1989: 46; see also 2000) has noted: "Communication ethics, like other forms of professional ethics, has developed with only remote connections to systematic moral philosophies and with only a vague sense of fulfilment of a broader moral order."

White associates the formation of journalistic ethics with the professionalisation process. He argues that "communication ethics has emerged out of the ethos of professionalism that characterises the rise of middle classes in the formation of modern technical societies" (ibid.). Indeed, the development of the journalistic profession shows how the system of common values emerged and consolidated in the process where journalists became a distinct category of communications professionals (Carey 1997/1969, Chalaby 1998, Schduson 1978). It is noteworthy that this system of ethical values was generated as part of the process where the journalistic profession became aware of itself as a specific occupational group. Therefore, journalists' ethical codes, in their purest form, are a statement of acceptable professional conduct as understood by the profession (Heinonen 1995, 2003). By investigating journalists' ethical attitudes in the era of new communications technology, we are also surveying the possible new features of journalists' professional identity.

ONLINE (R)EVOLUTION IN JOURNALISM

One of the implications of attaching journalism ethics to the development of the journalistic profession is that journalistic norms and values are not constant but variable. As journalistic practice and the social functions and the environment of the profession change, so too do the normative guidelines of professional conduct. In the case of online journalism, we are dealing with a highly dynamic phenomenon that is both a vague concept and an ongoing process. To give a context for this paper, it is necessary to begin by looking at journalists' reactions in general. Based on the literature on the impacts of digitalisation, the Internet, the World Wide Web and most recently mobile communication technology on journalism (see e.g. Boczkowski 2004, Hall 2001, Kawamoto 2003, Pavlik 2001) and drawing on empirical studies among Finnish journalists (Heinonen 1999), we can identify two main inclinations in how journalists seem to be responding to the challenges of the Information Age.

The first approach sees the Internet and what it represents (digital communication, interactivity, globality) as a turning-point in the history of journalism. This can be called a revolutionary inclination which foresees drastic changes in the professional role and identity of journalists. The traditional task of journalists as information brokers and gatekeepers will diminish if not altogether disappear in the wake of new communication practices. The other approach stresses the continued need for journalistic professional expertise even in the Age of the Net. This attitude can be called the evolutionary inclination. From this viewpoint, the Internet as an icon represents change but one that does not require dramatic re-evaluations of basic journalistic conventions including ethical values. Rather than diminish, the social role of the journalistic profession may gain in importance because of the overflow of information in the Information Society (ibid).

These two approaches are useful analytical tools in exploring the changing professional ethics in this era. Both inclinations acknowledge that the Internet – again in a symbolic sense – is a catalyst of change in journalism. As Cooper (1998) has noted, the new situation may have amplifying, transforming or mixing effects on the ethical issues of communication. Although Cooper refers mainly to the effects of new technology, this view is also applicable in the wider context because it highlights the dynamic nature of the current phase of journalism. Moreover, the approaches advise us to be careful in anticipating the possible directions of change. Predictions about the death of journalism heard during the hype of the late 1990s were silenced when the new economy bubble burst at the turn of the century and now the prevailing attitude regarding the future of journalism seems to be one of anticipation and expectation (see Berkman and Shumway 2003, Dahlgren 2001, Deuze and Yeshua 2001, Digital Journalism...2002, Rosen 2003). Here I shall look at how professional journalists in one country, Finland, define the issues for journalistic ethics of online journalism.

THE RESEARCH SETTING

The study in question was carried out in 2003 as part of the New Media Journalism masters programme at Tampere University. To understand the attitude of journalists working in established media towards online journalism, the students[1] conducted a series of in-depth interviews with new media journalists working for traditional media institutions. The focus was on the ethical aspects of online journalism and we covered the topic with five broad themes in 22 interviews. The interviewees can be considered to form an expert panel in that they were hand-picked on the basis of their experience both in journalism and online journalism. The dataset gathered proved to be a rich one and confirmed the topicality of the issue. Two major themes with several sub-categories emerged from the interviews. I will begin by briefly introducing the most common theme which I call constant issues, although the main focus will be on the other theme called emerging issues.

CONSTANT ISSUES

Generally, the interviewees took the view that journalism will manage well in the new online environment by adhering to its traditional ethical values. It was pointed out that an established journalistic institution is in itself a guarantee of ethical performance online. This trust in the brand was brought up like an automatic reflex, typically in the early stages of the interviews; among traditional media this is a common attitude towards new media. It was also pointed out that from an ethical point of view the problem was not the traditional media but rather the newcomers, "the others" (see Heinonen 2003). Nor was the new environment, as such, a problem but the lack of journalistic traditions among the newcomers.

The biggest problem is precisely this — that the quality of online journalism outside of these traditional media is so varied. And it can be unreliable because it does not rely on the old traditions.

In line with this emphasis on traditions and also in accordance with the generally firm ethical attitudes of Finnish journalists (see Heinonen 1995; Harju 2002), the interviewees stated that the ethical issues in online journalism are largely the same as in offline journalism.

These same...journalistic criteria are valid online as well...The same journalistic criteria as usual, but they are highlighted online.

As Cooper (1998; see also Deuze and Yeshua 2001) has pointed out, there are "perpetual" ethical questions that remain largely the same regardless of the changes in the technological setting of communication. In our study, these issues were typically presented as a list of features defining virtuous journalism, consisting of such attributes as truthfulness, accuracy, reliability and credibility. On the other hand, it was admitted that some constant values may be highlighted in the online environment. Two issues were mentioned more often than others in this regard, namely plagiarism and the blurring borders between journalistic and non-journalistic contents. It was felt that both of these issues were becoming a growing problem.

...a local radio station runs our stories complete with spelling mistakes on their web-site. They mark [the text], and then it's control + c and control + v; that's how it works.

In addition, many of the interviewees made the point that the increasingly hectic nature of journalistic work in the online environment may highlight problems of accuracy. As journalists are pushed from already tight deadlines to the 24/7 publishing flow, the risk of incorrect or otherwise un-ethical journalism increases.

...this is fast and short...we are working here with breaking news which is often real-time...there is a chance that you take too many shortcuts and there certainly is the temptation to publish too early without thinking, just fast.

EMERGING ISSUES

Perhaps the most interesting data in our study, however, dealt with issues that do not conveniently fit into any of the categories above. Conventional "vocabulary" was of little help in describing them, but they may represent quiet signals of future trends in professional ethics. It was possible to identify three loose and heterogeneous groupings of emerging ethical issues.

Firstly, regarding the technological issues, it was mentioned that the expanded time-span of online journalism may raise intriguing ethical considerations. In contrast to the print media, and to an even greater extent traditional electronic media, online journalism is theoretically eternal. Its electronic archives can easily be accessed many years from now and many newspapers are, in fact, hoping to make a business out of selling old news online. Additionally, any online site may be copied and archived in one of the Web archives around the globe. And search engines will easily find that otherwise forgotten information, true or false, from these archives.

One day we were contacted by someone who asked if we could remove a story from our archives in which he was mentioned in a not-so-positive light. There were no inaccuracies in the story but he felt uncomfortable about the story being brought up by search engines... I said we were not going to change history.

One of the problems presented by this eternal nature of online journalism concerns the question of how to correct mistakes. In print you publish a correction next day and both the false information and the correction are archived as such, albeit separately. Online, it is not as clear how to proceed.

A very important, indeed an essential principle is that although the story is published online you don't doctor it afterwards ... so if there are any mistakes these are corrected in a separate story, that is with a correction. To me, this is an essential issue which creates credibility and reinforces ethical values for the online medium.

Closely related to the expanded time-span of online journalism is the issue of the timeliness of contents. One interviewee made an interesting comment in this respect:

You often notice that the stories have not been updated. Or you don't know when a certain story has been created.

Another interviewee said:

You often see material left online that has lost its currency... there is a need for constant updating.

What these interviewees are implying is that it is crucial in the online environment to update contents. Secondly, information about updates should be made available to the public.

In the print media there is the problem of not following through the processes, giving just a snapshot instead. In these new mediums this is an even bigger problem.

Another issue that can be associated with the technological dimension of online journalism was the concern expressed by our interviewees about the effects of electronic interfaces on the quality of journalistic reporting.

Because of the [screen] resolutions and things like that, the [Inter]net favours short presentations ... Especially when you are reading from the screen, there are special requirements for the text and that will begin to affect the text. You have to spice up the text to make it juicier and that leads easily to bending the truth...

A second group of comments in this category of emerging ethical issues may be labelled (perhaps somewhat provocatively) as a clash of cultures. Scholars like Manuel Castells (1996) have pointed out that although the Internet originated for the purposes of the establishment, it has always contained a flavour of anti-establishment culture. According to this netizen culture, the Internet should be a free place in the both meanings of the word.

Journalism, on the other hand, is a very hierarchical, controlled and mostly profit-oriented institution. Therefore, when journalism enters the online world or when netizens meet journalism online, tensions may rise.

One of the specific issues brought up was that of anonymity. Even before journalism entered the Internet, there were numerous forums where you could and still can communicate under a pseudo-identity. But online journalism is considered to have a different set of rules although some allowances were made and opinions were somewhat divided.

It is entirely compatible with the spirit of the net, completely suitable that you can remain anonymous in discussions and chats … But as far as journalistic contents are concerned, that of course doesn't apply — that's a totally different matter.

A third grouping of emerging ethical issues deals with the relationship with the audience. Some new media advocates have demanded that the public be brought into journalism in the online world not as an audience but rather as partners in creating journalism (see e.g. Bowman and Willis 2003). Our interviewees did not go as far as that but they did make note of some new interesting possibilities regarding the position of the audience. One of these was the possibility of using hypertext in directing the readers to original sources.

If there has been a major crime and the police send us a press release, and we prepare a short news piece, then we sometimes add a link that takes you to this press release.

Interactivity, which is one of the most appreciated features of online communication, did not seem to be of particular interest to our interviewees, although it was not totally ignored either. It was pointed out that this is something journalism was still learning.

DISCUSSION

Considering that at least in so-called western countries journalistic culture and professional identity are characterised by largely common underlying norms, it can be assumed that our findings may be applicable also beyond this data. Not only our study in Finland, but also debates elsewhere have confirmed that the new media is, indeed, a catalyst for ethical considerations in journalism. Yet the main ethical issues online seem to be largely the same as offline. But although the new media do not seem to constitute a revolution in journalism ethics, the data suggests that in the online world proper journalistic conduct may have to change to be compatible with both the requirements and possibilities of the new medium. As institutional journalism everywhere is increasingly influenced by the global netizen culture, journalistic ethics may encounter issues to which the prevailing codes of conduct provide no or little guidance.

NOTE

1   The study was designed and carried out as part of the master's course on New Media Journalism Ethics and Law. The students contributed to every step from initial planning through interviewing to the preliminary analysis of the data. My thanks to Marja-Liisa Hakanen, Tauri Kankaanpää, Olli Kariniemi, Tero Kekki, Eeva Kiiskinen, Terhi Kinnunen, Liisa Kirves, Jenni Kivessilta, Risto Koivuniemi, Jukka Lehtinen, and Harri Mäkinen.

REFERENCES

Berkman, Robert I. and Shumway, Christopher A. (2003) *Digital Dilemmas: Ethical Issues for Online Media Professionals*, Ames, Iowa State Press

Boczkowski, Pablo J. (2004) *Digitizing the News: Innovation in Online Newspapers*. Cambridge, Massachusetts, MIT Press

Bowman, Shayne and Willis, Chris (2003) *We Media: How Audiences Are Shaping the Future of News And Information*. Availble online at http://www.ndn.org/webdata/we_media/we_media.htm

Carey, James (1997/1969) "The Communications Revolution and the Professional Communicator", Munson, Eve Stryker and Warren, Catherine A. (eds.), *James Carey. A Critical Reader*, Minneapolis, University of Minnesota Press

Castells, Manuel (1996) *The Rise of the Network Society. Volume I, The Information Age. Economy, Society and Culture*, Oxford, Blackwell

Chalaby, Jean K. (1998) *The Invention of Journalism*, Houndmills, Macmillan

Cooper, Thomas W. (1998) "New Technology Effects Inventory: Forty Leading Ethical Issues", *Journal of Mass Media Ethics* 3:(2) pp 71-92

Cooper, Thomas W. (1989) "Global Universals: In Search of Common Ground", Cooper, Thomas W., Christians, Clifford G., Plude, Frances Forde and White, Robert A. (eds.), *Communication Ethics and Global Change*, White Plains, Longman pp 20-39

Christians, Clifford G. (1989) "Ethical Theory in a Global Setting", Thomas, W., Christians, Clifford G., Plude, Frances Forde and White, Robert A. (eds) *Communication Ethics and Global Change*, White Plains, Longman pp 3-19

Dahlgren, Peter (2001) "The Twilight of Virtuous Journalism? – On Pinning One's Hopes on the Net", Porter, Vincent (ed.) *Ethics and Mass Communication in Europe*, London, Centre for Communication and Information Studies, University of Westminster pp 9-26

Deuze, Mark and Yeshua, Daphna (2001) "Online Journalists Face New Ethical Dilemmas: Lessons for the Netherlands" *Journal of Mass Media Ethics*, 16 (4) pp 273-292

Digital Journalism... Digital Journalism Credibility Study (2002). Online News Association. Available online at http://www.journalists.org/Programs/Research.htm

Hall, Jim (2001) *Online Journalism. A Critical Primer*, London, Pluto Press

Harju, Auli (2002) *Journalistisen työn sääntely ja ammattietiikka* [*The regulation of journalistic work and professional ethics*], Tampere. A research report by Tampere Journalism Research and Development Centre

Heinonen, Ari (2003) "Journalistic Ethics in the Age of the Net. Outlining an Approach for Studying Journalists' Changing Professional Identity", Salaverría, Ramón and Sádaba, Charo (eds): *Towards New Media Paradigms*, Pamplona, Ediciones Eunate

Heinonen, Ari (1999) *Journalism in the Age of the Net. Changing Society, Changing Profession*. Tampere: Acta Universitatis Tamperensis 685. Available online at http://acta.uta.fi/pdf/951-44-5349-2.pdf

Heinonen, Ari (1995) *Vahtikoiran omatunto. Journalismin itsesääntely ja toimittajat* [*The conscience of the watchdog. The self-regulation of journalism and journalists*], Tampere: University of Tampere, Department of Journalism and Mass Communication, Publications A84

Kawamoto, Kevin (ed.) (2003) *Digital Journalism: Emerging Media and the Changing Horizons of Journalism*, Lanham, Rowman and Littlefield Publishers

Pavlik, John (2001) *Journalism and New Media*, New York, Columbia University Press

Rosen, Jay (2003) "Terms of Authority", *Columbia Journalism Review*, 5/September. Available online at http://www.cjr.org/issues/2003/5/alt-rosen.asp

Schudson, Michael (1978) *Discovering the News. A Social History of American Newspapers*, New York, Basic Books

White, Robert A. (2000) "New Approaches to Media Ethics: Moral Dialogue, Creating Normative Paradigms, and Public Cultural Truth", Pattyn, Bart (ed.), *Media Ethics. Opening Social Dialogue*, Leuven, Peeters.

White, Robert A. (1989) "Social and Political Factors in the Development of Communication Ethics", Cooper, Thomas W., Christians, Clifford G., Plude, Frances Forde and White, Robert A. (eds) *Communication Ethics and Global Change*, White Plains, Longman pp 40-65

Ari Heinonen is Professor of New Media Journalism in the Department of Journalism and Mass Communication, University of Tampere, Finland. Previously, he was the Director of the Tampere Journalism Research and Development Centre and journalism lecturer after a career as a practising journalist. His research focus is the changing nature of professionalism in journalism, including the effects of new media on the role and identity of journalists in society. Contact details: Prof. Ari Heinonen, Dept. of Journalism and Mass Communication, FIN-33014 University of Tampere, Finland. Tel. +358-3-2157031, e-mail: ari.a.heinonen@uta.fi.

'What moral universe are you from?' Everyday tragedies and the ethics of press intrusion into grief

John Tulloch

Nowhere is the conflict between the professional values of journalists and the values of ordinary people more apparent in the UK than in press coverage of families grieving for victims of accidents or crimes. Attempts from the beginning of the 1990s to forbid press intrusion into grief or shock have been steadily resisted by the British Press Complaints Commission whose voluntary Code of Conduct requires journalists to make inquiries and publish material with "sympathy and discretion". Editors argue that such in inquiries are in the interests of accuracy and may be welcomed by relatives but this chapter argues that the voluntary code fails to address the problems posed by sensational journalism and its lack of compassion and empathy for grieving families.

Keywords: media ethics, press conduct, grief, intrusion, compassion

The quote in the title was attributed to Labour MP and Minister for Europe Denis McShane. It was allegedly spoken to a journalist who tried to question him and his former partner Carol Barnes as they arrived, in obvious distress, at Melbourne airport in March 2004 following the death of their daughter Clare in a skydiving accident. Later that week the *Sun, Daily Mirror, Daily Express, Daily Mail, Evening Standard* and *Daily Telegraph* printed long-lens photographs of the couple grieving in the field where Clare Barnes' body had been discovered (Greenslade 2004).

Do journalists inhabit a different moral universe to the person in the street? It is a truism in debates about media ethics that journalists experience a conflict between the canons of generally accepted moral behaviour assumed to apply to all reasonable "ordinary people" in western societies and a body of practices and values based on the assumption that journalists have a unique role and mission in society. As Stephen H. Daniel put it: "The values of truth-telling, honesty and fairness which we apply to communicators in general fail to exercise a compelling force over many journalists other than in the codes to which they give lip-service. This is not to say that journalists have no ethical standards; rather it says that the working ethical standards of the journalist are determined by what he [sic] sees as contributing to his own (and ultimately, the public) good through the survival of his paper, television station or job" (Daniel 1992: 51-52). To this list of values which fail to exercise "compelling force" might be added compassion and the ability to empathise with another human being. Many journalists are suspicious of the claims of compassion as a form of post-modern narcissism which prioritises feeling over analysis in a populism of shared emotion. According to the investigative journalist Tessa Mayes:

> *The implication is that news reporters are less humane or fail to empathise with victims of tragedies if they attempt to be forensic in gathering the news. Sadly, news reporters are more likely to be judged on their personal morals and what they feel about an event, rather than on the qualities of factual accuracy and analysis (quoted in Keeble 2001: 140).*

By implication, empathy and humanity are placed in the sphere of "personal morals" against the professional requirements of "factual accuracy" and "analysis". Of course, although Mayes assumes she is standing against a tide of woolly thinking, her position has the support of most accredited codes of journalistic conduct, including the Code of Practice operated by the British Press Complaints Commission, where the first clause is not about respect for human rights or press freedom, but accuracy:

> *The Press must take care not to publish inaccurate, misleading or distorted information, including pictures... (PCC 2004b)*

HUGE CHANGES IN ATTITUDES TO GRIEF
Within the lifetime of today's pensioners, huge changes have occurred in our public attitudes towards grief and mourning and our social practices may seem impoverished when compared to the past. Geoffrey Gorer's

profoundly influential study of attitudes to death and grief in the early 1960s was based on a survey of 1,628 people undertaken in May 1963. Nothing had changed about the emotional experience of grief, which he described as "a deep, complex and long-lasting psychological process with physiological overtones and symptoms" (Gorer 1965: 53) but its social expression had altered out of recognition. He concluded that, compared to their grandparents, "the majority of British people are today without adequate guidance as to how to treat death and bereavement and without social help in living through and coming to terms with the grief and mourning which are the inevitable responses in human beings to the death of someone they have loved" (ibid: 110).

This was a huge change from the position at the beginning of the last century when, with few exceptions "everybody knew how it would be appropriate for him or her to behave and dress when they suffered a bereavement and how to treat other mourners" (ibid: 63). Writing a few years later, the French historian Philippe Aries observed that, in Britain and northern Europe, funeral rites had been reduced to "a decent minimum... necessary to dispose of the body", that ceremonies were "discreet and...avoid emotion" and that, in agnostic England, "too evident sorrow does not inspire pity but repugnance; it is a sign of mental instability or of bad manners: it is morbid" (Aries 1976: 90).

This still remains broadly true, despite the explosion of support groups, charities and the counselling industry since Gorer and Aries completed their studies and despite the Diana phenomenon of mass popular mourning. As a society we still observe a recognisable body of practices and have a general sense of what constitutes proper behaviour, even if the rites themselves are maimed, truncated and partially evacuated of meaning. We offer "sympathy" and "support" by means of cards, notes, brief calls and flowers. We offer help, even without the expectation that it will be accepted. We don't want "to intrude" unless invited. In fact, we may practise avoidance by crossing the road. We try to speak well of the dead. We may take part in a public ritual – in agnostic Britain about the only time now that most of us enter a church or temple. We are careful of the feelings of the bereaved. We practise discretion. We may not wear a black tie or dress at the ritual but our choice of colours will be muted and our dress will be whatever we recognise as formal. Appearances are still important. And we can recognise behaviour that appears to breach these mores and register distaste or revulsion.

For the press, the most dangerous debates about conduct (in the sense that they may involve widespread public distaste and revulsion and the threat of legislation) occur when journalists are seen to be transgressing a deep-rooted, popular social more. During the controversy about press self-regulation versus privacy legislation in Britain in the early 1990s, one battleground was grief. Both the Calcutt Committee and the House of Commons National Heritage Committee heard harrowing evidence of systematic harassment and doorstepping by reporters and photographers of the relatives of accident or crime victims. The MPs reserved their harshest language to describe the treatment of the families of servicemen killed in Northern Ireland:

"Despite the provision in the [Press Complaints Commission] code... the press started telephoning at 11 o'clock at night and kept the phone going all night. The family was also subjected to persistent doorstepping. And, in what seemed to the committee to be a callous and totally unacceptable breach of the code, as well as more general canons of decency and compassion, the new widow, having been persuaded to give an interview in order to reduce press pressure, was asked by the accompanying photographer to 'look like a grieving widow'" (National Heritage Committee 1993).

"Callous", "unacceptable" and breaching "decency and compassion"... why does the demand "look like a grieving widow" (which sounds too neat, too convenient to be an actual quote) draw such moral obloquy? After all, although lacking in discretion, as a good professional the photographer was surely visualising what the reader would see and aiming to get the appearance to conform to the presumed reality of widowhood. Of course, the crass imperative quality of the demand ("hurry up here") certainly seems like an appalling lapse of manners and decorum. But another reason for revulsion is presumably that the demand seems to doubt the authenticity of the feeling undergone by the subject ("you don't really look like a grieving widow"). This tension between the surface of appearances and an inward state of pain that cannot easily be communicated without the suspicion of insincerity or play-acting brings an early, angry response from Hamlet when his mother suggests that death is "common" and that he really ought to start getting over the death of his father:

> "Tis not alone my inky cloak, good mother,
>   Not customary suits of solemn black,
>   Nor windy suspiration of forced breath,
>   No, nor the fruitful river in the eye,
>   Nor the dejected haviour of the visage,

Together with all forms, moods, shapes of grief,
That can denote me truly. These indeed seem,
For they are actions that a man might play,
But I have that within which passes show;
These but the trappings and the suits of woe."
(Shakespeare 1963 Act 1, Scene ii lines 77-86)

Hamlet's fierce rejection of "seemings" suggests a third motive underlying both: a revulsion against being "played" upon and turned into a stereotype as someone else's subject or thing for the interest and profit of an audience — a vivid example of that process known as reification.

M40 CRASH CONTROVERSY

Another controversy over media intrusion into grief arose in November 1993 following a crash on the M40 involving the death of 11 pupils from Hagley Roman Catholic High School. The morning after the crash the press were on hand outside the school to document the explosion of grief as the pupils learnt of the death of their friends. This was not, by all accounts, a media scrum but a successful exercise in disaster management, with the press corralled a respectful distance from the school and a team of counsellors drafted in by the education authority to do what they could to handle the distress. A media strategy was in place – the press was kept at arms length and didn't get a scoop but in return was supplied with a story salted with some heartrending personal details and extremely powerful images. Most of the national newspapers carried a particular iconic and strangely impersonal image of grief – one pupil, her face almost a literal representation of the ancient mask of tragedy, clutching a friend to her. Alongside a mosaic of smiling school shots of the victims, released by the authority, the effect was overwhelmingly sad. But some people found the fashioning of two young people into an icon of grief not just distasteful, but a cynical invasion of privacy. One *Guardian* reader was revolted and wrote a stinging letter:

If the publication by the Mirror Group newspapers of 'those' photographs of the Princess of Wales [working out at a gym] is held to be an unacceptable and unwarranted invasion of the privacy of the subject, by what twisted set of moral values is it possible to justify the publication of a large close up photograph of two (clearly identifiable) young schools girls as they hear of the death of 11 of their friends in the M40 minibus crash? (20 November).

Any journalist could fashion a reply. The story raised genuine public interest issues about road safety, accident black spots, teachers taking on additional duties and the need for new guidelines for school trips, such as having a relief driver. Across the nation, millions of people were shocked and saddened and anyone who had waited for a child to return from a school outing could identify with the families. If catharsis was needed, the press had fashioned a masterly image.

But whatever the merits of allowing the nation to sympathise vicariously, the unanswerable fact remained that the image was based on two pupils whose consent to become a brief national icon could only be notional. Why should their grief become a public possession? In the light of abundant evidence of much worse behaviour, Calcutt had drawn up a stringent clause for the editors' Code of Conduct in 1990 which forbade *any* intrusion into grief or shock (Robertson and Nicol 2002) and was designed to hold editors to account for sending reporters to question relatives. Unsurprisingly, the MPs of the 1993 National Heritage Committee investigating privacy and media intrusion (National Heritage Committee 1993) supported his recommendation that the clause dealing with grief in the Editors' code should state: "The press should not intrude into personal grief or shock, in particular in the aftermath of accidents and tragedies."

GRIEF: THE STICKING POINT

But this has proved to be, alongside a privacy law, one of the great non-negotiables for the British press. Hotlines for complaints, lay members on the PCC to sit alongside editors, limited third party complaints, tough guidelines to protect children – all have been conceded over the last 10 years. But grief has proven to be a sticking-point that editors have refused to countenance. In fact, the Editor's Code Committee of the Press Complaints Commission has stuck by a clause which states the opposite: "In cases involving personal grief or shock, enquiries must be carried out and approaches made with sympathy and discretion."

Enquiries and approaches *must* be made. So far the only change to this clause (now Clause 5 in the revised code) was added in January 1998 in the febrile period following the death of Diana, Princess of Wales, when what seemed like a change in public sensibility, the appearance of mounting popular support for privacy legislation and widespread public revulsion against paparazzi exacerbated the already calamitously low public esteem in which newspaper journalists were held. The emotional climate is memorably recollected by Neil Ascherson, wandering down the Mall:

> *It was…one of the worst moments for Britain's tabloid press. The people on the Mall had no doubts about who had killed Diana. 'She was hounded to death by the media,' they told me over and over again…But you could not find a syllable of this huge popular verdict in the tabloid newspapers. Terrified, the editors suppressed it and changed the subject to the failings of the Royal Family (Ascherson 2002: 126-130).*

One consequence was a series of panicky revisions to the code. These included an extension of the accuracy clause to deal with photo manipulation, a revision to the clause on harassment to include paparazzi-style persistent pursuit and an extension to the clause on the protection of children's privacy to all children while at school (with Princes William and Harry in mind). The PCC argues that collectively these revisions led to "perhaps the toughest set of press regulations anywhere in Europe". (PCC 2003b) One sentence was added to Clause 5 to cover publication: "Publication must be handled sensitively at such times, but this should not be interpreted as restricting the right to report judicial proceedings." But this clause has been seen as a blank cheque by journalists who have opened it up to a wide range of interpretation. Take, for instance, the evidence from this ruling:

> *Mrs Dorothy Yeomans…complained to the PCC that an article published in the Rhondda Leader on 15 January 2004 headlined 'Starving pet starts to devour pensioner' was insensitive at a time of grief in breach of Clause 5…The article reported the recent death of a man who had collapsed in his home. His sister complained that the article was distressing and included unnecessarily sensationalist details. The newspaper appreciated that the complainant was obviously distressed by her brother's death. However, it said that its enquiries – which were based on information provided by a member of the public and then confirmed by two sources – were made with sympathy and discretion. Given the unusual circumstances of the case, it would have been easy to publish a sensationalised article, but the newspaper believed that the construction of the story and its headline had been handled sympathetically and with appropriate sensitivity. (PCC 2004a).*

Describing the headline as sensitive strained the credulity even of the Press Complaints Commission and the *Rhondda Leader* was duly rebuked for "the overall tone...and...gratuitous inclusion of some of the detail" in the article. The PCC upheld the complaint under Clause 5 but qualified the judgement by noting that the article was published before the funeral – implying that a longer time lapse would have led to a different judgement. A further qualification was that the details had not been put into the public domain — implying that if there had been an inquest the newspaper would have been covered by its right to report judicial proceedings unless instructed otherwise.

This judgement and others like it under Clause 5 prioritise grieving family members as "victims" – members of a class of vulnerable people which includes children, patients in hospital, victims of crime and discrimination — and such protection is described by the PCC as being "at the heart of the Code of Practice". (PCC 2003b: 13,) This has evolved as a consistent rhetorical strategy. Whatever its merits as an accurate description of the function and operation of the code, the rhetoric serves two extremely useful purposes: i) it implies that people who have a problem with the press are a minority: a vulnerable species who must be shielded by a friendly public-spirited body; a body "with a heart" and ii) it tends to deflect the argument that such people might have rights as citizens. The continuing political agenda here is to defeat proposals for a privacy law and slow the evolution of judicial interpretations of the Human Rights Act in the direction of a judge-built law of privacy. This political project is part of a general strategy the PCC has developed in acting as a propagandist for voluntary regulation and against legal restrictions on the press. Its current chairman, Sir Christopher Meyer, described this role as "acting as a shock absorber between a free press and a fractious establishment" (PCC 2003c).

RISING NUMBER OF COMPLAINTS
OVER INTRUSIONS INTO GRIEF
In fact, the number of complaints to the PCC about intrusion into grief or shock had been rising from a low level before 1998 but in that year jumped significantly from 2 per cent to 3.3 per cent out of a total of around 2,500 (see Table 1). Meanwhile there had been a marked decline in complaints about accuracy – down from 73 per cent of all complaints in 1993 (PCC 1993) to 56.3 per cent in 2002 — and an increase in complaints under all the clauses covering privacy (including Clause 5 along with Clauses 3-4, 6-7, 9-10 and 12 of the code) to 23 per cent (PCC 2002). The commission claims that more than 90 per cent of complainants are "ordinary people". (PCC 2003a) However, as the PCC's mission is expressly to mediate, only a tiny fraction of these

Table 1: Complaints about press intrusion into grief or shock 1994-2003

Year	Total complaints	% Complaints re intrusion into grief	Adjudicated complaints re intrusion into grief	Upheld
1996	3023	1.3	2	1
1997	2944	2.0	4	1
1998	2505	3.3*	8	5
1999	2427	5.6	4	3
2000	2275	4.5	6	2
2001	3033	4.1	2	0
2002	2630	6.0	2	1
2003	3649	5.7	2	2

Source: Press Complaints Commission

complaints are actually adjudicated by the commission (see Tulloch 1998). During the *annus mirabilis* of 1998 an unprecedented total of eight complaints about intrusion into grief were pronounced on and five upheld. Over the next two years a further ten complaints were adjudicated and five upheld. Although the total proportion of complaints under Clause 5 has continued to increase (up from 1.6 per cent in 1996 to 5.7 per cent in 2003) the number of adjudicated complaints has now fallen back to just two a year from 2001.

After this flurry of activity, the PCC, having seen off a law on privacy, now appears to feel that it has established a form of "case law" covering complaints, including intrusion into grief. Indeed, in 2004 for the first time it began to print a list of "relevant precedents" beneath each adjudication. The following principles governing intrusion into grief have been enunciated:

- newspapers and reporter must not break news of death to relatives (McKeown vs *Newcastle Evening Chronicle* 1997);
- reporters must not step into a property without permission (Clement vs *South Yorkshire Times* 1998);
- recent deaths must not be treated in a flippant or gratuitously humorous way (Napuk and Gibson vs *FHM* 1999);

- "recent" seems to mean a lot less than a year (Judith Tonner vs *News of the World* 2002);
- close relatives of deceased people are particularly vulnerable in the "immediate aftermath" of a death and certainly before the funeral (Yeomans vs *Rhondda Leader* 2004);
- while it is acceptable for newspapers to publish criticisms of the recent dead in obituaries, newspapers should ensure they are not handled in an "insensitive fashion" (Kellner vs *BMJ* 2004) (PCC 2004).

Clause 5 and its accompanying "case law" is now seen by the PCC as a mature statement of principle and the most that the press should concede. In Clause 5 cases the PCC stubbornly defended the principle of contacting families (see for example Clement vs *South Yorkshire Times*, Maude vs *Derby Evening Telegraph* PCC 2004a). Thus, a robust defence was mounted when editors gave evidence to the House of Commons Culture, Media and Sport Committee in February 2003. This attacked the "widespread misconception...that all approaches by the press to the bereaved are inherently intrusive" (Editors' Code of Practice Committee 2003 paras 4.19-4.21).

DEFENDING THE DEATH KNOCK
Defending Clause 5 and the practice of contacting bereaved relatives – known in the profession as the "death knock" — the editors argued that:

- death can allow relatives "to honour the life that has been lost" and a report can be a kind of memorial;
- many details of a person's life can only be known by their closest family, particularly where that person is not a public figure;
- funeral directors and clergy often get facts wrong – talking to close family is the only way to ensure that details are accurate;
- although some families may find the press intrusive, others (particularly older people) may welcome reporters who make inquiries sensitively.

Are these weasel words? The editors' argument captures some real dilemmas for the conscientious reporter. It eschews sensationalism and focuses on the caring celebration of a life by means of a report or obituary rather than the exposure of disreputable or upsetting detail. It invokes community and a world of responsible local newspapers. To an interesting extent the editors' position is backed up in Geoffrey Gorer's study: in the general collapse of formal mourning practices, he found a continuing role for the local newspaper in acknowledging a life: "When anything had been written about the deceased in the local newspaper this was always referred to with gratification" (Gorer op cit: 62).

What it fails to address is the messy world of the accident or tragedy, the seizing on details and graphic images, the pursuit of relatives of crime victims, the relentless doorstepping of families. In other words – the world of contemporary sensational journalism. It is a world away from the *Rochdale Observer* reporting a murder in 1999:

> *The complainant explained how upsetting the description of the deceased injuries had been to the family, to whom the chosen wording, including three references in a short article to 'stomach cut open' and two to 'guts hanging out' had been cruel and insensitive (Mrs Joan Harvey vs Rochdale Observer, 6 January 1999; PCC 2004).*

The PCC upheld this complaint as well.

CONCLUSION

There are roughly four overlapping positions one can take on the issue of press behaviour:

> *The journalism is a "rough old trade" argument. Journalists are special and should not be subject to ordinary ethical codes – their mission is to get the story and get it right. Codes have no role in this and the best journalists may not be "virtuous" in any meaningful sense. Intrusion and insensitivity is the price of press freedom. The PCC Code is primarily a public relations exercise, a deal with the political class to buy off political pressures (Tulloch 1998).*

The "virtuous journalist" argument: Journalists should be subject to ordinary ethical codes but virtuous behaviour can only be based on the operation of individual conscience. Training can support this and so can open discussion in newsrooms and more tolerance in news organisations (Kovach and Rosenstiel 2003: 179-194) if individual journalists decide not to intrude. Journalists should be able to appeal to the PCC direct if they are being asked to transgress the code.

The "cultural meliorism" argument: Voluntary codes can "improve the culture of journalism" gradually via training and contracts. For example, the

PCC claims that by 2003 six national newspaper groups referred to the code in staff contracts and two more were considering including it. Legal controls will not work because newspapers will fight and the danger to freedom of expression outweighs the benefits (PCC 2003a).

The "structural determinism" argument: Codes and conscience will count for little in a newspaper industry run by media combines to maximise profit. Media concentration leads to abuse of power, the pursuit of larger circulations and "dumbing down". Grief is one ingredient that sells newspapers. It is futile to rely on voluntary regulation – the statutory nettle of a privacy law must be grasped (O'Malley and Soley 2000).

My own prejudice would be to support the virtuous journalist argument but this is only feasible if journalists establish a right to refuse instructions that breach the code. This recommendation for a "conscience clause" was made by MPs in the Privacy and Media Intrusion report last year. (Culture, Media and Sport Committee 2003). With scarcely veiled disdain, the PCC claimed it had:

> no evidence that journalists are asked to undertake ...assignments that would breach the code in the absence of any public interest. This would in any case seem to be a matter for the employer and employee...(Culture, Media and Sport Committee 2004)

It undertook to ask the Editors' Code Committee to consider the proposal. Unsurprisingly, when the editors published a much-heralded revision to the code in April, they found no reason to undermine their own authority.

REFERENCES

Aries, Philippe (1976) *Western Attitudes towards death: from the Middl Ages to the present,* London, Marion Boyars

Aries, Philippe (1981) *The Hour of Our Death*, London, Allen Lane

Ascherson, Neil (2002) *Stone Voices: The Search for Scotland*, New York, Hill and Wang

Calcutt, Sir David (1993) *Review of Press Self-Regulation,* London, HMSO Cmnd 2135

Culture, Media and Sport Committee (2003) *Fifth Report. Privacy and Media Intrusion.* HC 458. London, Stationery Office Ltd

Culture, Media and Sport Committee (2004) *Privacy and Media Intrusion: Replies to the Committee's Fifth Report*, 2002-03. HC 213, London, Stationery Office Ltd

Daniel, Stephen H. (1992) "Some Conflicting Assumptions of Journalistic Ethics", Cohen, Elliot D. (ed.) *Philosophical Issues in Journalism*, New York, Oxford University Press pp 51-52

Editors' Code of Practice Committee (2003) *Privacy and Media Intrusion: Evidence to the House of Commons Culture, Media and Sport Committee*, February

Gorer, Geoffrey (1965) *Death, Grief, and Mourning in Contemporary Britain*, London, the Cresset Press

Greenslade, Roy (2004) "Long lenses, hard hearts", the *Guardian*, 22 March

National Heritage Committee (1993) *Fourth Report Privacy and Media Intrusion Session 1992-93*, London, HMSO, 16 March

Keeble, Richard (2001) *Ethics for Journalists*, London: Routledge

Kovach, Bill and Rosenstiel, Tom (2003) *The Elements of Journalism*, London, Atlantic Books

O'Malley, Tom and Soley, Clive (2000) *Regulating the Press*, London, Pluto Press

Press Complaints Commission (1993) *Press Complaints Commission Review* (covered 1 January 1991 to 31 December 1993)

Press Complaints Commission (2002) *Annual Review*

Press Complaints Commission (2003a) *Submission to the Culture, Media and Sport Select Committee*, February

Press Complaints Commission (2003b) *Annual Review*

Press Complaints Commission (2003c) Society of Editors' Annual Lecture by Sir Christopher Meyer, PCC chairman, 12 October 2003. Available online at http://www.pcc.org.uk/press/detail.asp

Press Complaints Commission (2004a) *Reports of past decisions 1996–2004* Available online at http://www.pcc.org.uk/reports/details

Press Complaints Commission (2004b) Code of Practice, http://www.pcc.org.uk

Robertson, Geoffrey and Nicol, Andrew (2002) *Media Law*, London, Penguin Books, Fourth Edition

Shakespeare, William (1963) *Hamlet*, Hubler, Edward (ed), New York, New American Library, Signet Classic Edition

Shannon, Richard (2003) *Evidence submitted by Professor Richard Shannon to Culture, Media and Sport Committee. New Inquiry: Privacy and Media Intrusion*, February

Tulloch, John (1998) "Managing the Press in a Medium-Sized European Power", *Sex, Lies and Democracy: The Press and the Public*, Stephenson, Hugh and Bromley, Michael (eds) London/New York, Longman pp 63-83

John Tulloch is Professor of Journalism and Head of the School of Journalism, University of Lincoln, launched in November 2004. Previously he was chair of the Department of Journalism and Mass Communication at the University of Westminster. Recent work includes jointly editing, with Colin Sparks, *Tabloid Tales* (Maryland: Rowman and Littlefield 2000) to which he contributed the essay "The Eternal Recurrence of the New Journalism". He has written on press regulation, official news management and popular television. He is currently working on studies of the popular press and the journalism of Charles Dickens. Contact details: Lincoln School of Journalism, Faculty of Media and Humanities, University of Lincoln, Brayford Pool, Lincoln LN6 7TS, UK. Tel: +44 (0) 1522 882000. Fax: +44 (0) 1522 886021; email: jtulloch@lincoln.ac.uk

Secrecy, communications strategy and democratic values

Jerry Palmer

This chapter examines the relationship between the strategically oriented analysis of communications and the democratic value of the unimpeded flow of information. The focal points of the relationship are the role of secrecy in strategy construction and the role of stakeholders in communications flows. The first part analyses the strategic role of secrecy through a series of examples of typical situations such as leaks, kite flying and the use of off-the-record briefings. These are followed by examples in which the role of the passage of time in strategy construction is related to information control in the form of secrecy. It is argued that even where disclosure of information is mandatory, temporary enclosure of information serves strategic purposes. In the final section, the democratic possibilities of the stakeholder relationship are examined through the centrality of dialogue in stakeholder communications. Habermas's theory of communicative action and its extension in his subsequent analysis of law constitute the theoretical underpinning of this section.

Keywords: democracy, strategy, censorship, confidentiality, ethics, stakeholding

INTRODUCTION

The subject of this chapter is the relationship between secrecy, communications and democratic values across a range of domains of activity. It is central to its purpose that communication in several domains of social activity is analysed, as the theoretical concerns addressed lose coherence if they are applied to a single zone of activity. In particular, it explores the role of secrecy in communications planning, especially its relationship to the strategic, self-interest-oriented dimension of the latter and the extent to which this is compatible with certain fundamental democratic values. It sets out to show that despite its apparently anti-democratic nature, a central element of communications strategy may serve to resolve the contradiction in question.

The starting point of the analysis is a paradox: that secrecy is an integral part of communication, indeed — put at its strongest — that secrecy is the basis of all strategically organised communication. This is a paradox in that conventional definitions of communication include a public dimension, insofar as it involves the transmission of a message from a sender to a receiver. Yet it is not, in fact, communication that is public in this sense but the emission of the message: everything that precedes the act of emission may be enclosed and fall outside the public realm. This is clearly shown by the most commonly cited elements of the planning dimension of communication strategy:

In Table 1 we see that secrecy (the enclosure of information) at the point in time when the message does not yet exist has the function of ensuring that the eventual public act of communication serves communicator interests. We also see that stakeholders are an integral part of the planning process. The definition of stakeholding, across a wide range of activities, is an integral part of the argument advanced here.

Enclosure of information is central to models of the organisational space of communication (Table 2). Here, the distinction between the back and front spaces of an organisation is presented in terms of who has right of access to information. In the front (or public) space, public access to information is guaranteed as of right and any restriction of this access constitutes censorship; restriction of information to which the public has no right of access correspondingly constitutes (normal) secrecy. The process of disclosure of information to which the public has right of access is what constitutes publicity whereas the disclosure of information whose circulation is normally restricted constitutes confiding in someone, or "leaking".

In the processes summarised in these two analyses we see clearly the strategic function of the enclosure of information (or secrecy): it is there to underpin the sender's capacity for maximising the usefulness of the act of communication. Certainly there is a "public space of communication" corresponding to the enclosed spaces. However, the role of enclosure is to ensure that what passes into the public space serves the interests of the

Table 1: Components and Stages of Communications Planning

Time	Component	Enclosed/Public
1	Stakeholder analysis	Enclosed
2	Targeting	Enclosed
3	Budget	Enclosed
4	Co-ordination	Enclosed
5	Media planning	Enclosed
6	Publication/implementation	Public

4 & 5: order may vary

Table 2: Organisational Space and Forms of Communication

	Enclosure	Disclosure
Front space	Censorship	Publicity
Back Space	Secrecy	Confidence/leak

Adapted from Ericson, Barabck and Chan (1989: 9-11).

communicator. In particular, the role of stakeholders in this process is both crucial and ambiguous: stakeholders are those with whom communication is necessary, in other words those who must be able to access the public space of communication. Here the role of secrecy is to allow their selection according to the communicator's criteria rather than anybody else's and to allow a decision about whether to treat them only as targets or to engage with them in a more open-ended, dialogic relationship. This ambiguity is central to arguments about secrecy and democracy.

SECRECY AND DEMOCRACY

The enclosure of information consists essentially of two elements: the right to silence and the choice of forms of communication. If there is no obligation to publish, there is a right to silence or to partial disclosure where the protected enclosure of information leaves a margin of initiative to those so protected (how much to say, when and how). Downing (1986) shows how the function of state secrecy legislation is to create and preserve this margin of initiative. However, it is important that legislation alone is unlikely to suffice: the capacity to inspire loyalty (in part, no doubt, inculcated by fear based upon the threat of prosecution) is an equally important part of the preservation of this margin (Sigal 1973: 145-147). Although these authors speak only of the state, similar protections apply to commercial organisations. Where permanent silence is not protected the strategist still retains control of the forms of communication: the choice of time, media and personnel, also the choice between being on and off-the-record, which amounts to taking public responsibility for the statement in question.

The role of secrecy in this process — whether permanent or temporary — is protected by law, in various forms, in modern western societies: by official secrets legislation, by the ownership of information and the right to confidentiality. The terms which are used in arguments about this process and in the formulation of laws in this domain are varied: secrecy, confidentiality, privacy, for example. All these involve the enclosure of information within boundaries set by someone who controls the process whether it is through a legal protection or some other mechanism or both. As is well known there have been extensive debates surrounding these protections and the extent to which they are justified. The countervailing force commonly alleged in these debates is the democratic right and need for transparency in public processes. For example:

> *Good government requires the participation of citizens. For citizens to participate effectively the electorate must be well informed and this means access to the facts about government activities. A free flow of information about what the government is doing on behalf of its citizens and how taxes collected from citizens are spent is essential for accountable government …These views are the conventional opinion in most western liberal democracies …* *(Routledge et al. 2000: 1).*

In such commonplace arguments it is government activities which are specified. However, elsewhere similar arguments are applied to corporations. In the aftermath of the Enron and WorldCom scandals in the USA, the US Government passed the Sarbanes-Oxley Act which both places extra duties of transparency upon corporate directors, lawyers and accountants and requires regulatory bodies to create new rules to this purpose (or tighten the application of existing ones) (Huber et al. 2002; Quinn and Jarmel 2002; Reich and Wirtner 2002). Indeed, there is a general (but far from uncontested) pre-supposition that in a democracy secrecy is at best a compromise between an ideal of transparency and the recognition that practicality demands some measure of enclosure of information. As Ollivier-Yaniv comments (2003: 39): "At worst, [secrecy] is widely considered as dissimulation; at best, it is a by-product of the process of decision-making."

Nonetheless, it is clear that there are elements in the basic structure of democracy that constitute a principled defence of the right to secrecy: for example, the European Convention on Human Rights gives protection to privacy (Article 8) and restricts freedom of expression in the interest of various public goods, including confidentiality (Article 10, para.2). To the extent that we accept that the right to privacy and confidentiality are fundamental elements of a democratic order, we must accept that secrecy is not intrinsically incompatible with democracy. While the nature of such protections no doubt varies from jurisdiction to jurisdiction, the principle is not in doubt. Thus, in the absence of an argument to the effect that such protections are an aberration in a democracy, the conclusion must be drawn that democratic values demand some balance between the right to the enclosure of information and the demand for transparency in public affairs.

Such a balance already exists in various forms. In the first place, the right to secrecy is balanced in many domains of activity by the obligation to disclose information: for example, laws which are in the process of being formulated by governments must be made publicly available for discussion before becoming law. Corporations are also obliged to issue information concerning their finances at regular intervals — from this point of view, the Sarbanes-Oxley Act is a re-assertion of the validity of an already agreed principle and the strengthening of its application. Secondly, in the domain of individual rights, the right to privacy is balanced by public interest, in, for example, the European Convention on Human Rights, Article 8, para. 2.

UK research reports, commissioned by various media regulatory and policy-making bodies, found that privacy was recognised as a fundamental right by the public, that revelation in the public interest was a well-recognised justification of media intrusion and that the necessity of balance between the two was also recognised (Kieran et al 1997: 82-95, 122-34; Morrison and Svennevig 2002). Recent UK cases illustrate this attempted balance. The model Naomi Campbell sued the UK tabloid *Daily Mirror* under the right to privacy for revealing that she had attended Narcotics Anonymous. The paper's defence was that there was a legitimate public interest in this matter as she had denied using narcotics. Similarly, the Belgian brewing company Interbrew sued various UK newspapers to retrieve documents sent anonymously to the press which purported to show that the company was going to try to take over another brewer, SAB; the purpose of the retrieval was to identify the source of the leak. The papers refused to comply both with the request and with the initial court decision to oblige them to do so on the grounds that journalists' refusal to reveal their sources was a precious element of their ability to report matters in the public interest and, therefore, was itself a part of the public interest. Discussions of the extent to which corporations ought to be obliged to reveal their affairs are part of the same attempt at balancing private and public interest (e.g. Warner 2002; Reich and Wirtner op cit).

Thus it is clear that, on the one hand, there is a pressure, driven by the nature of communications strategy, to preserve the enclosure of information or to maintain secrecy and, on the other hand, a balance which is struck between the right to secrecy and legitimate transparency in the public interest. This debate applies as much in the area of family life and the commercial arena as it does to political life in a democracy largely because the principles involved transcend the division of society into different sociologically, politically and legally defined arenas. Moreover, in this process, either the outcome of debates and reforms is subject only to the play of interests and power or there is some underlying principle involved, to which recourse is possible. The principle, it will be argued, lies in the domain of communications strategy itself, namely in the role of stakeholders in strategy formation and it is the same principle that transcends the sociological divisions referred to above.

SECRECY AND STRATEGY

This section of the paper argues that analysis of the strategic use of secrecy clearly shows that it is self-interest oriented: its purpose is to maximise the usefulness of communication for the communicator and this is possible even where there are substantial obligations to disclosure. Nonetheless, it is important to bear in mind the central role of stakeholding in communications strategy. However much the function of secrecy may be to maximise the usefulness of communication to the communicator, the nature and role of the stakeholding audience acts as a guiding principle in the goal-oriented calculations made in communications planning and using the possibilities opened up by the enclosure of information.

In the examples to be analysed here, we shall see devices by which communicators attempt to turn the communications process to their own advantage, trying to circumvent or undermine the part that stakeholding plays, or can play, in this process. In terms of communication theory, they attempt to restrict communication as far as possible to the primarily monologic, linear process emphasised in traditional empirical models of communication (e.g Gerbner 1956). Stakeholding stresses the dialogic nature of communication and it is here (it will be argued) that the democratic potential of the communications process is to be found.

Where secrecy is absolutely protected, for example by official secrets legislation or confidentiality agreements, there is a right to silence. More importantly, as Downing (op cit) argues, such protection enables those who are protected in this way to decide what to communicate, when and how. As Mrs Thatcher's former press secretary has said, authorisation to disclose information protected by official secrets legislation is a normal part of the workings of such a law, with the result that he found it necessary to "break it every other minute of every working day" (Ingham 1991: 348). The use of the margin of initiative derived from this protection can be seen in features of both political and corporate communication via the mass media that are well established in both academic literature and journalists' memoirs. The best known examples are leaks, kite flying and the use of off-the-record briefings.

Leaks are defined as the unauthorised release of information. Such release both gives additional value to information and protects the source through disguise. However, as is well-known, many if not the majority of leaks are, in fact, false in the sense that they are authorised and in this instance the apparent desire to protect anonymity may be no more than a way of increasing the value of the information (Palmer 2000: 9-10; Lemieux 2000: 65).

Kite flying is a more complex process. For example, it is publicly indicated that such-and-such an organisation — government is a good example — is planning to introduce a policy or is considering a range of alternative options in some policy context. The indication may be largely anonymous, with the purpose of pre-testing public response to an idea without anybody being obliged to take responsibility for the process. It may be that there is uncertainty about what the public response is likely to be or it may be that it is anticipated that the preferred policy will arouse controversy. A deliberately controversial possibility may be allowed to be known in order to be subsequently denied in favour of a "less controversial" option which was, in fact, the preferred one anyway (le Bohec 1997: 73; Franklin 1994: 17). In a really delicate situation, an intermediary body such as a charity or a pressure group may be persuaded to air the possibility in question to test the water without the risk of too close an association between the real author of the proposal and a potentially risky reaction (Schlesinger and Tumber 1994: 61; Palmer 2001:

246-7). Clearly such techniques can only work on condition that the identity and the motive of the real author remain hidden. This can be achieved either by sending documents anonymously (but this may cast doubt on the authenticity of the proposal), through an off the record briefing or by persuading a journalist to co-operate by hiding the identity in question.

Speaking off the record achieves a level of risk reduction in public communication: the speaker does not have to take responsibility for what (s)he says. Additionally, since the identity of the speaker is a key component of meaning, non-attributed messages have degrees of ambiguity which allow processes such as dual meaning — one meaning for the general public, another for the select public which can make a good attempt at identifying the speaker and his or her reasons for speaking. UK government briefings to journalists were for many years conducted entirely unattributably; in recent years, the system has been modified, but much government communication to journalists remains unattributable (Hennessy and Walker 1989; Select Committee 1999). Significantly, the recent UK government Phillis report (January 2004) into the government's communications services recommends making Government briefings fully attributable.

The choice between on and off the record communication is not of course absolute, depending on the nature of the situation: the briefing may be a mixture of the two and the mixture may be either implicit or explicit. Off the record, moreover, is not a single entity but an escalating range of degrees of unattributableness. At the "shallow" end, it consists of publishing detailed information without identifying the source, except perhaps generically. At one level deeper it involves withholding some information, perhaps on the grounds that it might enable others to identify the actual source; deeper still it involves total silence (Sigal op cit: 112-115).

Choices depend upon two factors: the level of delicacy of the situation and the relationship between the speaker and the receiver of the information: in particular, the degree of trust (or complicity) between the two parties to the transaction. Journalists are, therefore, faced with a choice which is partly based on news values: the off the record nature of the information potentially increases its value in this respect. And the choice is partly based on moral values: to what extent does accepting the non-attributability imply complicity and acceptance of being manipulated? Information may be given to a journalist off the record deliberately to prevent its use in case the journalist is able to get it from another source that might give it on the record (Morrison 2003).

THE BASIS OF TRUST: THE POSSIBILITY OF SECRECY

The basis of this trust is the possibility of secrecy, in the sense that a journalist who fails to respect non-attributability is likely to find themselves in arid territory thereafter, cut off from profitable sources of information. Even where there is an obligation to publish, there is no obligation to entrust any individual journalist with any information other than the minimum which is obligatory and which gives the journalist no competitive professional advantage. This principle underpins all source-journalist interactions as soon as there is any measure of trust involved. Mrs Thatcher's press secretary's memoirs include this analysis of the situation, inspired by pressure put on him to modify the attribution rules in government briefings:

> *I would say what I wanted to say and unless I could say them [sic] on my terms I wouldn't say a word. What is more, my retribution would be wonderful to behold if [journalists] agreed to my terms and then dishonoured them... (Ingham 1991: 200)*

This relationship should be understood as part of the process by which political personnel both trade favours with media personnel and pressure them to produce mediated profiles of events that suit their purposes. Such pressure commonly takes the form of demanding corrections to stories deemed incorrect and threats of withdrawing co-operation (see for example le Bohec 1997: 21-8; Lemieux op cit: 146-8; Rawnsley 2000: 265-6, 322; Tumber and Palmer 2004: 147)

These examples (leaking, kite-flying, non-attributability) illustrate the fundamental principle analysed here: they are devices whose purpose is to undermine or circumvent the democratic possibilities of stakeholding in the interests of communicator goal-orientation. In these instances, the stakeholders are citizens; we shall see that the universality of citizens' stakeholding creates some theoretical problems.

Even where none of the above factors come into play and where the obligation to publish is substantial, secrecy plays a central role in the form of the passage of time, i.e. the temporary enclosure of information. One tactic is to publish bad news at a time when other matters are likely to dominate news (Palmer 2000: 56) — as UK ministerial aide Jo Moore in/famously suggested on 11 September 2001 that it might be a good day to get out some bad news. Subsequently her supposedly confidential email making this suggestion to some colleagues was leaked, presumably in an effort to discredit her. This tactic depends on the enclosure of information up until the time when the publication decision is taken. As Table 1 (the components and stages of communications strategies) showed, everything involved in the construction of a message and the manner of its publication remains enclosed until the act of publication. Therefore, whatever obligations to publish may be in force, until the time which is prescribed for it, secrecy operates; thus even a strong obligation to disclosure always contains an element of choice deriving from the period of time preceding publication, during which information is enclosed.

There is clearly a strategic role for secrecy: it is to further communicator interests. Legislation plays a key role but so does power and the capacity to inspire loyalty, also the ability to avoid factional disputes which may lead to competitive use of information in the form (for example) of genuine leaks. Crucially, secrecy-based communications strategies are largely compatible with the obligation of disclosure since the obligation maintains a margin of discretion regarding communication tactics and especially the use of the passage of time. With these devices, communicators attempt to turn communication into a monologic flow in which the impact of communication in relation to pre-determined goals can be gauged in advance. In so far as stakeholders figure in this process, they are targets (as Table 1 suggests) rather than partners in dialogue. However, it is crucial to the argument advanced here that the stakeholding relationship is compatible both with reduction to the status of target and with the status of partner in dialogue. This is true across the boundaries of the domains of activity analysed and it is for this reason that it is the location of the fundamental principle for which this article is arguing.

STAKEHOLDING, DIALOGUE AND ETHICS

The purpose of secrecy is to further the interests of those who seek to enclose information by allowing them an enlarged measure of control over the communication process, incorporated in strategy. However, we have seen that strategy involves the identification of stakeholders who may be defined as those who have an interest in the matter at hand and with whom, therefore, communication is either mandatory or prudential to the point of necessity. The contention of this chapter is that the nature of the stakeholder relationship is capable of being the basis of ethical judgement about the role of secrecy and to this extent is capable of resolving the dilemma noted at the beginning: that while transparency is fundamental to democracy, it is also the case that some forms of the enclosure of information are compatible with a democratic framework. This contention demands analysis of the

Table 3: Stakeholder communication, interest and power

Level of Power		Level of interest	
		Low	High
	Low	Minimal effort	Keep informed
	High	Keep satisfied	Key players

Source: Johnson and Scholes (1999: 216).

stakeholder relationship.

Conceived as no more than a relationship with those with whom one is obliged to maintain dialogue, communication with stakeholders does not go beyond the bounds of self-interested strategic calculation. This can be seen in a diagram of stakeholder communications planning taken from a business strategy textbook (Table 3).

Table 3 recommends levels of communicative effort appropriate to different stakeholder groups as a function of the level of interest they have in the topic in question but also the level of power their position gives them in the matter in question. Such a model applies across a wide range of situations and activities: for example, the communication of financial performance by corporations, government policy consultation, corporate re-organisation and employee relations or the development of policy by non-profit organisations. In all of these situations, in so far as actors follow the planning outlined in this model, it is clear that the choice of tactics corresponds directly to the balance of usefulness/threat that is implied in the relationship between the strategists and the stakeholders. To the extent that stakeholder communications are based purely in strategic interests, an analysis of secrecy conducted in these terms will not go beyond the structure of strategic use outlined above and manifest in the various commonplace "tricks of the trade" shown in the examples.

However, the relational basis of stakeholder identity implies that the analysis can also be inverted and done from the point of view of the stakeholder. From this side, the relationship lays out grounds on which claims can be made to inclusion in particular circuits of information (but not all circuits of information since the right to inclusion is based in the particularities of a relationship). Conceived in this way, the stakeholder relationship is dialogic since the relationship gives stakeholders the right to make demands concerning information. This model of communication is often called the "two-way symmetrical" model of communication management (Grunig 1992; Grunig and Hunt 1984). Grunig distinguishes

Table 4: Grunig's hierarchy of communicative excellence

HIERARCHY OF EXCELLENCE	MODEL	CHARACTERISTICS
	Press Agentry Model	One-way positive publicity to create awareness; avoid negative publicity
	Public Information Model	Persuasive one-way communication to provide truthful messages with altruistic motives
	Two-way Asymmetrical Model	Use feedback from relevant publics to design persuasive messages to manipulate the behaviour of the publics. No change results in communicating organisation.
	Two-way Symmetrical Model	Achieve mutual understanding with publics, negotiate mutually acceptable resolution to conflicting interests. This changes the communicating organisation.

Source: adapted from Grunig (1992: 286-90)

four models of communication with different organisational characteristics which he arranges in a "hierarchy of excellence" (Table 4).

In these models, stakeholders only occupy a recognised place in the two-way versions and in the asymmetrical two-way model they are still no more than targets, as in Table 1. However, in the symmetrical model, they are partners in dialogue. This model is argued to be the best because the three asymmetrical models are associated with organisations that are static and unreceptive to changes in their environment, whereas symmetrical models are associated with organisations that are open, receptive and adapted to change (Grunig and White 1992: 38-44). While it is not relevant to our purposes to assess whether this is an adequate model of organisational communication practice, we may notice something which is omitted: who nominates the stakeholders? If they are nominated by the communicator, then the model is always open to the charge that publics are functionally selected according to strategic calculations, which reduces the claim of symmetricality (cf. L'Etang 1996: 93-9). If they are self-nominating, then the symmetricality of the dialogic relationship is increased.

The ethical impact of this process can be assessed by using Habermas's model of communicative action (which is explicitly an ethical model). The grounds on which inclusion may be demanded are always in effect claims of legitimacy: to say "these are the reasons why I should be included" is always to lay claim to the legitimacy of that inclusion since the reasons imply an external framework of justification of some sort. That is to say, a claim is made in a dialogue in which reasons are given and debated, reasons which must be acceptable — if the claim is to succeed — to people other than the person who advances them; they must make sense in a framework which transcends the purely subjective interests of the claimant. Such reasoning is subject only to the rules of reasoning that govern all communicative action: to this extent the partners in the dialogue are equal as partners.

This process includes recognition of the strategic purposes of the parties to the dialogue, judged in terms of means-ends rationality, as well as judgements concerning their appropriateness and sincerity. The process of communicative action includes what Habermas claims are the principal elements of subjectivity — namely purpose, normative judgement and self-presentation — as well as the implicit recognition that one is entering a process of negotiation in which the rules of reasoning are applied. In this process, means-ends rationality (in other words, strategic calculation) is necessarily transcended in so far as dialogue is maintained. Of course, on many occasions this situation breaks down and participants must (ultimately) have recourse to strategic action (Habermas 1996: 21). However, in so far as people do remain in dialogue, the reasoning process is in place, and it is integrally trans-subjective. In other words the same reasoning would apply to anyone else in specifiable circumstances and to this extent the grounds underpinning the negotiation are universalisable (ibid: 15-18; Habermas 1984: 85-106).

In a discussion about stakeholder inclusion in the circuit of information, a convincing argument would show how a conduct of the relationship satisfactory to all parties would depend upon inclusion in the circuit of information. This fulfils the criteria demanded by the process of communicative action: the immediate strategic purpose of the claim is the inception or maintenance of a relationship (no doubt there would be further purposes, which need not retain us). It is appropriate to the extent that such a relationship is part of the normal conduct of affairs in our society and it constitutes a sincere presentation of self in so far as the intention to begin or maintain the relationship is genuine. That is to say, to the extent to which stakeholder claims are based in a genuinely dialogic framework they are fully ethical entities because they are universalisable in the manner Habermas envisages. Such a dialogue seems to fulfil Habermas's fundamental criterion that a norm is valid only if "all affected can accept the consequences and the side effects its general observance can

be anticipated to have for the satisfaction for everyone's interests ..."
(Habermas 1990: 65).

WHO NOMINATES STAKEHOLDERS?

However, there are weaknesses in applying this model to the type of situation in which communications strategies are developed and which derive from the principle of universalisation quoted here. In particular, the nature of strategic action in our context raises the question of who nominates stakeholders. It is relevant because it affects who is recognised as a participant in dialogue and it opens up the question of power differentials in the process of this recognition: if the communicator nominates their stakeholders, then the relationship is only partly dialogic (or symmetrical, to use Grunig's terms). If stakeholders are indeed self-nominating, then symmetrical dialogue is indeed installed.

However, on what grounds would a stakeholder nominate themselves? They would need access to sufficient information about the situation to know that stakeholding was a relevant option. But such information is likely to be enclosed by the communicating organisation or to have been communicated for reasons of strategic self-interest. If the former is the case, the stakeholding option is nul for lack of information; if the latter, it is effectively the communicating organisation which has nominated the stakeholder in question. In either case no advance has been made in relation to the ethical possibilities of stakeholding which can only be realised if potential stakeholders are alerted to the possibility of this option. Moreover, the exclusion is operated by power in the guise of enclosure of information.

Although the Habermasian model recognises the role of strategically oriented action and explicitly makes it compatible with the overall framework of communicative action by being integrated into it (Habermas 1984: 85; Habermas 1996: 18-21), the latter presupposes that actors do have sufficient knowledge of situations to enter into dialogue in the first place; yet this is problematic and the problem arises from the nature of strategic action and especially the role of communication within it. Optimistically, one could say — with Grunig — that excellent organisations will spontaneously recognise the necessity of openness.

However, firstly, there is no guarantee that all organisations will do so[7]; secondly, in so far as they do, it is largely for strategic reasons and the ethical route is again blocked off. Another way of phrasing this objection — more in line with the generality of Habermas's reasoning — is to say that without a commitment to solidarity, potential dialogue participants would have no reason to enter the process (see Gimmler 2002: 4). The nature of strategic action pulls in exactly the opposed direction to solidarity and thus even the best organisations are in a position characterised by a basic tendency away from dialogue participation. This induces scepticism about the real-life applicability of Habermas's principle under the circumstances in question.

The resolution of this problem can be attempted by using the developments Habermas proposes when he confronts the role of law in relation to ethics and strategic action (Habermas 1996). Indeed, the theory of law as developed here is grounded in the explicit recognition of the tension noted above. Building on his previous analysis of social differentiation in the period of modernity, Habermas (1987: 113-97) recognises that among other implications of the changes in question is a limit on the efficacy of communicative action in achieving social co-ordination — in other words agreement among social agents over validity claims. The main reasons for this limitation, he says, are:

- the abolition of the consensual value systems based in sacred authority, brought about by "disenchantment";
- the agreements constituted in membership of a common lifeworld are not translatable across the whole of the social order because of the massive differentiation of lifeworlds and their partial colonisation by systemic structures, especially the state and the economy;
- the massive increase in the scope of strategic, or purposeful, action released by modern economies and governed by means-ends rationality.

HABERMAS ON THE 'NORMATIVE REGULATION OF STRATEGIC INTERACTIONS'

If communicative action is no longer capable of creating and maintaining agreement about validity claims among social agents, then some other instance must be available for this purpose. Habermas characterises it as a process in which actors come to an understanding about the "normative regulation of strategic interactions":

> *For self-interested actors, all situational features are transformed into facts they evaluate in the light of their own preferences, whereas actors oriented toward reaching understanding rely on a jointly negotiated understanding of the situation and interpret the relevant facts in the light of intersubjectively recognised validity claims. However, if the orientations to personal success and to*

> *reaching understanding exhaust the alternatives for acting subjects, then norms suitable as socially integrating constraints on strategic interactions must meet two contradictory conditions that, from the viewpoint of the actors, cannot be simultaneously satisfied. On the one hand, such rules must present de facto restrictions that alter the relevant information in such a way that the strategic actor feels compelled to adapt her behaviour in the objectively desired manner. On the other hand, they must at the same time develop a socially integrating force by imposing obligations on the addressees — which, according to my theory, is possible only on the basis of intersubjectively recognised normative validity claims. According to the above analysis, the type of norms required would have to bring about willingness to comply simultaneously by means of de facto constraint and legitimate validity (Habermas 1996: 26-27).*

This type of norm is law since it applies *de facto* constraint and claims legitimate validity whose basis can be demonstrated. In a democratic society, Habermas argues, communicative action is built into the process of law formation. Therefore law is the one instance which reconciles the positivity, or facticity, of sets of arrangements whose validity cannot be settled in the validity claims pursued in the lifeworld alone, with the legitimacy of arrangements whose validity is settled in this way (ibid: 37-38).

If we apply this argument to the case in question here — stakeholders' right to information — then we can see that this implies a legally guaranteed framework of rights. In the case of market information, such a framework exists, although the recent US market scandals show how fallible it has been in the absence of robust regulatory powers, real compulsion and powerful sanctions. Such a framework is based in the recognition that the categories of stakeholders in question (market participants with economic interests expressed in the form of property) do have rights that demand appropriate channels of information, action and enforcement.

In a democratic society, these rights can be extended to all citizens in so far as their specifiable relationship to particular circumstances and agents demonstrates they are, indeed, stakeholders. Freedom of Information legislation recognises this principle in that its underpinning is the judgement that all government information ought to be available to all citizens unless good reason for its enclosure can be shown. However, stakeholding does not have, *per se*, the universality of citizenship. Therefore legislation guaranteeing stakeholder access to information cannot be based on citizenship except in so far as citizenship is in itself a form of stakeholding where certain categories of action are concerned. The guarantees of stakeholder access are rather categories of relevance of information to the form of stakeholding in question.

Guarantees of stakeholder access are an expression of public interest — since *ex hypothesi* everyone is a stakeholder in some context or other — and public interest demands an agency to enforce it. Moreover time is crucial in this question: even temporary enclosure of information may well be enough to serve strategic interests and act against other stakeholders' interest. This implies that any legally binding framework would need to be sufficiently robust to be capable of enforcing citizens' stakeholder rights within the time frame that makes enforced disclosure meaningful. It also implies a tightly drawn definition of the relevance of time frames and a robust enforcement mechanism.

Clearly, such a framework is fraught with difficulties. If the enforcement of such a requirement is to be left to the judicial process, this implies that it will always operate retrospectively, on the basis that a complaint has been lodged to the effect that stakeholders' rights have not been observed. Under these circumstances, the penalties would have to be severe if the judicial process were to have any impact. If the enforcement was assigned to some special office which was not forced to wait until after the event, then that office would acquire an enormous amount of leverage in public processes of every variety, and its own accountability would be problematic.

CONCLUSION

The nature and role of communications strategy gives a central place to stakeholders. Given the proviso that stakeholders are self-nominating, stakeholding is by definition reciprocity-based. However, the reality of the protection of information enclosure is such that this reciprocity is far from necessarily realisable in actual situations. The logic of Habermas's arguments suggests that it is only legally binding enforcement of disclosure that is capable of ensuring that the ethical possibilities of the stakeholder relationship are realized. However, this raises the question of access to information sufficient to know that the stakeholder relationship is relevant. At that point the legal enforcement becomes in its turn problematic; in particular, the nature of the enforcement agency is crucial.

The enforcement agency is the agent of the public interest (in the form of the universality of stakeholders' rights). Where the circulation of information is concerned, the traditional agency is the mass media. However, it is difficult to see how their nature, as currently constituted, could be compatible with the demands of stakeholder access as formulated here.

On the one hand, the media are one of the main conduits of information into and through the public domain, which arguably fits them for this role. From this point of view, "stakeholding" is only a variant terminology for traditional functions of the mass media as organs of information dissemination, opinion formation and surveillance of the state, in other words organs of the public sphere (see e.g. Curran 1996). On the other hand, the stakeholding relationship gives right of disclosure of information on the basis of the particularities of a relationship, whereas the mass media disclose information to the general public. To this extent, the mass media are not suitable organs for such disclosure except in those cases where the stakeholding relationship applies to all citizens.

Moreover, as competition-driven organisations run on decision-making criteria deriving from considerations alien to stakeholding (news values and other audience-oriented considerations), mass media in their traditional form may not be suitable vehicles for information disclosure based on the stakeholding relationship: their decisions about what information to disseminate and what to withhold bear no necessary relationship to stakeholding grounds. The implication is that the stakeholding relationship — seen as the basis of communicative ethics — demands forms of information circulation that do not conform to traditional conceptions of the role of the mass media and the public sphere but are grounded in narrow-cast dissemination and operate according to criteria of stakeholding need. This suggests that the mass media only serve as vehicles for stakeholder communications where the stakeholding is in the universal form of citizenship.

Finally, stakeholding has been presented here in terms of rights which are traditionally exercised by individuals and enforced through the state and the judicial process. It has often been pointed out that the exercise of rights makes no reference to forms of solidarity and critics of a rights-based conception of the social order argue both that consociation is, in fact, a prerequisite for a rights-based order to exist and that the exercise of rights is in practice inseparable from power differentiation. However, law — conceived in the fashion in which it is used here — is also an instrument for the enforcement of solidarity. It enforces behaviour, namely the circulation of information, that achieves two things: firstly, to the extent that the maintenance of power differentials depends upon exclusive access to specified information, it reduces their impact; secondly, it creates (or sustains) links which in sum become networks of solidarity, insofar as communication-based stakeholding is capable of being the basis of solidarity.

REFERENCES

Champagne, P. (1988) "Le Cercle Politique: Usages sociaux des sondages et le nouvel espace politique", *Actes de la Recherche en Sciences Sociales*, Nos. 71/2

Cockerell, M., Hennessy, P. and Walker, D. (1984) *Sources Close to the Prime Minister*, London, Macmillan

Curran, J. (1996) "Mass media and democracy revisited", Curran, J and Gurevich, M. (eds) *Mass Media and Society*, (2nd edition) London, Arnold pp 81-119

Downing, J. (1986) "Government secrecy and the media in the USA and Britain", Golding, P, Murdock, G. and Schlesinger, P. (eds) *Communicating Politics: Mass Communications and the Political Process*, Leicester, University Press pp 153-170

Ericson, R.V., Baranek, P.M. and Chan, J. (1989) *Negotiating Control: A Study of News Sources*, Milton Keynes, Open University Press

Franklin, B. (1994) *Packaging Politics: Political Communications in Britain's Media Democracy*, London, Arnold

Gans, H.J. (1980) *Deciding What's News*, London, Constable

Gerbner, G. (1956) "Towards a general model of communication", *Audio-Visual Communication Review* 4 (3)

Gimmler, A. (2002) "The Discourse Ethics of Jürgen Habermas", *Meta-Ethics Forum*. Available on at http://caae.phil.cmu.edu/Cavalier/Forum/meta/archive/archive.html

Grunig, J. (ed.) (1992) *Excellence in Public Relations and Communications Management*, Hillsdale, NJ, Lawrence Earlbaum Associates

Grunig, J. and Hunt, T. (1984) *Managing Public Relations*, New York, Holt, Rinehart and Winston

Grunig, J. and White, J. (1992) "The effects of worldviews on public relations theory and practice" Grunig, J (ed.) *Excellence in Public Relations and Communication Management*, Hillsdale, NJ, Lawrence Erlbaum Associates pp 31-64

Habermas, J. (1974) "The Public Sphere: An Encyclopaedia Article" (trans. Hohendahl, P.), *New German Critique 3*, New York, Telos Press pp 49-55

Habermas, J. (1984) *Theory of Communicative Action, Vol. I* (trans. McCarthy, T.) London, Heinemann

Habermas, J. (1987) *Theory of Communicative Action, Vol. II.* (trans. McCarthy, T.), Cambridge, Polity Press

Habermas, J. (1990) *Discourse Ethics: Notes on a Program of Philosophical Justification*, Cambridge, MA, MIT Press

Habermas, J. (1996) *Between Facts and Norms*, Cambridge, Polity Press

Hallin, D. (1986) The "Uncensored" War: *The Media and Vietnam*, Oxford, Oxford University Press

Harris, R. (1990) *Good and Faithful Servant: The Unauthorised Biography of Bernard*

Ingham, London, Faber and Faber

Hennessy, P. and Walker, D. (1989) "The Lobby", Seaton, J. and Pimlott B. (eds), *The Media in British Politics*, Aldershot, Dartmouth Publications pp 110-29

Huber, J.J. and Kim, T.J. (2002) The New Disclosure and Corporate Governance Regime: What Every Corporate and Securities Lawyer Must Know Now: The response to Enron: the Sarbanes-Oxley Act of 2002 and Commission Rulemaking, Practising Law Institute, Corporate Law and Practice Course Handbook Series

Ingham, B. (1991) *Kill the Messenger*, London, Fontana

Johnson, G. and Scholes, K. (1999) *Exploring Corporate Strategy*, (5th edition) London, Prentice Hall Europe

Jones, N. (1999) *Sultans of Spin*, London, Gollancz

Kahn, F.S. (2002) "Bombing Markets, Subverting The Rule Of Law: Enron, Financial Fraud, And September 11, 2001" (76 Tul. L. Rev. 1579) *Tulane Law Review*, June

Kieran, M., Morrison, D and Svennevig, M (1997) *Regulating for Changing Values*, Institute of Communication Studies, University of Leeds and the Broadcasting Standards Commission

Lamizet, B. (2002) "La Sémiotique du Secret", paper given at the conference Autour du Secret, University of Nancy II, May

Le Bohec, J. (1997) *Les Rapports Presse-Politique*, Paris, l'Harmattan

Lemieux, C. (2000) *Mauvaise Presse: Une sociologie compréhensive du travail journalistique et de ses critiques*, Paris, Editions Métailié

L'Etang, J. (1996) "Corporate responsibility and public relations ethics", L'Etang, J. and Pieczka, M. (eds) *Critical Perspectives in Public Relations*, London, International Thomson Business Press pp 82-105

Morrison, D. (2003) personal communication.

Morrison, D. and Svennevig, M. (2002) *The Public Interest, the Media and Privacy*, London, BBC/BSC/ICSTIS/ITC/IPPR/RA

Ollivier-Yaniv, C. (2003) "Avant-propos", in "Secret et pouvoir: les faux semblants de la transparence", *Quaderni*, 52 pp 39-41

Palmer, J. (2000) *Spinning into Control: News Values and Source Strategies*, London, Continuum Books

Palmer, J. (2001) "Les négotiations en amont: associations caritatives et médias en Angleterre", J.Walter (ed) *Télévision et Exclusion*, Paris, l'Harmattan pp 235-250

Quinn, L.C. and Jarmel, O.L. (2002) The New Disclosure and Corporate Governance Regime: What Every Corporate and Securities Lawyer Must Know Now: 781 MD and A 2002: Linchpin Of Sec Post-Enron Disclosure Reform (1335 PLI/Corp 781), Practising Law Institute, Corporate Law and Practice Course Handbook Series

Rawnsley, A. (2000) *Servants of the People: The Inside Story of New Labour*, London, Hamish Hamilton

Reich, A. and Wirtner, T. (2002) "What do you do when confronted with client fraud? To Disclose or not to Disclose is Becoming a Very Public Question", *Business Law Today* 39, September/October.

Rouledge, D., Barata, K. and Cain, P. (2000) Proceedings of the Information for Accountability Workshop, London, IRMT

Schlesinger, P. and Tumber, H. (1994) *Reporting Crime*, Oxford, Clarendon Press

Select Committee (1999) Proceedings of the Select Committee on Public Administration, London, Her Majesty's Stationery Office

Sigal, L. (1973) *Reporters and Officials*, Lexington, Mass, D.C.Heath

State of Ohio (n.d.) Case number 97CVH05 5114, Court of Common Pleas, Franklin County, Ohio. Available online at: http://stic.neu.edu/Oh/tobacco.doc

Tumber, H. and Palmer, J. (2004) *Media at War: The Iraq Crisis*, London, Sage

Tunstall, J. (1996) *Newspaper Power: The New National Press in Britain*, Oxford, Clarendon Press

Warner, E. (2002) "Secrets, leaks and insider gossip", the *Guardian*, 16 November

Wigand, J. (1995) Pre-trial deposition at Pascagoula, Mississipi. Available online at: www.jeffreywigand.com/insider/pascagoula.html

Dr Jerry Palmer is Professor of Communications at London Metropolitan University and Visiting Professor in the Sociology Department at City University. He has published seven books and numerous journal articles on aspects of popular culture and the mass media, of which the last two are concerned specifically with news and information flows. He teaches master's level courses in the area of communications strategy, communications ethics and communications policy. Contact details: Communications Studies, London Metropolitan University, 31 Jewry Street, London EC3N 2EY; tel: 020 7320 3030; email: j.palmer@londonmet.ac.uk.

Towards a definition of communication encompassing ethical dimensions*

Rolv Mikkel Blakar and Hilde Eileen Nafstad

This chapter aims to investigate whether prevailing definitions of communication address dimensions and distinctions that sufficiently sensitise us towards ethical, normative and value aspects of social behaviour and human interaction. Hence we focus on the communication side of the field of communication ethics. Communication and language use cannot be neutral in that special perspectives and interests are always reflected (Blakar 1979). Therefore, it is essential for researchers and professionals in the field of communication to adopt a concept of communication that sensitises us to the value issues that are necessarily embedded in communication.

Keywords: definition, communications, ethics, behaviour

INTRODUCTION

Communication theory is highly relevant to ethics and ethics is vital to communication. Every act of communication may be appraised from an ethical point of view. Furthermore, communication theory provides a fruitful perspective for assessing social processes with regard to values or ethics. However, it is essential that communication be defined in such a way that distinctions and dimensions relevant to ethics are encompassed and exposed rather than concealed.

A characteristic feature of our time is globalisation. For the individual as a social being, globalisation entails a variety of psychological implications. Two marked consequences are that individual human beings are exposed to

---

*We are grateful to Erik Carlquist for useful comments on an earlier version of this article.

a flow of information that is more complex than ever before, and that they meet other individuals with different culturally defined repertoires of behaviour. Both of these consequences contribute to an increasing complexity of social interaction, forcing us to face a variety of value dilemmas and ethical issues.

Traditionally, the focus of communication ethics has been on establishing ethical codes of conduct for various communication-oriented disciplines and professions, such as journalism, public relations and teaching. In all these fields there is the crucial task of promoting good practice and constraining malpractice. However, little effort has been invested in analysing whether various definitions of communication sensitise us toward values and ethical issues. Analysis of this kind should supplement the more traditional work on ethical codes.

Whenever ethical dimensions and value issues are explicitly addressed, implications of different definitions of communication may not be that essential and decisive. However, in most accounts of communication ethical issues will not be foregrounded. Under such "normal" conditions of activity it will, thus, be decisive whether the concept of communication adopted sensitises us towards distinctions and dimensions relevant to ethics, or whether such distinctions and dimensions are concealed.

PREVAILING DEFINITIONS

Hardly any other concept is used as often as communication when social behaviour, interaction and information processing are described and explained. Scientists, politicians, journalists and commentators as well as "ordinary people" turn to the concept of communication to explain all kinds of social phenomena. However, it is astonishing that a concept which is used so often by people to explain many different phenomena and processes has rarely been questioned and defined. Apparently the concept of communication has gained status as a kind of magic wand which may be used to explain almost everything. The danger, then, is that we witness a special game in which a "mystery" (for example, conflict) is explained by means of another "mystery" (communication, or deviant communication). In particular, when it comes to values, ethical issues and normative questions, explanatory concepts which function to conceal are counterproductive.

A first step to render the communication perspective into an analytically sharp and clarifying perspective with which to understand social phenomena, including ethical and moral issues, is to propose a fruitful definition. Our criticism of the concept of communication as used today may be summarised as follows: First, to the extent that communication is defined at all, the conceptual definitions are too broad and general. Second, in most communication studies, operational definitions or measurements of communication represent trivial oversimplifications which fail to grasp essential aspects of communication.

Concerning broad and general definitions, there are primarily three types:

- Communication is seen as synonymous to behaviour. An illustrating case is Watzlawick et al. (1967: 22) who, in the influential classic *Pragmatics of Human Communication*, state that "...all behavior, not only speech, is communication, and all communication – even the communicational cues in an impersonal context – affects behavior".
- Communication is regarded as a stream or flow of information. A classic definition of this category is given by Athanassiades (1974: 195): "Verbal and non-verbal communication, i.e. the flow of information, impressions, and understandings from one individual to others."
- Communication is used as synonymous to interaction. "Taken very broadly, communicative competence is the ability to interact well with others" (Spitzberg 1988: 68). Some, as does Larsson (1997: 21) include both information and interaction without this leading to particularly clear delineations and definitions of communication: "Communication is a very broad scientific concept which should be defined more precisely, especially in relation to the concept of information. A wonderfully short definition of communication is 'social interaction through messages' (Gerbner, in McQuail and Windahl 1995), where we allow ourselves to interpret 'message' as information in the widest sense."

As we shall see when analysing in detail examples of human interaction, such broad definitions function to conceal, as they cannot manage to grasp essential distinctions between apparently similar, but actually fundamentally different, social interaction situations. These distinctions are essential when ethical appraisals are to be made. Recently, the situation unfortunately has developed from bad to worse when it comes to use – not to mention misuse – of the communication concept.

This is due primarily to two mutually reinforcing developmental tendencies. First, the study of human communication has been divided into a range of specialised sub-traditions addressing themselves to limited sectors of human communication. But in this flowering of "experts" on political communication, (mass-)media communication, cross-cultural communication, rhetorical communication, international communication, doctor-patient communication, family communication, communication and leadership, communication on the Internet, communication over cell phones, to name but a few of the sub-areas, the basic task of defining communication has generally been neglected.

The other tendency is that modern digital technology has resulted in a variety of advanced computer-based methods which analyse different variables and parameters in communication in media, families, doctor-patient relationships and so on. The problem is, however, that the different variables of which the data programs give refined analyses are not grounded in general theory on human communication.

CRITICAL INQUIRIES

One may ask why one would need a concept of communication – and not least, why this concept is so central – if all behaviour, anyway, is communication? Why not just make do with a (perhaps somewhat more specified) behavioural concept? A science of the individual cannot be imagined without a concept of behaviour. Neither interaction nor information concepts are avoidable when one is to understand social interaction. Equally heretically, one may, therefore, ask this of those who conceive of communication as synonymous to interaction or flow of information. Hence, if communication and the flow of information are the same, we may be able to manage with only one concept.

Likewise if communication and interaction are perceived as identical. Conceptual redundancy is usually a sign of unclear and imprecise thinking. In order to use the concept of communication to explain something, it is necessary to show what the concept brings of understanding in addition to, or as differentiating from, the concepts of behaviour, interaction and/or information. When a concept such as communication is used without delineating it from other related and more or less overlapping concepts, it will be concealing instead of clarifying.

It is easy to demonstrate that such broad definitions which imply that "all behaviour is communication", that communication is synonymous to interaction or that communication is "flow of information" conceal a host of fundamental distinctions highly relevant to the analysis of social and ethical issues. If all flow of information is communication, then one cannot, for example, distinguish between receiving a message and receiving information.

For example: if you look out the window and see that it is raining, you then receive information about the weather. If someone comes into the room and says that it is raining, then you receive the same weather information. With regard to information flow, the two episodes are identical. However, normative and ethical issues (e.g. lying/misinforming) can only be involved in the latter episode. A further example: a seminar participant is in great pain, but does not want the others to know. Grimaces and jerks (i.e. behaviour) reveal this to the others anyway (i.e. flow of information).

It is essential to distinguish this situation from one in which the person tells the others that "today I'm in great pain". If you only have observed the pain, you are in a totally different way faced with a communicative-ethical judgement about if, and then when and in what way, you should show that you know about this. Definitions of communication should serve to reveal and grasp such distinctions and, in any case, not contribute to concealing them. It is critical that the communication concept functions to make us aware of and sensitive to such distinctions. If we do not reflectively distinguish between information about somebody received by observation, and information received by the person's self-report, conflicts and uneasy ethical situations will necessarily occur.

Our second criticism is that operational definitions of communication are usually oversimplified and commonplace. Variables of the type: who is speaking, who speaks to whom, duration of speaking, who interrupts whom and how often, how many and duration of pauses, how long and/or complete sentences each person uses — are typical variables in different types of communication analyses. In analyses of public communication, parameters such as who gets to speak, how often, and duration of speech in mass media, are much used. These are, of course, not uninteresting measures of how communication functions. But interpretation of such in themselves "exterior" variables are totally dependent on the current understanding of communication which, as we have seen, is based on lacking or vague conceptual definitions.

An interruption can, for instance, be an expression of a power struggle (I try to stop you). But it can also be an expression of perfect understanding (I have already understood/anticipated what you are about to say). What does one gain, then, from only counting interruptions? Different types of interruptions may carry different ethical implications. In the same way, incomplete sentences may be symptoms of inadequate verbal and communicative abilities. But they may also be an expression of perfect understanding, so that formally complete and elaborate sentences would be totally unnecessary, indeed would seem almost alienating. Confusing or mistaking such differences carries ethical implications. Interpretation of various variables used to describe communication under different conditions demands a far more finely meshed and well-developed concept of communication than those currently in use. Especially when social interaction is to be judged normatively and ethically, adopting a concept of communication sensitive to such distinctions is essential.

AN ILLUSTRATIVE CASE EXAMPLE

To present a more fruitful definition of communication, let us compare the following episodes:

(1) A boy is lost in the jungle. While he wanders around, he cannot help but break lots of branches and twigs because he bends these out of his way in order to go further. After he has been missing for a while, a search party is sent out. They find the broken branches, follow the trail and find the boy where he lies sleeping.

(2) A boy is lost in the jungle. When he realises he is lost, he thinks: "When they discover I'm gone, they will send people out to look for me." Therefore, he breaks lots of branches and twigs so that those looking for him will be able to see where he has walked. After he has been missing for a while, a search party is sent out. They find the broken branches, follow the trail and find the boy where he lies sleeping.

The outcome of the two episodes is, indeed, the same. In both episodes, the boy's behaviour has had communicative value, which supports the definition of communication as behaviour and that all behaviour is communication. For the sake of argument, we may assume that the behaviour, that is, the way the branches were broken, was identical in the two episodes. On video the two episodes would, indeed, be identical. In both episodes the search party also receives identical information on where the boy has gone. This supports the definition of communication as flow of information.

In spite of identical outcomes, behaviour and information, no one would disagree there still is an essential difference between the two episodes. The difference has to do with the boy's intention. In the first, the branches were broken because the boy wanted to move them out of the way so that he could go further. In the second, he breaks the branches because he wants to make a trail so that those who he anticipates will come to look for him will be able to follow it. We view this difference as essential when defining and delineating communication. We consider the second episode to be a prototypical case of communication.

In our view it is not fruitful, however, to operate with a communication concept that is so broad as to include also the first episode. In both, there is flow of information, in fact identical information. There is behaviour in both, for argument's sake identical muscular movements breaking the branches. Still, these two apparently identical interaction situations must psychologically and socially be described and analysed fundamentally differently.

Moreover, these psychological differences are decisive for ethical assessments of behaviour, interaction and information. Whereas the first episode scarcely involves any ethical issues at all, the second does. For example, it is possible for the boy in episode two to "lie" by making false trails and thus mislead the search party. In episode two, but not in episode one, it is relevant to ask evaluative questions about, for example, the efficiency of the communication. From the perspective of ethical analysis it is critical that prevailing definitions claiming that communication is behaviour and all behaviour is communication and definitions stating that communication is flow of information, are not able to distinguish between these two "identical" episodes.

TOWARDS A MORE FRUITFUL DEFINITION OF COMMUNICATION

The challenge when defining communication is to grasp the essential aspects of these universal human activities while simultaneously delineating communication from other processes that overlap with and/or resemble communication. The concept of communication must be defined and used in association with and relation to a host of other central concepts, notably interaction, information and behaviour. The word communication comes from the Latin, *communicatio*, which means "to make common". With this analysis as background, we shall now present what we regard as a fruitful definition of communication:

> *Communication: an intentional act to make something known to a certain receiver.*

In addition to this definition capturing the behavioural aspect (*to make*) from the first, the information aspect (*something made known*) from the second, and the interactional aspect (*from a sender to a receiver*) from the third of the predominant ways of conceiving of communication, this definition is based on communication being intentional. Even though the basic point of view is the sender's intentional message, it should be emphasised that communication is a dialogical process in which the participants in a mutual interaction create together and share responsibility for that which is made common, i.e. the mediated message (Blakar 1992; Rommetveit 1992; Wold 1992).

This definition explicitly anchors the concept of communication in the requirement that action (i.e. the exchange of information) has to be intentional. In the first place this requirement raises more problems than it solves. However, our task is not to simplify, rather to problematise the communication concept to make it a more fruitful analytical tool in the study of social relationships and human interaction, including ethics. We shall briefly point out some of the essential implications which follow from this. Importantly, with this point of departure one cannot in the same manner as mainstream psychology and social science limit oneself only to descriptive questions about the "what" and "how". One must also address the intricate question of the "why" of communication. The fruitfulness of such a communication concept in studying human relations, including ethical and normative issues, is illustrated by the fact that ethical and moral assessments must inevitably consider the "why" of human behaviour.

There are other essential implications of grounding the definition of communication in intentionality (Blakar 1984) which we will only mention briefly. First, when we adopt this communication perspective, we must continuously and systematically shift between an inner (empathic) and an outer (observing) perspective. Second, the concepts we use operationally to describe and analyse communication must be grounded in both (lived) experience and (observable) behaviour. Third, whenever we are explaining failures and problems of communication, we are forced to consider the question of whether this is due to the actors not being able to, or their not being willing to (e.g. lack of ability versus lack of willingness to take the other's perspective). Particularly the last, but also the other two points, take communication analysis to the core of ethical issues in social relations by sensitising us to questions such as: could you not, or were you not willing to understand/support/help another person?

CONCLUSION

We have attempted to define communication in a way that allows for distinctions essential for understanding human interaction and social relations, including ethical ones. As argued, the prevailing definitions are too broad and thus ignore or conceal distinctions that are fundamental for an ethical approach. On the other hand, there are certain distinctions which contemporary communication research makes too absolute or exaggerates the implications. One distinction that the definition we have presented minimises is that between verbal and non-verbal communication. Today, this distinction has been given so much weight that it, in fact, has resulted in separate traditions, separate journals and separate handbooks for non-verbal communication (as distinct from verbal communication).

According to our definition, this distinction has been exaggerated. It is of no consequence whether we call each other's attention to something by pointing (non-verbal), or by saying: "Look over there" (verbal). The central aspect in communication is that we make something known, not whether we do this verbally or non-verbally. Often, the verbal and non-verbal will be coordinated in that we both point and say: "Look over there." Ethically it is also irrelevant whether we deceive somebody by pointing or by saying: "Look over there."

Definitions in psychology and social science do not function neutrally (Nafstad 2002; 2003). That various concepts in psychology are not value-neutral but function normatively, makes it even more problematic that central concepts – in this case, communication – are often used without being defined. When professionals and laypeople use various concepts, such as communication, without defining them, it is impossible to know on the basis of which assumptions and values, normative evaluations of communication as, for example,. "good versus bad," "effective versus ineffective," "fruitful versus unfruitful" communication builds.

Communication which from the point of view of one definition (e.g. flow of information) may be characterised as successful because a manager efficiently distributes information, may from another definition's horizon be judged as unfruitful because the interaction does not allow for dialogue and feedback. From a normative point of view, therefore, it is essential to identify which dimensions of communication a chosen definition includes and which dimensions are eliminated or marginalised.

REFERENCES

Athanassiades, J.C. (1974) "An investigation of some communication patterns of female subordinates in hierarchical organisations", *Human Relations*, 27 pp 195-209

Blakar, R. M. (1979) "Language as a means of social power", Mey, J.L. (ed) *Pragmalinguistics: Theory and Practice*, Vol 85, Series Janua Linguarum, The Hague, Mouton pp 131-169

Blakar, R.M. (1984) *Communication: A social perspective on clinical issues*, Oslo, Universitetsforlaget

Blakar, R.M. (1992) "Towards an identification of preconditions for communication", Wold, A. H. (ed) *The dialogical alternative: Towards a theory of language and mind*, Oslo, Universitetsforlaget pp 235-252

Larsson, L. (1997) *Tillämpad kommunikasjonsvetenskap*, Lund, Studentlitteratur

Nafstad, H.E. (2003) "Area ethics: To integrate basic, applied, and professional ethics in a particular field of activity", proceedings from first international conference on teaching applied and professional ethics in higher education, Roehampton, London, 2-4 September pp 145-151

Rommetveit, R. (1992) "Outlines of a dialogically based social-cognitive approach to human cognition and communication", Wold, A. H. (ed) *The dialogical alternative: Towards a theory of language and mind*, Oslo, Universitetsforlaget pp 19-44

Spitzberg, B.H. (1988) "Communication competence: Measures of perceived effectiveness", Tardy, C. H. (ed.), *A handbook for the study of human communication: Methods and instruments for observing, measuring and assessing communication processes,* Norwood, N.J., Ablex Publishing pp 67-106

Watzlawick, P., Beavin, J.H. and Jackson, D. (1967) *Pragmatics of human communication,* New York, Norton

Wold, A. H. (ed.) (1992) *The dialogical alternative: Towards a theory of language and mind*, Oslo, Universitetsforlaget

Rolv Mikkel Blakar is Professor in Social Psychology at the University of Oslo. His field of research is communication and psychology of language. In particular he has analysed language as a means of social power. Currently he is analysing how societal ideology is reflected in the language. He has been dean of the Faculty of Social Science and pro-rector at the University of Oslo. At present he is head of the steering group of the Ethics Program at the University of Oslo. Contact details: University of Oslo, Department of Psychology, PO Box 1094 Blindern, 0317 Oslo, Norway. Tel. +47 92421444; email: r.m.blakar@psykologi.uio.no.

Hilde Eileen Nafstad is Associate Professor in Social and Developmental Psychology at the University of Oslo. She is affiliated with the Ethics Program of the University of Oslo as supervisor and is undertaking research on ethics in the professions as well as developing area ethics of psychology and the social sciences. Her most recent publications include: *The Caring Human Being* (ed.); *Ideological Shifts in Society* and *Assumptions in Psychology; and Area Ethics: To Integrate Basic, Applied and Professional Ethics in a Particular Field of Activity.* Contact details: University of Oslo, Department of Psychology, PO Box 1094 Blindern, 0317 Oslo, Norway. Tel. +47 22845155; email: h.e.nafstad@psykologi.uio.no.

Between trust and anxiety:
on the moods of Information Society*

Rafael Capurro

This chapter addresses the experience of information anxiety as a basic mood of today's networked information society. Following the analysis by Richard Wurman, information anxiety is considered as having two sources, namely information overload and the fear of control, surveillance and exclusion. In addition, the paper explores the distinctions made by Heidegger and Wittgenstein between "fear" and "anxiety".

Keywords: trust, anxiety, information society, moods, information overload

ON INFORMATION ANXIETY

We live in an information society. To be well informed means, if we trust our everyday experience, anxiety reduction. But today we are paradoxically plagued with information anxiety. According to Richard Wurman information anxiety has (at least) two sources, the first concerns our relation to information, the second our relation to each other. He writes:

> *Information anxiety is produced by the ever-widening gap between what we understand and what we think we should understand. Information anxiety is the black hole between data and knowledge. It happens when information doesn't tell us what we want to know (Wurman 2001: 14).*

Following this logic, the more the information the greater the

*An earlier version of this paper was presented at the Institute of Communication Ethics annual conference, University of Lincoln, 14-15 June 2004

hermeneutic challenge of making sense and, consequently, of anxiety reduction. As John Seely Brown and Paul Duguid rightly state:

For it is not shared stories or shared information so much as shared interpretation that binds people together. [...] To collaborate around shared information you first have to develop a shared framework for interpretation. 'Each of us thinks his own thoughts,' the philosopher Stephen Toulmin argues. 'Our concepts we share' (Brown and Duguid 2000: 107).

Information technology and information hermeneutics are two sides of the same coin. But as no human society can survive without information it can also be said that every human society is an information society. This historical perspective has, as Michael Hobart and Zachary Schiffman state, a liberating effect. They write:

The fundamental fact of information's historicity liberates us from the conceit that ours is the information age [...] It allows us to stand outside our contemporary information idiom, to see where it comes from, what it does, and how it shapes our thought (Hobart and Schiffman 1998).

Our present economy, policy, scientific research, technological innovation, and, last but not least, our everyday life are largely dependent on digital information. In this sense we can state that information anxiety and its counterpart, information trust, are the basic moods of today's digitally networked information society.

INFORMATION OVERLOAD

The Internet is, following Wurman, the "black hole" between data and knowledge. It does not tell us what we want to know. What we want to know depends on our situation, i.e. on our existential conditions, on our history and commitments, on our beliefs and desires. What we want to know is partly explicit but it remains implicit to a great extent. It emerges at the moment in which we become aware of the relevance of the gap between "what we understand" and "what we think we should understand". This awareness arises, for instance, when our critical spirit does not trust the present knowledge as a secure basis for the future. In our digital-based economy this attitude is being reflected globally and 24 hours a day in our finance markets, being constantly driven between the moods of trust and anxiety. Any kind of foreknowledge rests on assumptions that cannot be completely made explicit because this would imply an absolute knowledge that is unattainable for a finite being. There is no complete information for a human knower.

This trivial but basic assumption has been forgotten or was just ignored by some of our modern economic theories as they invented the *homo oeconomicus rationalis*. But, *hélas*!, there is no possibility for us to fill the gap between information and knowledge and, consequently, between trust and anxiety. There is no mood-free rational economy. Even more, moods are not the opposite to rationality but rationality itself is already in a mood of a knower who trusts (or not) sense data and his/her (imperfect) predicting capacity. According to David Hume: "Our actions have a constant union with our motives, tempers, and circumstances" (Hume 1962: 272).

Herbert Simon coined the concept of "bounded rationality", following the suggestions by Friedrich von Hayek in his 1945 paper *The Use of Knowledge in Society*, that it is the "pragmatic mechanism" with no promises of optimisation, and not the "ideal market mechanism", that fits the real world (Simon 1982: 41-43). Uncertainty and expectancy are the basic moods of the pragmatic market mechanism. According to Simon, we should remain sceptical assuming that people form their expectations about the future rationally and that firms and investors can thus predict the future of their business based on the permanent prevalence of such an assumption as in the case of Adam Smith's "invisible hand" and Hegel's "*List der Vernunft*".

Richard Wurman mentions another source of information anxiety that concerns our relation to each other in a network society:

> *Our relationship to information isn't the only source of information anxiety. We are also made anxious by the fact that other people often control our access to information. We are dependent on those who design information, on the news editors and producers who decide what news we will receive, and by decision-makers in the public and private sector who can restrict the flow of information. We are also made anxious by other people's expectations of what we should know, be they company, presidents, or even parents (Wurman op cit: 14).*

FEAR OF SURVEILLANCE, CONTROL AND EXCLUSION

While the first source of information anxiety has to do with information overload, the second one is related to the fear of surveillance, control and exclusion. While creating a global medium like the Internet we are confronted with exclusion or what we use to call the digital divide. Since 11 September 2001, but also since 11 March 2004 (when terrorist bombers struck Madrid), we are facing the reality of a web of trust becoming a web of surveillance. After the shock of March 11, Spanish voters sent each other text messages. Within a few hours several thousand of them met apparently spontaneously to protest against the official information policy. This makes clear the kind of synergy made possible by the mobile web, while at the same time the collective fear of, say, viruses attacks, privacy infringements, theft and pornography, make the idea of a net of control not only plausible but even desirable, at least from the viewpoint of some governments and pressure groups as stated by Lawrence Lessig (1999) and most recently also by liberal philosopher Richard Rorty (2004).

Net control is becoming a legitimate part of the "war against terrorism". But this war is an asymmetric "war" and cannot be won with a top-down strategy based on the mood of anxiety. This is exactly what terrorists want. The "war against terrorism" becomes, according to Rorty, a greater threat to western democracies than terrorism itself. The alternative seems to be between slavery within a "goodwill despotism" (Rorty op cit) and liberty under the threat of terrorism. In today's information society the price of trust is liberty and the price of liberty is anxiety. *Tertium non datur.*

Thomas L. Friedman, the *New York Times* columnist, reports of a wood-panelled room in Bangalore where the Indian software giant Infosys can hold a simultaneous global teleconference with its US innovators. Mr Nilekani, CEO of Infosys, explains: "We can have our whole global supply chain on the screen at the same time." The journalist comments:

> *"Who else has such a global supply chain today? Of course: Al Qaeda. Indeed, these are the two basic responses to globalization: Infosys and Al Qaeda" (Friedman 2004).*

GROWING COMMERCIALISATION OF THE INTERNET

Close to this anxiety in face of a net of control and/or of terrorism is the anxiety related to the growing commercialisation of the Internet. It leads to what John Walker calls "the digital imprimatur" (Walker 2003). This means no more and no less than the end of the Internet as we know it today when Big Brother and big media put "the Internet genie back in the bottle" through Trusted Computing, Digital Rights Management, and the Secure Internet on the basis of "micropayment" and "document certificates". This is, from a historical perspective, a victory of the hierarchic 20th century mass media. It is devoted to guaranteeing trust through control by equating freedom with anxiety on the basis of digital Leviathans. The principles stated and the actions started by the World Summit on the Information Society (WSIS) as well as by several civil society initiatives in favour of freedom of communication (Internet Commons Congress 2004) are at the opposite end of this vision.

ON MOODS

Anxiety is a mood. According to ordinary understanding moods happen inside our minds. In his famous dictionary of the English language Samuel Johnson defines anxiety as:

> 1. Trouble of mind about some future event; suspense with uneasiness; perplexity; solicitude.[...] 2. In the medical language, depression; lowness of spirits" (Johnson 1755/1968).

The *Oxford English Dictionary* puts it like this:

> The quality or state of being anxious; uneasiness or trouble of mind about some uncertain event; solicitude, concern (OED 1989).

Compare these definitions with Friedman's description of the intersection between Al Qaeda and information technology in Madrid on 11 March 2004:

> *Ever once in a while the technology and terrorist supply chains intersect – like last week. Reuters quoted a Spanish official saying after the Madrid train bombings: 'The hardest thing [for the rescue workers] was hearing mobile phones ringing in the pockets of the bodies. They couldn't get that our of their heads' (Friedman op cit).*

If we use the word anxiety for describing the mood of the Spanish officials in face of the unbelievable terrorist threat, we would *prima facie* agree with the conception of moods as something happening within their heads. But it is also evident that this interpretation of moods is one-sided since what is going on in the heads of the rescue workers cannot be dissociated from the whole situation in which they are embedded. In other words, we can speak of a terrible situation as a mood concerning only the heads of the rescue workers but, in fact, it concerns the whole situation within a train station, a city, a country and even the whole European continent. Moods are then related not just to private feelings but they pervade the situation in which subjects are inserted. Our states-of-mind cannot be dissociated from their circumstances.

This view is also the one developed by Martin Heidegger's phenomenological approach (Heidegger 1976: 134). According to Heidegger, moods are not primarily private feelings but they disclose a public experience, i.e. they concern the way(s) we are in a given situation with others in a common world. Being originally social our feelings do not separate us from each other but even in the case in which we speak of mood as a subjective state, this belongs already to the situation in which I am embedded implicitly or explicitly together with others. In his commentary on Heidegger's *Being and Time*, Hubert Dreyfus writes:

> *For example, when one is afraid, one does not merely feel fearful, nor is fear merely the movement of cringing; fear is cringing in an appropriate context (Dreyfus 1991: 172).*

The psychologist, Eugene Gendlin, remarks that Heidegger's conception of mood is more "interactional" than "intrapsychic" (Gendlin 1978). In his article on Heidegger's concept of *"Befindlichkeit"*, he writes:

> 'Sich befinden' *(finding oneself) thus has three allusions: The reflexivity of finding oneself; feeling; and being situated. All three are caught in the ordinary phrase: How are you? That refers to how you feel but also to how things are going for you and what sort of situation you find yourself in. To answer the question you must find yourself, find how you already are. And when you do, you find yourself amidst the circumstances of your living.*

Gendlin underlines another important difference of the Heideggerian conception of mood with regard to the traditional subjectivist view, namely the relation of mood and understanding, or, more precisely, the conception of mood as a specific way of understanding. Moods are not just affections colouring a situation but are an active although mostly implicit way of understanding a situation independently of what we actually say or not with explicit words. There is then, according to Heidegger, a difference as well as an intimate relation between mood, understanding and speech as the three basic parameters of human existence.

In *Being and Time*, Heidegger gives a famous analysis of two moods, namely fear (*"Furcht"*) and anxiety (*"Angst"*), borrowing insights from Kierkegaard's *Concept of Anxiety*. The key difference between these moods is that while fear is a mood in which one is afraid about something fearsome, anxiety, in contrast, faces us with our being-in-the-world itself in such a way that no intra-worldly entity is at its origin. But we are confronted with the very fact of the being there, with our existence in the world, and of the being of the world itself, without the possibility of giving an intrinsic reason for them. Dreyfus remarks:

> In anxiety Dasein discovers that it has no meaning or content of its own; nothing individualises it but its empty thrownness (Dreyfus 1991: 180).

Such an experience is not necessarily accompanied by sweating and crying but it is nearer to what we could call today a "cool" experience of the gratuity of existence. Ludwig Wittgenstein describes such a "key experience" (*"mein Erlebnis par excellence"*) in his *Lecture on Ethics* with the following words:

> This experience, in case I have it, can be described most properly, I believe, with the words I am amazed about the existence of the world. Then I tend to use formulations like these ones: 'How strange that something exists at all' or 'How strange that the world exists' (Wittgenstein 1989: 14, my translation).

But according to Wittgenstein we have really no appropriate expression for this experience –– other than the existence of language itself. On 30 December 1929 Wittgenstein remarked:

> I can imagine what Heidegger means with being and anxiety. Human beings have the tendency to run against the boundaries of language. Think for instance about the astonishment that something at all exists. [...] Ethics is this run against the boundaries of language (Wittgenstein 1984: 68, my translation).

ON THE MOODS OF INFORMATION SOCIETY

How are we doing in today's information society? What is our mood? In view of the difference between fear and anxiety we can answer that within the situation of being-in-the-network we are in the mood of fear and trust. We use the Internet in everyday life in such a way that not only the Gnostic perspective of cyberspace as something separated from the real world – as promulgated, for instance, by John Perry Barlow (1996) – has become outdated as mobile and miniaturised computing – we could call this the Vodafone effect – but it is now everywhere embedded in our everyday material life. Just the opposite of cyberspace mythology happened. This creates, indeed, a mood of (implicit) trust. But at the same time it gives rise to new types of fear as the pervasive connection of all things can also lead to disastrous outcomes.

And what about anxiety? It seems as if the network does create a kind of digital veil that conceals the type of experience addressed by Wittgenstein and Heidegger with the concept of anxiety. The network is more of the kind of instrumental grid called later by Heidegger *"Gestell"* (literally "enframing") i.e. of a collection of all kinds of positioning (*"stellen"*) or manipulation of things. We could use this term with regard to information society by calling information *Gestell* all forms of language production and manipulation (Capurro 2000).

But is today's experience of, say, ubiquitous computing, multifunctional cellular phones and permanent online accessibility, really at the opposite of the kind of affective understanding arising from our confrontation with the abyss of human existence as manifest in the mood of anxiety? Does the information *Gestell* create a kind of super human subject with all kinds of enhanced capabilities, as described for instance by MIT designer William J. Mitchell in his book *ME++* (Mitchell 2003). David Hume writes:

> *When I turn my reflection on myself, I never can perceive this self without some or more perceptions; nor can I ever perceive anything but the perceptions. It is the composition of these, therefore, which forms the self (Hume 1962: 283).*

In today's information society we form our selves through digitally mediated perceptions of all kinds. Interconnectivity does not mean the death of the modern subject as proclaimed by some popular postmodernists but its transformation into a "nodular subject" (Mitchell op cit) which means, paradoxically, a weakening of its manipulating ambitions. The power of networks does not lead necessarily to slavery and oppression but also to reciprocity and mutual obligation. The boundaries of language against which we are driven appear now as the boundaries of digital networks which not only pervade but accelerate all relationships between humans as well as between all kinds of natural phenomena and artificial things. But, indeed, the subject of the digital network is at the same time its creator and its object.

From a more radical perspective, if we follow the tendency not only to drive against the boundaries of language but also against the boundaries of the digital, we may be able to experience life in a networked world in a mood of anxiety. And we might then make a trivial statement like: "I am amazed about the existence of a digital networked world" switching for a while from fear, as the everyday mood of information society, into anxiety and calmness, giving ourselves an opportunity to perceive what Buddhists call "nothingness".

REFERENCES

Barlow, John Perry (1996) *A Declaration of Independence of Cyberspace*. Available online at http://www.eff.org/~barlow/Declaration-Final.html, accessed on 15 April 2004]

Brown, John Seely and Duguid, Paul (2000) *The Social Life of Information*, Boston, Ma, Harvard Business School Presso

Capurro, Rafael (2000) "Hermeneutics and the Phenomenon of Information", Mitcham, Carl (ed) *Metaphysics, Epistemology, and Technology. Research in Philosophy and Technology*, Vol. 19 pp 79-85. Available online at http://www.capurro.de/ny86.html, accessed on 15 April 2004

Dreyfus, Hubert L. (1991) *Being-in-the-world. A Commentary on Heidegger's Being and Time, Division I*, Cambridge MA and London, the MIT Press

Friedman, Thomas L. (2004) "Origin of Species", *The New York Times*, 14 March

Gendlin, Eugene T. (1978) *Befindlichkeit*: [1] *Heidegger and the Philosophy of Psychology. Review of Existential Psychology and Psychiatry: Heidegger and Psychology*. Vol. XVI, Nos. 1, 2 and 3, 1978-79. Available online at: http://www.focusing.org/gendlin_befindlichkeit.html, accessed on 15 April 2004

Hobart, Michael E.and Schiffman, Zachary S. (1998) *Information Ages. Literacy, Numeracy, and the Computer Revolution*, Baltimore and London, John Hopkins University Press

Heidegger, Martin (1976) *Sein und Zeit. Tübingen*: Max Niemeyer (English translation: *Being and Time*, by Macquarrie, John and Robinson, Edward, Oxford, Basil Blackwell 1987)

Hume, David (1962) "A Treatise on Human Nature", *On Human Nature and the Understanding*, Flew, Anthony (ed.), New York, Macmillan

Internet Common Congress (2004) 24-25 March 2004. Washington, DC http://www.internationalunity.org/

Johnson, Samuel (1755/1968) *A Dictionary of the English Language*, Hildesheim, Olms

Lessig, Lawrence (1999) *Code and Other Laws of Cyberspace*, New York, Basic Books
Mitchell, William J. (2003) *ME++ The Cyborg Self and the Networked City*, Cambridge MA and London, MIT Press

Rorty, Richard (2004) *Feind im Visier. Im Kampf gegen den Terror gefährden westliche Demokratien die Grundlagen ihrer Freiheit, Die Zeit*, 18 March No 13 pp 49-50
Simon, Herbert A. (1982) *The Sciences of the Artificial*, (2nd edition) Cambridge MA and London, MIT. Press
The *Oxford English Dictionary* (1989), (2nd edition) Oxford, Clarendon Press
Walker, John (2003) *The Digital Imprimatur*. Available online at http://www.fourmilab.ch/documents/digital-imprimatur/, accessed on 15 April 2004
Wittgenstein, Ludwig (1989) *Vortrag über Ethik*, Frankfurt am Main, Suhrkamp
Wittgenstein, Ludwig (1984) *Zu Heidegger*, McGuiness, B.F. (ed.) *Ludwig Wittgenstein und der Wiener Kreis. Gespräche, aufgezeichnet von Friedrich Waismann*. Frankfurt am Main, Suhrkamp
Wurman, Richard Saul (2001) *Information Anxiety 2*, Indianapolis, Indiana.

Professor Dr. Rafael Capurro is editor-in-chief of the *International Journal of Information Ethics* (IJIE): http://www.ijie.org. His recent publications include: *Ethik im Netz*. Stuttgart, Franz Steiner Verlag 2003; *Netzethik. Grundlegungsfragen der Internetethik* (Capurro, Rafael and Hausmanninger, Thomas, eds), München, Fink Verlag 2002. ICIE Series Vol. 1. Contact details: Hochschule der Medien, Stuttgart University of Applied Sciences, Wolframstr. 32, 70191 Stuttgart, Germany. Website: www.capurro.de; email: rafael@capurro.de

Paedophiles in the community: Inter-agency conflict, whistleblowers and the local press*

Simon Cross and Sharon Lockyer

This chapter explores the leaking of confidential information about convicted paedophiles being rehoused in prison accommodation. It argues that a politics of paedophilia has emerged in which inter-agency consensus on the issue of "what to do" with sex offenders has broken down. Accordingly, the paper situates media "outings" of paedophiles in relation to leaked information from official agencies. Findings are presented from a case study of whistleblowing by Prison Officer Association officials to a local newspaper in the East Midlands of England and the paper concludes with a discussion about what happens after the whistle has blown.

Keywords: paedophiles in the community, local press, naming and shaming, inter-agency conflict, whistleblowing

INTRODUCTION

In August 1997, 44-year-old David Moist heard unusual sounds coming from the stairwell of his council flat in Teignmouth, Devon, in south-west England. He went to investigate and was attacked by a large group of men. Moist was severely beaten and surgery to repair the damage took many hours. Following the attack, his flat was ransacked and the words "Beast Out" were daubed on the outside walls. According to the Association of Chief Probation Officers, who documented the incident, Moist was attacked

---

*An earlier version of this paper was presented at the Institute of Communication Ethics conference, University of Lincoln, Lincoln, 14-15 June 2004.

by an *ad hoc* group calling itself an "Unofficial Child Protection Unit" hours after being named in the local newspaper as a convicted paedophile. A neighbour of the beaten man reportedly claimed that only direct physical action could protect their children from paedophiles.

Later that day, a police spokesman confirmed that Moist's attackers would be prosecuted. He went further and condemned the attack as proof that public "outing" of sex offenders was irresponsible and led to vigilantism. However, ironically, it emerged that local police officers, worried that the man might be about to commit another offence against children but lacking sufficient evidence to detain him, had leaked details of the man's obsessive sexual interest in children to the local newspaper and other media in an attempt to get him removed from their area. It worked. After recovering from his extensive injuries, Moist was re-housed in a new location.

MEDIA AND MORAL POPULISM

Men like David Moist are pariahs. Their iconic status as "paedophiles-in-the-community" has come to symbolise the ultimate "neighbour from hell" (Kitzinger 1999). It assumes a particular representation of menace, however, as part of popular knowledge that there is "obvious" risk to the community by releasing paedophiles from prison (Collier 2001). While such "knowledge" is almost certainly misdirected, given the relatively low re-offending rates of convicted child sexual offenders (Silverman and Wilson 2002; cf. Soothill et al. 1998), public concerns about released paedophiles have become absorbed within a rhetoric of contemporary punitive populism reinforced by the popular press and other agencies (Evans 2003).

Thus, even normally liberal broadsheets have reinforced the figure of "the paedophile" as dangerous. An editorial in the *Independent* newspaper, arising from released paedophiles forced to seek police protection from vigilantes, is illustrative: "It is not the habit of liberal newspapers to stand up for the baying crowd [but] if a dangerous paedophile turned up at any neighbourhood slammer, free to walk, every local parent would be, to go to the root of the word, vigilant" (27 April 1998: 8). The conundrum this creates is neatly summed up by Andrew Marr (1998: 23): "We don't want to pay to keep them in police cells. But if they try to leave, we'll have their guts for garters."

The practice of releasing paedophiles from prison into the community underpins public perception that they receive "soft" forms of punishment (Silverman and Wilson op cit). A common assumption is that those involved in the management of paedophiles are unable to supervise their charges effectively because paedophiles are "driven" by the nature of their perversion to repeat their offences; *ergo* the only appropriate penal response is to jail them without the possibility of release. Another assumption is that paedophiles are beyond rehabilitation. However, as a number of commentators have argued (e.g. West 1996; Eldridge et al. 1997; Critcher 2000), such views are reinforced by media constructions of "the paedophile", which have the appearance of a recurrent moral panic over contemporary childhood.

Public concern about soft punishment for sex offenders has led the media to take the issue of the perceived threat paedophiles pose to communities into their own hands "because they perceive the statutory services as ineffective and unable to fulfil their statutory responsibilities" (Cowburn and Dominelli 2001: 414). The rape-murder of four girls in Belgium in 1995 by Marc Dutroux, a convicted paedophile released back into the community, amplified European media interest in the failure of national authorities to punish paedophiles properly. In Britain, media interest in paedophiles released from prison and allowed to live anonymously in the community was crystallised by the abduction and murder, in 2000, of seven-year-old Sarah Payne by a convicted paedophile, Roy Whiting.

USE OF MEDIA FOR INTER-AGENCY CONFLICT

Whiting's conviction gave British newspapers and "pro-child" pressure groups such as the NSPCC, an opening to argue that there existed a policy vacuum in which the authorities appeared uncertain about how to deal with re-offending paedophiles. It also gave them *carte blanche* to criticise statutory agencies involved in supervising paedophiles in the community and set in train "processes which led to the policy makers and 'the professionals' losing control of the ['paedophile-in-the-community'] policy agenda" (Kitzinger op cit: 212). And as Critcher (2002a: 530) points out, following the Whiting trial, the press agenda about paedophiles living anonymously in the community emerged as pivotal: "It mediates between policy and public agendas, constructs the public agenda and seeks to influence policy agendas."

This mediator role is exemplified by the activities of the mass circulation British newspaper, the *News of the World*. The paper's editor, Rebekah Wade, gained prominence by pursuing a "naming and shaming" campaign (Critcher 2002b; Bell 2002; Lawler 2002) that threatened to reveal the identity of all 110,000 known child sex offenders. In practice, the paper eventually published a "rogue's gallery" of 79 photographs of convicted paedophiles and a call for public help in tracking down and apprehending those pictured. Supported by the NSPCC, the paper also demanded "real" life sentences and new legislation referred to as "Sarah's law" (after the Sarah Payne case) giving communities the right to know if known or suspected paedophiles live in their area (Silverman and Wilson op cit; Cowburn and Dominelli 2001).

Criticism that this was a publicity stunt designed to increase falling sales (Greenslade 2000), did not deter Wade from continuing to publish the names and whereabouts (though not the exact addresses) of paedophiles. Her argument was that the paper was in tune with the public mood and that there was a distinction between the paper's vigilance and public acts of vigilantism. (Bell op cit; Evans op cit). Perhaps. But critics of "name and shame" campaigns, including the National Association for the Care and Resettlement of Offenders, warned of the dangers of unmanaged publicity leading to acts of vigilantism.[1] This issue received widespread media attention in 2000 following events on the Paulsgrove estate in Portsmouth, on Britain's south coast.

Community grievances sparked by the *News of the World*'s naming of a paedophile living on the estate, led to street-protests involving the estate's women and children (Bell op cit). Condemned by the broadsheet press for being "irrational" and the "wrong kind of mothers" (Lawler op cit: 108), protestors were represented as a working-class mob fuelled by vigilantism. Moreover, the Association of Chiefs of Probation argued that "outings" of sex offenders was not only stoking unwarranted fears about the extent of the "paedophile threat", but was undermining the work of those agencies closely involved in community supervision of paedophiles (Collier op cit).

Consequently, the *News of the World*'s claim that "community notification" protects the community from paedophiles is a moot point (Silverman and Wilson op cit). What is certain is that under the workings of the Sex Offenders Act 1997, sex offenders released from prison have the right to local authority housing but only a few probation professionals have the right to know where they live. As Critcher (2002a: 525) points out: "Local newspapers gave voice to these grievances and sought to defend their communities". Indeed, it is salient to point out that the *News of the World* borrowed the idea of naming and shaming from anti-paedophile "outing" campaigns originally conducted in the southwest of England and reproduced in other parts of the country.

VIGILANTE JOURNALISM

In 1996, the *Bournemouth Echo* in Dorset made use of confidential files on sex offenders living in the region and published 38 photographs and last known addresses of convicted paedophiles. In 1997, the *Manchester Evening News* "outed" 28 convicted paedophiles and other sex offenders living locally, while in 1998, both the *Hartlepool Mail* and the *Oxford Mail* argued that it had a public duty to notify its readers of any convicted paedophiles known to be living in their area. Many other local newspapers keep informal registers of sex offenders, often with photographs supplied from police records (Travis and Ahmed 1998) which are then used by anti-paedophile campaign groups to identify individuals (Birkett 1997).

"Outing" campaigns highlight the close relationship between national and local press agendas as well as the potential of the local press to frame the terms of populist debate. As Kitzinger (op cit: 20) puts it: "Many of the national stories about paedophiles began life on the front page of local papers and some neighbourhood protests were sparked by local press reports rather than vice versa." Campaigns manifest apparent consensus on the need to protect communities from "dangerous outsiders". Thus, while anti-paedophile newspaper campaigns represent "the paedophile" as the classic "outsider", deserving symbolic removal from the community, anti-paedophile vigilantes advocate literal physical removal.

This point is illustrated by the case of two paedophiles, Sidney Cooke and Robert Oliver, convicted for the killing of a teenage boy. Their conviction had occurred before the 1997 Sex Offenders Act which otherwise would have required their movements after release to be supervised[2]. Both men had received death threats while in prison and were in fear for their lives. Efforts to house the men in probation and bail hostels in the West Country had resulted in more than 40 public disorder incidents ostensibly caused by local newspaper demands that they be removed from their area. The extent of public protests was also picked up by national media, keen to tell the story of paedophiles being chased from town-to-town by a posse of anti-paedophile protestors.

In seeking to make sense of such events it is important to recognise how popular notions of retribution and just desserts coalesce around the perceived inability of statutory services as ineffective when it comes to protecting the public from paedophiles. Media intervention (including the framing of the probation service's work with offenders as persistently negative: see Aldridge 1992) in managing the threat paedophiles pose to communities is now a major concern of agencies working with sex offenders (see Silverman and Wilson op cit). Their concerns are unlikely to be met with popular support, however, because the obsession with knowing where paedophiles are housed has become enmeshed with the idea that we will be safe from them so long as they are not our neighbours.

But neither is this a straightforward "not in my back yard" reaction towards those "outsiders" perceived as a threat to the moral and social order. In the local media environment, where journalists specifically champion local grievances, the "outing" of sex offenders constitutes a "coming together" of media and community activism in the face of (usually) political or policy grievances caused by the world external to those communities.[3] And as Silverman and Wilson (op cit) point out, growing hostility to official agencies' practice of habitually housing paedophiles in estates without local consultation is a consequence of community grievances about this practice residing on the margin of the agenda for police, probation services, councils and other agencies. [4]

However, the naming of sexual offenders presents an ethical dilemma for journalists/editors over the choice between outing sex offenders in their backyard and working with the authorities and other professionals. In their attempts to give journalists direction on this issue, the Press Complaints Commission (PCC) have issued guidance notes (in 2001) for editors when handling sex offender campaigns.[5] The PCC now advises that "while it is not the role of the Commission to proscribe the publication of material that is legitimately in the public domain, it would urge editors to think carefully before embarking on public campaigns of this nature" (Press Complaints Commission 2001). It also recommends that editors should consult with representatives from the probation and local police services before publication.[6]

HOUSING PROBLEMS – AND A LOCAL SOLUTION

Nevertheless, sex offenders must live somewhere and the majority are free to live in the community (Wing 1998). Addressing the media's role in usurping this basic right, the Head of Communications for the National Probation Service described the impact of media "outings" on the management of sex offenders post-sentence: "Where sex offenders were being identified in local communities, local newspaper editors were taking an editorial decision to expel these people from their areas. The media, and it's the local media doing this, were getting into a real hunt mentality. The problem we had in housing sex offenders in the community was all local media-driven."[7]

This comment helps make sense of a decision, taken by the Home Office in 1999, to use Crown property sites to house paedophiles considered at risk from vigilantism. The benefit of using Crown property in this way is that secure accommodation can be provided without the need for any official, lengthy, public consultation process — and the concomitant dangers of public disorder. Amongst Crown property identified as secure enough to house paedophiles deemed to be at risk from vigilantism was Nottingham Jail, in the East Midlands of England. Housing paedophiles inside a prison can therefore be seen as an attempt to find a stable solution to the increasingly difficult problem of where to house convicted paedophiles released from prison.[8]

However, because the majority of the British mainstream press are united in seeing the concerns of anti-paedophile groups as (generally) legitimate, a tight Home Office cabal maintained secrecy over plans to house paedophiles inside Nottingham Jail.[9] According to a Chief Probation Officer seconded to the Home Office: "There is now a sort of neurosis within the Home Office that if we let outside agencies know about our plans, then they're going to leak it to the press. You know there are very real temptations out there, both for money but also to get it out of their patch. If you look at a lot of news coverage about where these leaks [about paedophiles] come from, you can detect they come from official sources."[10] Indeed, of all the government departments, the Home Office suffers the highest number of critical leaks, which reflects the degree to which it must engage with "permeable external bodies" such as the prison service (Walker 2000).

Accordingly, there was no attempt to consider a public communication strategy and press offices, nationally and locally, had no knowledge of what was being planned. A senior press officer on the Home Office criminal justice press desk commented: "That is one of the reasons why the Nottingham prison, police and probation services were kept in the dark and under-informed by the Home Office. They were only brought into the loop at the last minute. It explains why information about the prison [plan] was not widely shared around the Home Office and it certainly wasn't something that we on the press desk were aware off until information came out from a leak inside the prison. That all happened without our involvement. If we'd known about the unit, we would have advised strategies for putting information into the public domain."[11]

FRAMING THE WHISTLEBLOWERS' FEARS

As implementation of the Home Office plan proceeded and as more agencies were included in local planning, policy disputes could not be maintained within the parameters of Home Office secrecy. Thus, in May 1999, *Nottingham Evening Post*[12] received information from whistleblowers in the local Prison Officers' Association (POA) branch that the Home Office were secretly building a paedophile unit inside the grounds of the local jail.[13] It reported: "Stunned prison officers contacted the *Evening Post* after being told about the plans at an internal briefing." It continued: "Neil Mason, secretary of the Nottingham branch of the Prison Officers' Association, said: 'They could not have picked a worst place. It is dangerous for us and for the local people and their children.'" (20 May 1999: 1).

Two days later, under the headline, "Fear in the heart of a community", the paper outlined the conflict between the POA and the Home Office: "Neil Mason, secretary of the Nottingham branch of the Prison Officers' Association, said: 'Why should a prison look after civilians who have served their sentence?' He criticised the move saying: 'How can we have open government when there is no consultation on plans like these? No one in the community was told a thing. They tried to get as far down the road as they could before anyone found out'… Another warder, who asked not to be named said: 'We have been told this has to be up and running as soon as possible. Our concern is that Nottingham will become home to some of the worst paedophiles from around the country. We also don't know how much access some of the current prisoners who are on duties such as gardening will have access to them. It could present a lot of problems and we are far from happy about it.'" (22 May 1999: 3).

A third *Evening Post* feature, "Staff's fear on paedophile bid" (25 May 1999: 2), linked POA and local community concerns about their non-consultation in the Home Office plan. It quoted both national and local POA officials: "Yes, the paedophile problem must be dealt with. But to dump them together in the heart of a residential area must be counter-productive. Paedophiles feed off each other's sick fantasies … We support the community's right to be consulted on this radical and potentially dangerous proposal." At this juncture, however, the local paper's interest in the POA dispute with the Home Office began to be reframed within its partisan promotion of community concerns and grievances about the housing plan.

Thus, within days of disclosing information about Home Office building plans, the POA found itself located outside the *Evening Post*'s developing news frame. Building on what the paper referred to as "secret" Home Office plans to house paedophiles "only yards from a primary school" (22 May 1999: 1), the paper quickly developed a new interpretative frame concerning growing anger and hostility in the community towards the Home Office based on the authenticity of the POA leak. However, the paper's attention was now wholly directed towards challenging the Home Office on their non-consultation with the local community. In short, the POA whistleblowers no longer figured within the paper's "local injustice" news frame.

AFTER THE WHISTLE HAS BLOWN: RESISTANCE MEETS REALITY

Whistleblowing in organisations is always a high-risk strategy. This is evident in organisations since it can and often does lead to discipline and sacking. However, whistleblowing has another less obvious side-effect since the very act of leaking information to the media is always intended to cause a degree of 'mischief' (Jaworski et al. 2004). Thus, even if the quality of leaked information is good (not to say in the "public interest" and deserving of being discussed in the public sphere) there is often no easy way for the recipient of information (usually journalists) to trust the whistleblower as a future source of information. Paradoxically, the act of whistleblowing can lead to the whistleblower's own exclusion from subsequent public debate their actions have initiated (Fellows 1996).

The POA blew the whistle on Home Office plans to undermine their efforts to extend prison officers' responsibilities to include care of ex-prisoners. Faced with this prospect, the POA had few practical resources with which to resist beyond publicising (and puncturing) a secretly developed Home Office policy. However, whistle blowing can offer a significant advantage: i.e., the achievement of symbolic capital such that it creates a preferred representation of reality (Jaworski et al. 2004). This is by no means an insignificant point. Powerful organisations like the Home Office keenly protect their internal activities from disclosure by constant policing against outside (especially journalists') intrusion. As Downing puts it: "Secrecy is not used as an impermeable shield blotting out all communication, but as a device to allow the pinnacle of the power structure to communicate when and how it prefers" (1986: 157).

However, the leaking of confidential information to the media has a high news value within news production (Schlesinger and Tumber 1994) and, by blowing the whistle to the press, POA officials intended to obstruct the Home Office "power structure" in the hope that it would generate useful publicity for their opposition to block government plans to extend their role. However, POA quickly came up against the local newspaper's role as an "effective change agent" in the community (see Aldridge 2003). As the Deputy Editor of the *Evening Post* put it: "We only run campaigns if we're confident we're going to win. We don't like to run campaigns that we're going to lose because it looks bad. A local newspaper's reputation has to be the ability to change things and we couldn't offer a credible alternative to where the paedophiles should be housed."[14]

The POA's decision to leak confidential information about Nottingham Jail's paedophile unit was not authorised at the highest level of the organisation. In fact, the decision to whistleblow was taken further down the hierarchy, at the local branch level, by elected officials representing prison officers concerned about the impact of such a unit on their established work practice. However, a planned second leak of details concerning extensions to the unit was given to the press via a formal news release issued from the national POA executive replete with ready-made quotations from senior and local POA officials. According to the *Evening Post* journalist who made particular use of this "formal" news release: "The national POA clearly had nothing to lose given that the Nottingham branch had already blown the whistle".[15]

The Home Office's strategy of secrecy was also compromised by conflict between official agencies. With hindsight, perhaps, it could not have worked without all local and national players involved maintaining a commitment to uphold confidentiality. The decision by the POA to blow the whistle on Home Office plans thus reveals the complexity of "elite dynamics", at least when it comes to the vexed and conflict-ridden issue of "what to do" with convicted paedophiles post-sentence. Nevertheless, for all the discomfiture POA whistleblowing caused the Home Office, the policy was enacted and the paedophile unit received its first residents within two months of the POA leak. It remains *in situ* inside the jail.

CONCLUSIONS

This case study of inter-agency conflict surrounding the Home Office's secret attempt to build paedophile housing inside the grounds of Nottingham Jail is more than just a parochial inflection on a national issue. It illustrates how the politics of paedophilia is rooted in a breakdown of professional consensus on how to deal effectively with paedophiles in the community. And at the centre of local interest in the whereabouts of paedophiles is the mundane reality that official agencies are involved in leaking confidential information to local media for their own promotional interests. This insight into the pragmatics of whistleblowing is hardly new but it underpins the point that anti-paedophile vigilantism could not occur without collusion between the local (and national) press and public protection agencies.

However, such collusion reflects the strategic importance of information and news management in our mass-mediated society. With this in mind, it is salient to note that the press are deeply immersed in anti-paedophile campaigns and demonstrations as a key element in their commercial survival. This has led Harold Lockwood, chair of the Association of Chief Probation Officers, to criticise newspapers' "heavily editorialised coverage [that] has only served to excite public disorder" (Travis and Ahmed op cit: 6). Amongst the association's concerns is that commercial imperatives incite lynch mobs which, in turn, make probation officers' work with sex offenders more difficult.

In response, local newspapers have defended themselves against charges of whipping up public hysteria for commercial gain. An editorial in the *Hartlepool Mail* is typical. It said: "We make no apologies for blowing the whistle on a convicted paedophile. We would argue that it is grossly unfair to the people living in an area that someone like this should be placed among them in secret" (ibid).

Reporting paedophiles in the community is certainly fraught with ethical difficulties and journalists/editors tread a fine line between acting with professional vigilance and inciting public vigilantism. The *Nottingham Evening Post* is currently committed to a "Protect Our Children" campaign calling for mandatory "real" life sentences even for first-time child sexual offenders and arguing that concerns over physical attacks (and the occasional lynching) meted out to paedophiles could be easily resolved by not releasing them from prison. While this is a legitimate view, the absence of consensus on where and how paedophiles should be housed post-sentence means that "naming and shaming" is likely to reappear in some form. What is less certain is whether children are safer as a result of whistleblowing journalism.

NOTES

1   Wade is now editor of the *Sun*, Britain's biggest selling tabloid daily. She has continued to "name and shame" selected groups, most recently in the paper's "Shop a Yob" campaign (2003). Here, readers are invited to name and shame teenagers who are subject to anti-social behaviour orders. Again, inter-agency disagreement over the newspaper's intrusion into penal matters is illuminating. On the one hand, it is supported by the police and some "pro-child" agencies including the NSPCC. On the

other, it is opposed by the National Association of Probation Officers and more than 180 other organisations (Byrne 2003).

2 Since 1997, persons convicted of a sexual offence in England and Wales are legally required to sign the Sex Offenders Registers (Scotland and Northern Ireland have similar requirements). It gives police, probation and other relevant statutory agencies details of names and addresses and other personal information to help track the identities and whereabouts of released sex offenders.

3 Kitzinger (op cit) suggests how local newspapers do not galvanise communities with absence of purpose but connect to local issues and concerns to survive. Underpinning this practice is the local press' special role as symbolic representatives of community (Aldridge 2003).

4 Responding to community grievances, the Government introduced a Criminal Justice and Court Services Act (2001), with a statutory requirement for criminal justice agencies to consider community responses and concerns when making their decisions regarding management of sex offenders. Further, in December 2001, home secretary David Blunkett highlighted a commitment to local community involvement in Multi-Agency Public Protection Panels (MAPPS) where police, probation service, social services share information about high-risk offenders living in the local area to manage the risk from released sex-offenders (Silverman and Wilson op cit).

5 The PCC acted after receiving a formal complaint from chief probation officers worried about the growth of newspaper "paedophile registers" and campaigns to "out" child sex offenders.

6 Following consultations with the Association of Chief Police Officers, the Association of Chief Officers of Probation and the Society of Editors, the PCC has also now updated its Code of Practice to include sex offender reporting guidelines to ensure accuracy of allegations (including swift correction of inaccuracies), necessary apologies to injured parties, respecting the private lives of sex offenders' relatives and friends, and ensuring that victims of sexual abuse remain unidentified.

7 Interview, 24 January 2001.

8 The paedophiles who opted to live in this unit were subject to a tenancy agreement which included giving prison authorities 24 hours' notice of intention to leave the unit and those who did so agreed to be accompanied by uniformed police officers. The tenancy agreement also contained strict criteria on the age, identity and criminal background of visitors.

9 Similarly, in December 2000, a local housing officer in South London leaked information to the local newspaper, the *Wandsworth Guardian*, that the Home Office was planning to re-open a hostel to house high profile paedophiles and sex offenders. As in the Nottingham Jail plan, it was made without any consultation with the local community. This caused outrage within the local community and led to an ultimately successful campaign to overturn the decision (for details see Silverman and Wilson op cit).

10 Interview, 12 February 2001.

11 Interview, 12 February 2001.

12 Owned by Northcliffe Newspapers Group Limited, *Nottingham's Evening Post* is part of a stable of 106 regional titles. It is Nottingham's only paid-for local newspaper and

so has a monopoly position in a city and region of about 350,000 inhabitants. It is currently ranked 13th in the Newspaper Society's 2004 top UK regional evenings ranked by circulation http://www.newspapersoc.org.uk/facts-figures/circulation/ evecirc.html, accessed 12. July 2004.

13   The POA also simultaneously leaked details of the plan to *The Times* whose coverage detailed POA concerns about a policy of housing paedophiles near to a school and residential area (albeit inside a jail).

14   Interview, 25 January 2001.

15   Interview, 25 January 2001.

REFERENCES

Aldridge, Meryl (1992) "The probation service and the press: the curious incident of the dog in the night-time", *British Journal of Social Work*, Vol 22 (6) pp 645-661

Aldridge, Meryl (2003) "The ties that divide: regional press campaigns, community and populism", *Media, Culture and Society*, Vol 25 pp 491-509

Bell, Vikki (2002) "The vigilant(e) parent and the paedophile: The *News of the World* campaign 2000 and the contemporary governmentality of child sexual abuse", *Feminist Theory*, Vol 3(1) pp 83-102

Birkett, Dea (1997) "Monsters With Human Faces", the *Guardian Weekend*, September 27 pp 22-26

Byrne, Ciar (2003) *"Sun's* anti-yob campaign raises 'lynch mob' fears", the *Guardian*, October 20 p. 18

Collier, Richard (2001) "Dangerousness, popular knowledge and the criminal law: a case study of the paedophile as sociocultural phenomenon", Alldridge, Peter and Brant, Chrisje (eds), *Personal Autonomy, the Private Sphere and the Criminal Law*, Oxford and Portland, Oregon, Hart pp 223-243

Cowburn, Malcolm and Dominelli, Lena (2001) "Masking Hegemonic Masculinity: Reconstructing the Paedophile as the Dangerous Stranger", *British Journal of Social Work*, Vol 31 pp 399-415

Critcher, Chas (2000) "Government, Media and Moral Crisis: Paedophilia in the British Press in the Summer of 2000", paper presented to the conference on Communication in Crisis: The Media, Conflict and Society, 1-2 December, University of Naples

Critcher, Chas (2002a) "Media, Government and Moral Panic: the politics of paedophilia in Britain 2000-1", *Journalism Studies*, Vol 3 (4) pp 521-535

Critcher, Chas (2002b) "The Politics of Paedophilia", paper to a conference on Media and Politics sponsored by the Political Studies Association, Loughborough University, September 22

Downing, John (1986) "Government secrecy and the Media in the United States and Britain", Golding, Peter, Schlesinger, Philip and Murdock, Graham (eds), *Communicating Politics: Mass Communications and the Political Process*, Leicester, Leicester University Press pp 153-170

Eldridge, John, Kitzinger, Jenny and Williams, Kevin (1997) *The Mass Media and Power in Modern Britain*, Oxford, Oxford University Press

Evans, Jessica (2003) "Vigilance and Vigilantes: Thinking psychoanalytically about anti-paedophile action", *Theoretical Criminology*, Vol 7 (2) pp 163-189

Fellows, James (1996) *Breaking the News: How Media Undermine American Democracy*, New York, Vintage Books

Greenslade, Roy (2000) "Vigilance and vigilantes", the *Guardian*, July 31 p 23

Jaworski, Adam, Fitzgerald, Richard and Morris, Deborah (2004) "Radio leaks: Presenting and contesting leaks in radio news broadcasts", *Journalism*, Vol 5 (2) pp 183-202

Kitzinger, Jenny (1999) "The ultimate neighbour from hell? Stranger danger and the media framing of paedophiles", Franklin, Bob (ed.), *Social Policy, the Media and Misrepresentation*, London, Routledge pp 207-221

Lawler, Steph (2002) "Mobs and monsters: Independent man meets Paulsgrove Woman", *Feminist Theory* 3 pp 103-113

Marr, Andrew (1998) "The paedophile that haunts our imagination", the *Independent*, April 9 p 23

Newspaper Society (2004) "Top UK Regional Evenings Ranked by Circulation". Availabel online at http://www.newspapersoc.org.uk/facts-figures/circulation/evecirc.html, accessed 12 July 2004

Schlesinger, Philip and Tumber, Howard (1994) *Reporting Crime: The Media Politics of Crime and Criminal Justice*, Oxford, Oxford University Press

Silverman, Jon and Wilson, David (2002) *Innocence Betrayed: Paedophiles, the Media and Society*, Cambridge, Polity

Soothill, Keith, Francis, Brian and Ackerley, Elizabeth (1998) "Paedophilia and Paedophiles", *New Law Journal*, June 12 pp 882-883

Travis, Alan and Ahmed, Kamal (1998) "Worry over 'outing' of paedophiles", the *Guardian*, May 21 p 6

West, David (1996) "Sexual Molesters", Walker, Nigel (ed.) *Dangerous People*, London, Blackstone Press pp 51-69

Walker, David (2000) "Pssst...I've Got Something to Tell You', the Guardian Online. Available online at http://www.guardian.co.uk/analysis/story/0,3604,345185,00.html, accessed 13 July 2004

Wing, Arthur (1998) "Housing and Sex Offenders", *Child Abuse Review*, 7 pp 449-452

Simon Cross lectures in Media Studies at the University of Lincoln, UK. He has worked at the School of Political Science and Communication, University of Canterbury, New Zealand and at the Centre for Mass Communication Research, University of Leicester, UK. He studied for a PhD on representations of mental illness in British TV current affairs at Loughborough University. Previously published research includes: "Hearing Voices: Mental Illness and Cultural Recognition", *Inter/Sections*, 2002; "Public Images and Private Lives: The Media and Politics in New Zealand" in *Parliamentary Affairs*, 2004; "Visualising Madness: Mental Illness and Public Representation", *Television and New Media* (August 2004). He is currently preparing material on partisan journalism in the local press and also fictional representations of paedophiles in British television drama. Contact Details: Dr Simon Cross, Faculty of Media and Humanities, University of Lincoln, Brayford Pool, Lincoln, LN6 7TS, UK. Tel. +44 (0)1522 886797; email: scross@lincoln.ac.uk

Sharon Lockyer is a lecturer in Media Studies in the School of Media and Cultural Production at De Montfort University, Leicester, UK. Research interests include sociology of journalism, humour studies and social science research methodology. Previously she taught at Loughborough University where she was awarded her PhD on the ethics of humour. Published work includes "Dear Shit-Shovellers: Humour, Censure and the Discourse of Complaint", *Discourse and Society*, 2001 (with Michael Pickering). She has received prizes for her academic work on humour. She is currently co-editing a collection (with Michael Pickering) entitled *Beyond A Joke: The Limits of Humour* to be published by Palgrave Macmillan (2006). She is the convenor of the British Sociological Association (BSA) Sociology of Media Study Group. Contact Details: Dr Sharon Lockyer, School of Media and Cultural Production, Faculty of Humanities, De Montfort University, The Gateway, Leicester, LE1 9BH, UK. Tel. +44 (0)116 255 1551 Ext 7393; email: SLockyer@dmu.ac.uk

Partisan, empathic and invitational criticism: The challenge of materiality

Omar Swartz

Implicit in the theory of invitational communication is a critique and rejection of partisan criticism. In this chapter, I challenge this rejection and articulate a defence of the partisan ethos in rhetorical theory and criticism. The first half of the chapter articulates my defence of partisan criticism and the second half compares this defence against assumptions and claims of empathic and invitational communication. My claim is that because the invitational paradigm undervalues material conditions within the context of communication, it risks importing a metaphysics into communication scholarship that obscures the need for transformative political and social criticism that helps all people, feminists and non-feminists alike.

Keywords: partisan criticism, empathic communication, invitational communication, rhetoric, materialist ideology, feminist theory

Eleven years ago, Celeste Condit (1993) cautioned against what she called partisan criticism. She argued that partisan criticism propagated a mythical "oppressor-oppressed" narrative that was unreasonably reductionist and simplistic. Fundamental to her argument was her claim that "it is no longer so easy to identify single categories of victim and victor" (ibid: 187). By perpetuating such categories, Condit asserted that critics advance over-generalisations and moralisations unconnected to real-life politics.

In contrast to partisan criticism, Condit offered what she called empathic communication. Such communication "begins in the recognition of the tenet, held by many human groups, that the central value is care for all living things" (ibid). According to Condit, this view "does not encourage the critic to adopt a partisan stance that favors some human groups and dismisses others" (ibid). A core assumption Condit made is that "there are very few happy, empowered oppressors. Even the average American white male of the upper middle class is a tortured unhappy beast" (ibid). Social change occurs less from confronting such "beasts" than from understanding and working with their fears and needs in a language that they understand.

Condit's perspective is given a renewed emphasis in other scholarship by Sonja K. Foss, Karen A. Foss, and Cindy Griffin, among others such as Gearhart (1979) and Freeman, Littlejohn and Pearce (1992). Collectively, these scholars advance a theory of invitational communication. Implicit in this theory is a critique and rejection of partisan criticism. In this essay, I challenge this rejection and articulate a defence of the partisan ethos in rhetorical theory and criticism. My claim is that because the invitational paradigm undervalues material conditions within the context of communication, it risks importing a metaphysics into communication scholarship that obscures the need for transformative political and social criticism that helps all people, feminists and non-feminists alike.

A DEFENCE OF PARTISAN CRITICISM

The word "partisan" has roots in French, Italian, and Latin. The Italian *partisano* (*parte* means "part") comes from the Latin, *participatio*, meaning "participation" or "participant" (Pinkerton 1982). In Latin, *participium* means "that which takes part". In 1658, the French word *partifan* was defined as "a partaker or partner" (Phillips 1658/1969). In context, partisan was a descriptive term for a person who stood for some ideal, party or value related to the good of a community; to be partisan was to make common cause with others to fight, resist and transform an inequitable status quo. In the 19th century, Noah Webster (1828/1970) defined the English word *partisan* as "a person able in commanding a party, or dexterous in obtaining intelligence, intercepting convoys or otherwise annoying an enemy". The most notable example of Webster's definition is the partisan resistance movement to the Nazis throughout occupied Europe during the Second World War (Simpson and Weiner 1989).

In short, to be partisan has come to mean being oppositional, joining with others with a deep commitment to be a part of a counter-force to normative power (Ayto 1990). The term "partisan", however, is commonly understood as denoting a person who speaks on behalf of a political machine and carries connotations of a person being imbalanced, unreasonable, zealot, pathological or biased (*Oxford American Dictionary of Current English* 1999). Here, I reject this sense of the term and embrace the heroic tradition of partisan that suggests political resistance and social redescription. In the context of this essay, partisan criticism is an attitude — a will to create, invent and reduce the suffering of people resulting from their political, legal and economic alienation. Partisan scholarship embraces a deep commitment to a cause and the championing of an ideal — social justice.

Fundamental to social justice from a communication perspective is what Dana L. Cloud (1994) calls a "materialist ideology of criticism". As Cloud argues, the point of criticism is its material effect — that is, criticism's ability to help people in the material world. In such a world, most human groups do not, contrary to Condit, "care for all living things". Furthermore, in this world, the conditions of material oppression render prudent our favouring of some human groups and our dismissal of others (e.g. siding with the Jews against the Nazis and siding with the Chinese against the Japanese during World War Two). If the upper middle class, white males of this world feel tortured, unhappy and beastly, as Condit suggests, that is unfortunate. However, it is unlikely that the two-thirds of the human beings on earth who live in a structured lethal poverty shed tears for these people. Famine, which is often grounded in a politics benefiting upper class, white males and their colleagues in the developing world, is "the most common form of violence in today's world" (McCaughan 2001: 40).

Many people in the world also feel no pity for the "suffering" of the privileged upper-class. If this sounds harsh, that is unavoidable. Moreover, this claim is far less harsh than the material conditions that the wealthy and privileged have created for the bulk of humanity. As Perry Anderson writes: "In the global ecology of capital today, the privilege of the few requires the misery of the many, to be sustainable" (1992: 352-353). If the wealthy were to extend solidarity to the poor, then I would reconsider this position: the poor and dispossessed do not despise the wealthy because the wealthy have money; rather, they despise the wealthy because the wealthy are responsible for creating and sustaining poverty. The onus, therefore, is on the rich to do something to abolish poverty.

Moreover, the critical attitude of partisan scholarship is, in practice, human. As Philip Wander and Steven Jenkins note: "If the critic is willing to speak of things outside the language of his essay and beyond the academic boundaries of criticism, he becomes less a role player and more of a human being" (1972: 446). Although empathy is an important part of being human, moral indignation, rage, vengeance and a sense of a consuming struggle are, at times, equally important. As Brenda J. Allen, Mark P. Orbe, and Margarita Refugia Olivas observe, it is often necessary to "embrace our emotionality as a central component of scholarship" (1999: 406). To be empathic is to understand a situation fully, and such understanding is often not possible in the messy struggles of everyday politics. Of prime importance is to act against injustice and not waste time in coming to terms with why the oppressor feels justified in perpetuating his/her oppression or support for the economic inequities of the status-quo.

THE DANGERS OF TEXTUAL FETISHISM

As scholars, what we have to work with are texts. Texts are useful because they provide the raw material for analysis. However, textual fetishism, what Thomas Farrell (1993) identifies as the "textualisation of politics" (148) obscures the fact that, arguably, the point of criticism is to have a material influence — that is, to help people (particularly poor people). Although discourse practices, indeed, constitute many of our problems, we should not forget that people do the suffering. As Cloud insists:

> It is not only discourses and codes from which many people need liberation. A politics of discourse, even where the project is grounded in the critic's commitment, assumes that those who are oppressed or exploited need discursive redefinition of their identities, rather than a transformation of their material conditions as a primary task. The project of ideology critique, modernist as it may be, is the only critical stance that suggests discourse may justify oppression and exploitation, but texts do not themselves constitute the oppression (1994: 157).

Engagement with social texts, however, can be part of the liberation, a point that is fundamental to the task of criticism. Although criticism is political, the critic is not necessarily an urban guerrilla. As discussed by critical legal scholar David Fraser:

> A law review article is hardly a car bomb, leaving violence and destruction in its wake, but it is one of the few forms of 'armed propaganda' open to those of us who believe in a fundamentally different world and who live and work in the heart of the legal academy. In a very real sense, legal scholarship, as an act of

'interpretation' is an act of calculated and relentless violence. It is an imposition of meaning, a will to power in a world of the word. (1990: 778)

In other words, legal interpretations, as well as other textual interpretations, do matter:

A judge articulates her understanding of a text, and as a result, somebody loses his freedom, his property, his children, even his life. Interpretations in law also constitute justifications for violence which has already occurred or which is about to occur. When interpreters have finished their work, they frequently leave behind victims whose lives have been torn apart by these organized, social practices of violence. Neither legal interpretation nor the violence it occasions may be properly understood apart from one another (ibid: 779).

Likewise, the partisan critic realises that language does matter — that language supports material conditions in which people are not treated equally and are, indeed, seriously mistreated — and takes a side. After all, moral violation often assumes literary form (Lang 1988: 350). To condemn injustice is to condemn the agents of injustice, as well as the instruments of injustice and the mute or compliant witnesses. When injustice is tangible, when the materiality of suffering cannot be denied, then criticism is just when criticism acts as moral critique.

A CRITIQUE OF THE INVITATIONAL PARADIGM

In contrast to the above discussion of partisan criticism and its assumptions of social chance, Foss and others advance the view that certain rhetorical styles (or communicative stances) are more appropriate than others for increasing the quality of community life. They argue that "invitational rhetoric" (discourse that addresses social problems through the creation of relationships as opposed to positing an antagonistic resistance to already established relationships) is an example of such discourse:

If you want the world to be an environmentally sound place, for example, you seek out, appreciate, and encourage instances where you see sound environmental practices going on around you. If you want a world where workers are paid equitable wages, you look around and find examples where workers are being paid fairly.

You applaud and affirm these cases when you find them. You use these examples to try to recreate these conditions when you have opportunities in other places (2003: 19).

Implicit in this understanding of invitational communication are a number of assumptions, two of which are relevant to my critique. First, communicators who engage in this form of discourse approach communication as an attempt to achieve a level of understanding with another person (ibid: 9). The idea is to learn as much as possible about the other to appreciate how that person views the controversy; to do so involves refraining from judgement of the other person's moral choices. Such an assumption is often useful, as when a divorcing couple negotiates child-rearing responsibilities in a situation in which the lifestyle of one parent is considered abhorrent by the other.

Arguably, the most famous example of this situation is Palmore v. Sidoti, a 1984 child custody case. At issue in Palmore was whether the state could divest a fit, Caucasian mother of custody of her young child on the grounds that her marriage to an African American man was "harmful" to the psychological development of the child. In Palmore, the Caucasian ex-husband and father of the child took offence that his daughter was being raised in the home of an African American. In more recent years, cases such as Palmore have been typical in family law when the issue is not race but homosexuality (i.e. Bottoms v. Bottoms 1995, in which a lesbian mother was divested of custody on the grounds of her active homosexuality; and Roe v. Roe 1985, in which a father was declared "unfit" because his homosexuality was held to impose a psychological burden on his child).

Under such circumstances as found in the above cases, a confrontational approach will not easily lead to a productive resolution of the conflict. Although one party may receive custody, the other party is, correspondingly shamed, denigrated as a human being and removed from the community of those "equal before the law". The children of these legal battles also are injured severely, often, in part, because the ostracised "deviant" parent is, in fact, the better or more committed parent. These cases turn on the fact that but for the presumed "deviancy," the defendant parent otherwise would retain custody of the child.

Further, confrontational or partisan rhetorical strategies often result in a polarised community. Families and larger social groups cannot help but experience strain when they suffer a legal inequality based on another's moral condemnation. Unfortunately, the case law in family litigation is filled with such tragic, divisive and hurtful examples. Thus, an invitational or empathic rhetorical strategy can be useful to help all sides to understand the subjectivity and uniqueness of the others. Doing so would help each side of the conflict to perceive how the other side feels and, thereby, focus concern on the most important issues, such as the best interests of the child. For example, one party can ask what he or she can do to help the other feel more comfortable in believing that the child will not be hurt by his/her homosexuality. Invitational or empathic communication suggests that conflict can be avoided when parties learn to speak to the concerns of the other, differentiating between those concerns and the stereotypes in which the concerns are expressed.

A second requirement for an invitational or empathic communication involves equality in that to be successful, both parties must be equal in areas that are deemed important to the parties (ibid: 9). In the family context, for instance, expecting this perception of equality is not (or should not be) unreasonable. Beyond this context, however, it is not clear whether invitational or empathic theorists privilege a formal equality at the expense of a substantive equality in which important differences between people preclude a genuine equality. Invitational communication assumes a liberal, formal equality, one in which all individuals are presumed equal by virtue of their inherent agency, and that such agency is perceived to be sufficient to overcome any material limitations of that person's ability to actualize his or her goals. This notion of equality, which is dominant in the United States, may not be enough for true social justice to flourish in our society.

WHY FORMAL EQUALITY IS NOT ENOUGH

In the feminist legal literature, for instance, the existing legal regime of formal equality has been criticised from the point of view of substantive equality. Central to formal equality is the constitutional mandate that similarly situated individuals or groups should be treated similarly (Reed v. Reed 1971). On its face, this position is reasonable, as formal equality did not exist for women before 1971 in the U.S. and is not an achievement at which to be scoffed. However, formal equality is not enough. Many feminists and critical scholars have pointed out that a *de facto* inequality may become masked by an apparently neutral and formally equal relationship.

For example, contract law treats all parties alike, glossing over the fact that an immigrant farm worker does not come to the contract with the same degree of power as does a multinational corporation. Although both have the same rights before the law with regard to the contract, few people would argue that the bargaining power of the immigrant worker is equal to that of the corporation. The formal equality guaranteed by the federal constitution is not violated by this arrangement, because the equal protection clause does not guarantee that a law be equitable in its impact.

In Personnel Administrator of Massachusetts v. Feeney (1979), the Supreme Court upheld a state law giving hiring preferences to veterans for state jobs, even though the preferences had the effect of permanently denying promotions to the plaintiff, a female state employee with high seniority. The plaintiff made a concerted effort to attain a higher paying position but, in each instance, the position was filled by a newly hired male veteran, each of whom had fewer objective qualifications. The court reasoned that the purpose of the law was not to discriminate against women; therefore, the disparate impact against women was not a violation of equal protection. The purpose of substantive equality is to avoid this kind of legal conclusion; however, because substantive equality may interfere with principles of formal equality, principles of substantive equality have only a marginal influence in US jurisprudence. This can be contrasted with Canadian jurisprudence which, in the last two decades, has been much more proactive in establishing a commitment to substantive equality (Bavis 1999).

The advantage of substantive equality is that the perspective considers the results or effects of a relationship. In other words, we cannot assume that A and B are equal because the law states they must be treated as if they were equal. More essential to an understanding of the relationship between A and B are the substantive differences in the relative power of each. The goal is to avoid outcomes that are patently unfair because they involve a gross inequality in bargaining power. For example, African Americans have been granted formal equality but few would agree that, on a substantive level, African Americans in the aggregate have the opportunity to compete equally with white people for social resources.

Constitutional law is unconcerned about the condition of the black community, as long as no black plaintiff can point to a specific instance of government-sponsored discrimination. Therefore, a commitment to substantive equality would lead a person to support affirmative action and other ameliorative policies (contrary to formal equality) intended to create a society in which all people could compete equally for a respectable place in the national community. To take another example, dominance theory, as articulated by Catharine MacKinnon (1987), explores the imbalances of power between men and women, which become encapsulated in social and legal norms. She then criticises in partisan terms the unseen or taken-for-granted assumptions in our society that place individuals in hierarchical relationships, usually at the expense of women.

ON THE LIMITS OF EMPATHY

In sum, understanding, empathy and dialogical heart-to-heart interaction with people in power does not necessarily lead to the type of social transformation that theorists such as Condit or Foss, Foss, and Griffin would like to see. Thus, it is surprising that these theorists contrast invitational communication with these more malignant coercive or confrontational rhetorics (Foss and Foss op cit: 7-9). Certainly, theoretical distinctions in this area exist and naming them is useful. It is less useful, however, to assume, even implicitly, that there is something wrong with coercive, confrontational, or, in other words, partisan persuasion. These scholars, however, disparage such a rhetorical stance, in part, on the grounds that such an approach may exacerbate conflict.

They also suggest that the motives of such a critic may be compromised. As Foss and Griffin claim: "Embedded in efforts to change others is a desire for control and domination" (1995: 3). While this critique has some validity, the condition is unavoidable when much of society (for example, in the U.S.) suffers from alienation and resists social edification and emancipation from economic or other materialist oppression. As Richard Boyd acknowledges, any "real project of teaching for critical democracy must be done against the wishes of most students [who resist change], and that means I must presume to tell them not only what they need to know, but who they should become" (1999: 398).

Invitational rhetoric, unlike confrontational or partisan rhetoric, seeks to generate what Foss and Foss suggest can be a "genuine understanding" among people who hold potentially incommensurable positions. As noted by Foss and Griffin: "Change may be the result of invitational rhetoric, but change is not its purpose" (op cit: 6). Although this position clearly has merit, there are times when social change is not about understanding people who think differently. Conflict is often necessary for significant moral growth and change (Stewart, Smith, and Denton 1989: Chapter 7). Materiality is often separate and distinct from rhetorical action. In the material world, individuals and communities often pursue narrow self-interest and take advantage of others to effectuate that goal (through rhetoric and/or otherwise).

Weak parties, in turn, often seek to persuade stronger parties to treat them better but find their efforts wasted when the hearts of their oppressors are closed to them. As a result, persuasion must be supplemented by strategic coercion to create the impression that, until the weaker party is treated fairly, that party will agitate, sabotage, bomb or otherwise disrupt the peace enjoyed by the stronger, oppressing group. For instance, what the State of Israel, George W. Bush, Tony Blair, and, increasingly, Vladimir Putin disingenuously label "terrorism" is often the dramatisation of Arab or Islamic oppressed groups' frustration and their attempt to destroy the complacence (what the dominant group calls peace) by which the world ignores their displacement. As Esther Madriz argues: "The only way to win this 'war' against terrorism is to manifest respect for the integrity of innocent lives and to reinforce this respect with a truthful commitment to the promotion of social justice" (2001: 40). So-called terrorists may be no more guilty for their actions than the larger society that calls forth the cultural conditions that make terrorism a sensible option for a significant subgroup.

My suggestion that "terrorism" is a morally more complex notion than the simple marginalization of terrorist actors as horrible criminals follows the work of Johan Galtung, who theorized the important distinction between "direct" and "structural" violence. Direct violence involves flagrant and affirmative acts of aggression, such as the United State's invasion of Iraq. Structural violence, on the other hand, denotes a form of violence imbedded in the systematic ways in which a society's organization prevents individuals from achieving their full potential. An example of this is the neo-liberalism of the post-Cold War economic environment in which poverty, disease, and hunger have become preventable phenoemona, but are now increasing because they are considered by economic and political leaders a "normal" part of world society and a "natural" reflection of market and geo-political reality. To demonise subgroups that resist the growing inequality of the world (all human beings should resist such conditions), to blame them for their non-invitational communication patterns when they are excluded from full membership in the human community, is simply to condemn them to and for their oppression.

CONCLUSION

As suggested above, partisan rhetorical strategies diverge most clearly from the view of Foss and Foss that invitational rhetoric may be more effective for creating conditions for potential change than confrontational communication styles. As a "soft" claim, their point is undoubtedly correct. To engage, in their words, "the larger world is to make an extra effort to understand those perspectives that are repugnant or distasteful" (op cit: 18). By engaging in this extended effort to understand what the "other side" believes, conditions grow more likely that groups in conflict can come to address their problems in a productive and creative manner (ibid). Foss and Foss give an example of how their position can work in a delicate context:

If you can come to an understanding of why a neo-Nazi perspective might make sense to someone, you are more likely to understand the conditions that are likely to produce such a perspective. You then can help to create different kinds of environments in which that viewpoint has less opportunity to flourish. By understanding how perspectives that are abhorrent to you make sense and are attractive to someone else, you can set about creating an environment in which individuals are likely to make other choices (ibid).

All of the above is reasonable, even preferable, particularly in an idealistic world in which materialistic resources were fairly distributed. Yet, as Foss and Foss clearly acknowledge, we live in a non-invitational world in which equality is seldom achieved and justice is often determined by the amount of money a person possesses. Hierarchy and oppressive social relationships are the norm and non-invitational communication habits dominate our social life. However, Foss and Foss go a step further and argue (the "hard" claim) that these non-invitational communication habits are, in fact, the cause of the oppressive realities that many people experience:

A number of scholars and activists from different fields suggest that creating what you want is much more effective than resisting what you do not want. They explain that resistance and opposition are ineffective options for creating change because what we resist persists. To resist something grants it life and establishes it more firmly in place. Whatever you give your attention and energy to in the form of communication thrives and grows. Communication is creative — it generates or produces the nature of the reality in which we live. When you talk about what you do not want, you create more of it in your reality. By communicating about it and bestowing your belief on it, you reinforce it as reality, you strengthen it, you become its accomplice, and it remains a part of your life experience (ibid:19).

In other words, although Foss and Foss qualify their theory by acknowledging that confrontational and aggressive rhetorical strategies are "legitimate and valuable options that help achieve particular communication goals in many situations" (ibid:16), this is only because material success in this world entails their use. It is better, they argue, to change this material condition by first changing our communicative patterns:

Because we most often choose conquest and conversion rhetoric as default modes of communication, we create and experience a particular kind of world. Communication isn't just words and sounds and gestures that reflect our world. It is the means through which we create that world. By the choices we make in our use of communication, we create our reality (ibid: 7).

In terms of the philosophy of communication, Foss and Foss are correct: rhetoric is epistemic and communication does contribute to the creation of social reality. Nevertheless, the reality created by communication is often material, deadly and is not reducible to the communicative practices of any particular human being. Although individuals such as Martin Luther King, Jr. and Mahatma Gandhi influenced human culture by advancing an invitational communication paradigm, both faced insurmountable obstacles when they tried to reinvent community life.

Despite their accomplishments, both King and Gandhi largely failed as invitational speakers because material conditions in society during their lifetimes allowed for only a certain type of moral and spiritual evolution. Both men were inspiring and effective in certain areas, yet neither achieved the type of world that their teachings advocated. To acknowledge this is not a sign of disrespect. Rather, it is to note that invitational rhetoric, although important for many tasks, is not the answer for every political and/or critical task. In sum, invitational rhetoric is not a substitute for traditional persuasion or practical partisan rhetorical discourse.

REFERENCES

Allen, B., Orbe, M.P. and Olivas, M.R. (1999) "The complexity of our tears: dis/enchantment and (in)difference in the academy", *Communication Theory* 9 pp 402-429

Anderson, P. (1992) *A zone of engagement*, London, Verso

Ayto, J. (1990) *Dictionary of word origins*, New York, Arcade Publishing

Bavis, C.D. (1999) "Vriend v. Alberta, Law v. Canada, Ontario v. M and H: The latest steps on the winding path to substantive equality", *The Alberta Law Review* 37 pp 683-714

Bottoms v. Bottoms, 457 S.Ed.2d 102 (Va. 1995)

Chowaniec, M. (1998) Virtual town committee website (http://www.burlingtongop. org/defining.htm)

Cloud, D. (1994) "The materiality of discourse as oxymoron: A challenge to critical rhetoric", *Western Journal of Communication* 58 pp 141-163

Condit, C. (1993) "The critic as empath: Moving away from totalizing theory", *Western Journal of Communication* 57 pp 178-190

Farrell, T. (1993) "On the disappearance of the rhetorical aura", *Western Journal of Communication* 57 pp 147-158

Foss, S.K. and Griffin, C.L. (1995) "Beyond persuasion: A Proposal for an Invitational Rhetoric", *Communication Monographs* 62 pp 2-18

Foss, S.K. and Foss, K.A. (2003) *Inviting transformation*, Prospect Heights, IL, Waveland Press

Fraser, D. (1990) "If I had a rocket launcher: Critical legal studies as moral terrorism", *Hastings Law Journal* 41 pp 777-804

Freeman, S., Littlejohn, S., and Pearce, W.B. (1992) "Communication and moral conflict", *Western Journal of Communication* 56 pp 311-329

Gearhart, S.M. (1979). "The womanization of rhetoric", Women's Studies International Quarterly 2 pp 195-201

Lang, B. (1988) "Language and genocide", Rosenberg, A and Myers G. (eds.) *Echoes from the holocaust*, Philadelphia, Temple University Press pp 341-361

Madriz , E. (2001) "Terrorism and structural violence", *Social Justice* 28 pp 45-47

MacKinnon, C. (1987) *Feminism unmodified: Discourses on life and law*, Cambridge, MA, Harvard University Press

McCaughan, E.J. (2001) "Violence, inequality, and the 'civilized' world", *Social Justice* 28 pp 39-41

Oxford American Dictionary of Current English (1999), New York, Oxford University Press

Pinkerton, E.C. (1982) *Word for word*, Detroit, MI, Verbatim

Palmore v. Sidoti, 466 U.S. 429 (1984)

Personnel Administrator of Massachusetts v. Feeney, 442 U.S. 256 (1979)

Phillips, E. (1658/1969) *The new world of English words*, Menston, England, the Scolar Press Limited

Reed v. Reed, 404 U.S. 71(1971)

Roe v. Roe, 324 S.E.2d 691 (Va. 1985)

Simpson, J. and Weiner, E.S. (1989). *The Oxford English Dictionary*, (2nd edition) Oxford, Clarendon Press, Vol 11

Stewart, C., Smith, C.A., and Denton, R. (1989) *Persuasion and social movements*, (2nd edition) Prospects Heights, IL, Waveland Press

Wander, P. and S. Jenkins. (1972) "Rhetoric, society, and the critical response", *Quarterly Journal of Speech* 58 pp 441-450

Webster, N. (1828/1970) *An American Dictionary of the English language*, New York, Johnson Reprint Corporation

Dr Omar Swartz is assistant professor in the Department of Communication, University of Colorado at Denver, Plaza Building, Suite 102M, Campus Box 176, P.O. Box 173364, Denver, CO 80217-3364, USA, (303) 556-5660. Email: Omar.Swartz@cudenver.edu. He is the author of five books and more than 50 articles, including: "On social justice and political struggle", *Human Nature Review* 4 (2004) pp 152-163; "Toward a critique of normative justice: Human rights and the rule of law", *Socialism & Democracy* 18 (2004) pp 185-209; and "Codifying the law of slavery in North Carolina: Positive law and the slave persona", *Thurgood Marshall Law Review* 29 (2004) pp 285-310.

Communication and the machine of government

Anne Gregory

This chapter examines the Interim Report of the Government Communication's Review Group, chaired by Bob Phillis, (known as the Phillis Review) and draws parallels between government communication issues and those in other public and private sector organisations. The paper then examines these issues theoretically from the public relations perspective, focusing on the relationship and advocacy models of communication practice. It concludes that the relational model with its deontological ethical base is the appropriate model for government communication practice. The terms "communications" and "public relations" are used interchangeably since both embrace a raft of communication tactics including marketing communications.

Keywords: Phillis, advocacy, relationship, public relations, communication, government

HOW SPIN HAS HIT THE HEADLINES

At the beginning of September 2003, the government published the Interim Report of the Phillis Review, announcing that it would implement the recommendations in full. So was launched a strategy which the government hopes will help restore the public's faith in its communication endeavours.

In 1997 the Labour Party came to power heralding an era free of sleaze and with a commitment to open government. Over time, however, it has become labelled as a government of "all spin and no substance" (Ingham 2003). Notable instances when spin has hit the headlines include the Ecclestone affair, when in 1996, Bernie Ecclestone founder of Formula One, donated £1 million to the Labour Party, shortly before the Government decided to exempt the sport from a tobacco advertising ban. The Labour Party later returned the money following accusations of sleaze. Jo Moore, Special Adviser to the then Trade and Industry Secretary, Stephen Byers, told government communicators that they should bury any bad news on 11 September 2001 in an attempt to hide potentially embarrassing announcements behind the larger news story. The handling of the Foot and Mouth crisis in 2001 led to many accusations that the government deliberately misled the public over the scale of the crisis until too late. In December 2002, after denials from Downing Street, it emerged that the Prime Minister's wife had bought property in Bristol through the fraudster boyfriend of her lifestyle adviser. Increasingly, "the public now expects and believes the worst of politicians and government even when there is strong objective evidence in favour of the government's position".[1]

The report identifies a "three-way breakdown in trust between government and politicians, the media and general public".[2] This has resulted from the reaction of the media to a rigorous and proactive strategy of news management by the government. Phillis suggests this adversarial relationship has led to a mistrust of information when it is perceived as emanating from "political" sources. Significantly Phillis concludes: "We consider it vital for the health of our democratic institutions that trust between the government, the media and the public is rebuilt".[3] Responsibility for the restoration of trust lies with politicians, the civil service and the media.

THE PHILLIS RECOMMENDATIONS
Phillis goes on to make a number of far-reaching recommendations:

The Integration of Communication with Policy-Making
First, he recommends that "communications must be strategic and integrated with the policy and delivery strategies both within departments and across government".[4] It is quite usual in government departments to split the policy making and communications functions. Furthermore, there is no uniform approach to communication in the various government departments. The "delivery" departments such as health and education tend to be more proactive and strategic in their communications largely because they have, by the very nature of their function, more of an end-user focus. Here, professional communicators are often involved at the policy making stage and are integrated within it. This is not always the case. Indeed a

number of communicators in certain departments have complained to the author that they are positively shut out from policy decisions and expected to perform the role of message deliverer at the end of the process. Often they have little briefing, little time and few resources to make any sensible communication effort and certainly are unable to either plan or deliver strategically. Phillis states that "communications should be an equal and equally respected third in the trinity of Government policy making, public service delivery and communications".[5]

The disjunction of policy making from communication is closely paralleled in industry and other parts of the public sector. However, while regularly complaining that they are often involved too late and end up being a crafter of messages about policies they know to be flawed "there's a far greater management appreciation of the needs to embed communications within what a company does" (Shawe 2003). Unfortunately, it often takes a crisis to force an organisation to recognise the importance of integrating communications into the policy-making debate as illustrated by Shell's re-appraisal of its communications following the Brent Spar incident (Le Jeune 2002). The same has been the case with government.

Furthermore, in business there are tensions when the communication function reports to another function that may not have a full appreciation of its role. For example, if public relations reports into marketing, it can be pressured into securing free publicity for a particular product, irrespective of whether that product enhances the corporate identity overall and irrespective of whether the information is of genuine interest to the press or the end user. The result is that the wider reputation of the organisation can be damaged, the public relations department's relationship with the press can be damaged and its role as an "honest broker", providing information and acting as an advocate with integrity is compromised. Parallel tensions can be observed when civil servants who are supposed to be politically neutral find themselves reporting to a political appointee, the Prime Minister's director of communications and strategy.

Structural issues

Phillis comments that current structures and processes make cross-departmental communications difficult to co-ordinate and cites the problems surrounding Foot and Mouth Disease where it was unclear how and which government departments should be communicating during the earlier stages of the crisis. Departments tend to operate in silos and the government's Information and Communications Service Unit does not provide a cross-government function – largely because it has neither the power nor resources to do so.

This problem also exists for many local authorities with cross-departmental issues such as social depravation to manage and for large corporates that have devolved communication functions. An obvious solution is to have an effective upward and downward referral system and a central, co-ordinating function with authority. Phillis partly tackles this with certain structural recommendations, but there are still areas of potential difficulty as will be expanded on later.

Special advisers and civil servants
Third, Phillis examines the role of special advisers and civil servants in some detail. In summary, the group states the role of civil servants as being to "explain minister's reasons and justifications for their decisions, actions and policies"[6] — this includes their reason for not taking alternative action and why they reject criticisms. So there is clearly an element of advocacy involved in the role. The group also re-iterates the duty of civil servants to make government information available on time and in an accessible form. Phillis defines the special adviser's role as being to explain and advocate the political dimensions of any issue, an important function both for the media and ministers. The distinction between the roles is seen to be vital, and Phillis expresses concern if special advisers can pressure civil servants into moving from their neutral stance. He also recognises that the roles of both specialists can become confused.

There are clear parallels here between central government and local district and county councils. The communication or public relations departments of councils exist to provide non-political information and advice to citizens and the press. They can find themselves under political pressure to support the party in power. There are few parallels in industry, but perhaps the closest is when a company makes a poor managerial decision and the communications department could well be asked to publicly support the board position while they know that other stakeholders will be opposed and where they feel there is little moral justification. A simple example is excessive increases in senior management pay, especially if the company is not performing well or where employee pay is being held-down.

Press spokespersons
The role of press spokesperson is singled out for special mention. Phillis recognises that their role is legitimate and that ministers need to have a high

level of trust in them. Such an individual needs to understand policy as well as being able to act as spokesperson and, as such, they form an important bridging role.

Again there are some parallels in industry. In some organisations individuals reporting directly to the CEO or chairman of the board, play a senior adviser role (Moss, Warnaby and Newman 2000). This individual may or may not be a member of the organisation's communications or public relations team, they may be a retained consultant. Either way, they are seen to be a trusted individual and can act in a senior spokesperson role with a great deal of autonomy. Their position within the organisation can be ambiguous and sometimes their focus on a particular crisis or issue can cause conflicts with the mainstream communication department and either derail or temporarily redirect their longer-term agenda. However, when the lines of reporting and communication are robust and roles clear – this individual can add major strength to the communication team.

The role of the centre
Phillis was asked by the Prime Minister to look specifically at the role of the central Government Information and Communications (GICS) function, as opposed to those within individual departments. Several issues were identified as needing to have a central focus:

- cross-government communication strategy and co-ordination of cross-cutting issues, e.g. anti-drug policies;
- leading on recruitment, training and career development;
- a centre of expertise for professional standards;
- support for No.10's communications, including the co-ordination of media handling;
- co-ordinating communications in crisis;
- monitoring the effectiveness of activity and expenditure;
- auditing civil servant and special adviser guidelines and arbitrating in disputes over them.

With this in mind, Phillis recommends that more power, authority, involvement and resource be given to the GICS. Phillis also observes the fact that the director of communications and strategy (who heads up both the special adviser and civil service function at No.10) is a political appointment and has "led to a perception, in some sections of the media and population at large, that, at the highest level, government communications are being driven by an overtly political agenda".7

To deal with these issues Phillis recommends a restructuring of communication within government and the appointment of three senior people:

- a permanent secretary who focuses on communication strategy across government;
- a deputy permanent secretary who will be both the Prime Minister's senior official spokesperson and leader of civil service communications at No.10;
- a director of communications, responsible to the Prime Minister who will lead the Prime Minister's political communications team at No.10 and assist Cabinet Ministers and their special advisers.

So the civil service and political dimensions will be seen to be clearly separate and the role that the former director of strategy and communications had in heading up the civil service operations, will cease.

Engaging the public
Phillis is keen to stress that government communication should be a dialogue. This means it should be more than media relations which essentially restricts opportunities for genuine dialogue with individuals. The group recommends a broad raft of communication techniques which, when integrated, "make a strategic contribution to the policy and delivery aims and objectives of each government department"8. "The group believes that to re-engage the public, more emphasis needs to be given to local and regional communications and this includes the vital role of the public service employees inter-facing direction with the public".9

Apart from these specific recommendations, Phillis lists a series of ideas under consideration which are effectively extensions and elaborations of the Interim suggestions. However, the Prime Minister has also asked the group to take into account any recommendation emanating from the Hutton inquiry into the death of Dr David Kelly and to reflect on the responsibilities that the media have in not creating barriers to the public's understanding of government and politics.

REFLECTIONS FROM THE PUBLIC RELATIONS LITERATURE
For some time concern has been expressed about the issues surrounding political communication (Maloney 2000; Michie 1998; Gregory 2002). These

have largely been from an ethical dimension, particularly over the role of political public relations consultants and special advisers and the nature of political communication discourse. However, as with the Phillis Review Group, concern has been voiced over the issue of disengagement from the political processes as the general public become increasingly cynical about political communication of all kinds.

Indeed, for some time the public relations literature has recognised that trusted communication is critical as a building block to constructing a genuine sense of community which reinforces democratic processes and encourages participative involvement (Kruckeberg and Starck 1988).

INTEGRATION OF COMMUNICATION WITH POLICY

A 15-year study of Excellence in Public Relations and Communication in the USA, Canada and the UK led by the American academic James Grunig[10] encapsulated much of the thinking on this. A key finding of the research was that public relations is not just a technical support function providing communication expertise for other management disciplines, but is in itself a management function that helps an organisation to interact with the social and political environment. Public relations used strategically helps to develop high quality relationships with stakeholder groups and individuals which directly contribute to organisational and societal effectiveness.

Communication professionals must not only be technically competent, but in a strategic role they identify those critical publics who can affect or who are affected by organisational decisions and who can cause issues or crises for those organisations (including government). Thus, communicators must be a part of the decision and policy-making process to be able to advise senior managers on the consequences of decisions on publics or stakeholders and their likely reaction to them. Communicators bring a unique understanding of stakeholders into decision-making because as organisational boundary-spanners, who frequently interact with the stakeholding environment, they will be researching and listening to those stakeholders before decisions are made (White and Dozier 1992). Excellent communication programmes include dialogue with critical stakeholders both before and after decisions are made in order to build good, sustainable relationships with them. Communicators who act as "message-crafters", delivering messages after decisions are made are not able to act strategically.

Furthermore, the study found excellent communication departments do not flourish in organisations that are authoritarian, mechanistic and where one-way communications are the norm. Excellent communication flourishes where the organisational culture is open and participative and a communicative culture helps to shape the organisation itself. Empowerment of the communication function is a key to communication success. Communicators should be either part of the power elite themselves or have easy access to those in power. In addition, their counsel on the communication dimensions of decision-making should be as respected as any other functional authority – the policy makers in government's case.

STRUCTURAL ISSUES

There is surprisingly little definitive advice in the public relations literature specifically on the structure of departments. Most of the standard texts[11] describe the options available and one is devoted specifically to departmental organisation (Beard 2001). Typically departments are structured along task (for example, publications, events, design, press relations) or functional (e.g. government relations, community relations, customer relations) lines. Options are also given for centralised and/or devolved functions. What is emphasised though is the requirement for strong links between communication functions and there is little doubt that the corporate or "head office" public relations function has power to enforce cross-cutting policy and co-ordinate communication across divisions where that is necessary. The standard texts mentioned reinforce the need to co-ordinate communication efforts so that stakeholders are not given conflicting information and so that they are not engaged in an ad-hoc way by a range of communicators within the same organisation – such at least, is the theory.

SPECIAL ADVISERS, CIVIL SERVANTS AND SPOKESPERSONS: THE ROLE OF THE ADVOCATE

While Phillis discusses the role of civil servants and special advisers, the more interesting debate is around the nature and extent of advocacy and this remains still to be addressed. This is at the nub of the debate about spin. Indeed, the government's vociferous advocacy and the attempted exclusion of opposing voices though the Rebuttal Unit, along with the "gloss" put on its position has caused much concern and is the root of the ethical question.

The public relations literature itself holds different positions on this issue. In summary there are two models of practice: the relationship model and the advocacy model. The relationship model, whose main historic proponent is James Grunig, is posited on the notion that organisations are part of a wider social and political system and to thrive they must seek mutual dependence, co-orientation, co-existence and the building of mutually beneficial relationships. The excellence model of public relations, explained earlier, states that two-way symmetrical communication, where an organisation is as open to being influenced by its publics as it is likely to influence them, is the ideal. While it is recognised that absolute mutuality is idealistic and that in reality both organisations and publics are purposive in intent, "nevertheless, negotiations and compromise permit organisations and publics to find a common ground – a win-win zone" (Dozier et al op cit) where each can co-exist with an acceptable level of comfort and discomfort.

Core to this idea of relationship building is dialogue to reach mutual understanding. The rules of engagement in dialogue are not simple and the rhetorical school of public relations scholarship has made a major contribution to understanding. The rhetorical school came to the fore in the 1990s, led by scholars such as Pearson, Heath and Toth[12] who themselves are reliant on the work of Kenneth Burke (1969). They suggest that public relations involves publics making sense of the symbols (verbal, written, visual and/or behavioural) produced by organisations. To make sense of those symbols, dialogue needs to be entered into so that there can be agreement on meanings. To rhetoricians, the *process* of communication is at the ethical heart of the matter. They advocate a set of rules of engagement based on Habermas (1984) which require that participants test and probe ideas that are proposed, have equal freedom to initiate and continue dialogue, to set the discussion agenda and to challenge or explain. To do this they must have freedom from manipulation and equality of power. In turn, all those participating in dialogue become accountable for ensuring they are understood, that they are factually accurate, their communication is appropriate for the recipients and that they are sincere.

In contrast, the advocacy model stresses organisational autonomy and envisages that an organisation will assert itself on its environment and exert a level of control (Barney and Black 1994). The rhetorical school supports advocacy in that they believe in the proposing and vigorous debate of particular arguments within the rules of engagement outlined above. The purpose of advocacy in this context is Aristotelian in origin: discover the truth through mutual agreement. The purpose is not to "win", but to ensure the best argument prevails. However, the more commonly accepted understanding of the word advocacy is overwhelming persuasive argument to a particular viewpoint with no sense of obligation to seek other views. The objective is quite simply organisational advantage – to "win" is very important.

Many practitioners would argue that their persuasion work is overtly partisan and therefore not unethical. It is for others to put a countervailing view. This view of advocacy is a popular model (Grunig and Hunt 1984) and it is easy to see why. First the employer pays and expects loyalty in return. Second many practitioners come from a journalistic background and the journalist's role is to get the story out. As Heath says (2001:2): "This has led to a focus on message design and dissemination to achieve awareness, to inform, to persuade – even manipulate." Thirdly, many practitioners believe advocacy should be encouraged in a democratic society where freedom to express opinions is cherished. Ultimately, it is up to "the public" to decide whether or not the arguments are acceptable.

There are problems with this position especially where the rules of ethical engagement for advocacy are not observed. Organisations sometimes act to suppress opposing voices with legitimate alternative views, for example, in the debate about genetically modified food. Furthermore, debate can be dominated by those with power, influence and resources.

Often communication advocacy is justified as being similar to legal advocacy. Clearly this is not the case since there is no judge to oversee fair play and no trained opponent with a guaranteed voice and equal resources. The divergence of opinion and tensions within the public relations literature is clearly reflected in the issues identified by Phillis. As previously mentioned, Phillis states that government communication should be regarded as a dialogue. However, he also says that advocacy is permissible, without saying how that advocacy should be conducted. The public relations literature does recognise that bounds have to be put on advocacy, for example Edgett (2002) has explicated a coherent case for ethical advocacy.

Phillis has gone part of the way to solving the problem by clearly separating the roles of special adviser and civil servants, and has recognised the unique position of the spokesperson as advocate, but he has not resolved or even addressed the issue of the nature of advocacy. Structural clarification will not resolve issues of content. However, it is clear that Phillis is trying to encourage a direction of travel towards relational and dialogical communication.

ENGAGING THE PUBLIC

Phillis recommends that government communicate through a whole raft of channels to engage with the public and specifically commends two-way communication channels. The Excellence Study mentioned earlier recognises that listening to publics is critical so that both the organisation's self-interest and that of publics is balanced. The purpose of communication is to manage conflict and build and enhance mutually beneficial relationships. The study suggests that this way public relations departments become the ethical conscience of the organisation and the *de facto* advocates of social responsibility.

CONCLUSIONS

The Phillis Review Group has identified a breakdown of trust between government, politicians and the media driven to a large extent by the adversarial nature of the relationship between government and the media. From the previous discussion it can be argued that the adversarial debate has its roots in the commonly understood meaning of the word advocacy. The government has sought to advocate its position and, the evidence suggests,[13] used both special advisers and civil servants to advance its political as well as governmental agenda.

Phillis proposes a move towards a relational model with its focus on mutuality and the responsibility to the wider public good. The author argues that this is best served by the mutual and relational model of communication. The ethical basis for this kind of thinking is deontological. Communicators of all kinds have an obligation or duty to do what is in the overall interests of society. Relationships of trust, of mutual benefit are "good" in themselves, but also benefit society at large.

The relational role of communication is vital because it serves a critical role in building and maintaining community – and that is the business of government. As Kruckeberg and Starck (1988: 53) say: "A community is achieved when people are aware of and interested in common ends. Communication plays a vital role as people try to regulate their own activities and to participate in efforts to reach common ends."

Note: The full *Interim Report of the Government Communications Reviews Group* along with membership of the group and full supporting evidence can be found at www.gics.gov.uk/review

NOTES

1. *Government Communication Review Group Interim Report* (GCRGIR). Available online at www.gics.gov.uk/access/review/interim-report-htm p.2, accessed 24.9.03
2. ibid p 1
3. ibid p 2

4.   ibid p 2
5.   ibid p 2
6.   ibid p3
7.   ibid p 5
8.   ibid p 4
9.   ibid p 4
10. This 15-year study has been reported in three books. The final report of the study undertaken by a variety of researchers in three countries is by Grunig, L., Grunig, J. and Dozier, D. (2002) *Excellent public relations and effective organisations: A study of communication management in three countries*, Lawrence Erlbaum Associates, Mahwah, NJ. This book was preceded by Dozier, D., with Grunig, L., and Grunig, J. (1995) *Managers Guide to excellence in public relations and communication management*, Lawrence Erlbaum Associates, Mahwah NJ which was an explanation of the theory and results of the study written largely for practitioners. The detailed literature review and conceptualisation of communication and management theory leading to the theory of excellence in public relations is contained in Grunig, J. (ed.) (1992) *Excellence in public relations and communication management*, Lawrence Erlbaum Associates, Hillsdale, NJ.
11. For example Grunig, J. E. and Hunt, T. (1984) *Managing Public Relations*, Fort Worth, Holt, Rinehart and Winston and Cutlip, S., Center, A. and Broom G. (2000) *Effective Public Relations* (8th Edition), London, Prentice Hall International
12. For a fuller explanation of the rhetorical position see Botan, C.H. and Hazelton, V. (eds). (1989) *Public Relations Theory*, Hillsdale NJ, Lawrence Erlbaum Associates Inc. and Toth, E. and Heath R. (1992) *Rhetorical and Critical Approaches to Public Relations*, Hillsdale, NJ, Lawrence Erlbaum Associates, Inc
13. Sixsmith, M. (2003) Evidence to Government Communications Review Group. Avaliable online at www.gc.review.gov.uk/evidence/martinsixsmith.doc, accessed 24.9.03

REFERENCES

Barney, R.D. and Black, J. (1994) "Ethics and Professional Persuasive Communication", *Public Relations Review,* Vol 20, No 3 pp 233-248
Beard, M (2001) *Running a Public Relations Department* (2nd edition), Kogan Page, London
Burke, K. (1969) *A Rhetoric of Motives*, Berkeley: University of California Press. Quoted in Heath (2001) *Rhetorical Enactment Rationale, Handbook of Public Relations,* Thousand Oaks, Sage
Edgett, R. (2002) "Towards an Ethical Framework for Advocacy in Public Relations", *Journal of Public Relations Research,* Vol 14, No 1 pp 1-26
Gregory, A. (2002) Public Relations and the Age of Spin, Annual General Meeting Inaugural Lecture, Institute of Public Relations, London
Ingham, B. (2003) Evidence to Government Communications Review Group. Available online at www.gcreview.gov.uk/evidence/bernardingham.doc p.2, accessed 24.9.03
Heath, R.L. (2001) "Shifting Foundations", in *Handbook Public Relations*, Heath, R.L. (ed.) Thousand Oaks, Cal, Sage
Grunig, J. E. and Hunt, T. (1984) *Managing Public Relations*, Fort Worth, Holt, Rinehart and Winston

Habermas, J. (1984) *The Theory of Communicative Action I: Reason and the Rationalisation of Society,* Boston, MA, Beacon Press

Kruckeberg, D. and Starck, K. (1988) *Public Relations and Community: A Reconstructed Theory,* New York, Praeger

Le Jeune, M. (2002) Managing Risk and Reputation in an era of Increased Media Scrutiny. Paper presented at Institute of Public Relations Conference, Manchester

Moloney, K. (2000) *Rethinking Public Relations,* London: Routledge

Michie, D. (1998) *The Invisible Persuaders,* London, Bantam Press

Moss, D. A, Warnaby, G. and Newman, A. (2000) "Public Relations practitioner role enactment at the senior management level within UK companies", *Journal of Public Relations Research*, 12 (4) pp 277-307

Shawe, J. (2003) "Spreading the Corporate Message", *Profile,* Issue 39, Institute of Public Relations, London p 1

White, J. and Dozier. D.M. (1992) "Public Relations and Management Decision Making", *Excellence in Public Relations and Communication Management* Grunig, J.E. (ed.), Hillsdale, NJ, Lawrence Erlbaum Associates Inc

Anne Gregory is the UK's only full-time Professor of Public Relations and Director of the Centre for Public Relations Studies at Leeds Metropolitan University, the largest department of public relations in the UK. Before moving into academic life, she spent 12 years as a full-time public relations practitioner, holding senior appointments both in-house and in consultancy. Still involved in practice on a consultancy basis, she is President of the UK Institute of Public Relations and editor of the institute's *Public Relations in Practice* series. Contact: Centre for Public Relations Studies, Leeds Business School, Leeds Metropolitan University, Bronte Hall, Beckett Park Campus, Leeds, LS6 3QS. Tel: 0113 283 7520; fax 0113 283 1751; email: A.Gregory@lmu.ac.uk.

The Phillis Review:
Government communication
under the spotlight

Anne Gregory

In the previous chapter (first published in Ethical Space Volume 1 No.1), Anne Gregory examined the Interim Report of the Government Communications Review Group, chaired by Bob Phillis and known as the Phillis Review. In this chapter (published in Ethical Space Volume 1 No. 2), *she looks at the full report, commenting on what's new and reflecting on some of the issues raised.*

PHILLIS'S STARTING POINT

In the *Interim Report on Government Communications* published in September 2003, the Phillis Review Group indicated there was "a three-way breakdown in trust between government and politicians, the media and general public".[1] This had been brought about by "a rigorous and proactive government news management strategy"[2] which had led to a "challenging and adversarial"[3] response from the media. As a result "the public now expects and believes the worst of politicians and government, even when there is strong objective evidence in favour of the government's position".[4] Phillis concluded: "It is vital for the health of our democratic institutions that trust between the government, the media and the public is rebuilt. This will require culture and behaviour change from all parties: politicians, the civil service and the media."[5]

The interim report made a number of observations and recommendations. In summary these were that:

- "Communications must be strategic and integrated with the policy and delivery strategies both within departments and across government".[6]

- "Current structures and processes make it difficult to co-ordinate communication across government"[7] because departments effectively operate in silos.
- There are legitimate roles for both politically appointed special advisers and politically neutral civil servants in communication, but that the roles are distinct and should have separate reporting lines. The group also recognised the unique role and importance of the official spokesperson. Phillis, therefore, recommended a restructuring that included the appointment of a permanent secretary who would focus on communication strategy across government and who would have overall responsibility for civil servants. A deputy permanent secretary would double up as the Prime Minister's official spokesperson and be leader of the civil service communication function based at No.10. The director of communications would be a political appointee, responsible to the Prime Minister, lead the special advisers' team at No.10 and assist cabinet ministers and their special advisers.
- Government communications "must be viewed as part of a dialogue"[8] and, therefore, it should go beyond media relations. "The full range of communication channels"[9] should be used "especially those with a so-called 'return path'."[10] In particular, the use of local and regional communications was encouraged.
- There was a key role for a central government communication function which includes development of strategy, standards setting, HR development and the co-ordination of cross-government communication activities.

THE FINAL REPORT

The *Final Report* confirms the interim recommendations and observations, in some cases puts more flesh on them and examines some new areas hinted at in the *Interim Report*. In introducing its report, the group makes a number of statements re-iterating its concerns about public trust and disengagement, but two fundamentals are also established:

- "The interests of the general public should be paramount in any programme to modernise government communication."[11]
- "We believe that modern government communication should be based on the following principles:
  - openness, no secrecy;
  - more direct, unmediated communication to the public;

- genuine engagement with the public as part of policy formulation and delivery, not communication as an afterthought;
- positive presentation of government policies and achievements, not misleading spin;
- use of all relevant channels of communication, not excessive emphasis on national press and broadcasters;
- co-ordinated communication of issues that cut across departments, not conflicting or duplicated departmental messages;
- reeinforcement of the civil service's political neutrality, rather than a blurring of government and party communication."[12]

The 12 final recommendations can be grouped into four themes:

Structure
Recommendation 2 confirms the new structure at the top of the communication function, and clarifies the role of the permanent secretary who will "lead the central civil service communications unit and provide strategic leadership for communication across government".[13] It is envisaged this unit will become a centre for excellence, supporting both government departments and the civil service team in No.10. This and Recommendation 7 recognises that there can be issues around the roles of special advisers and civil servants who often work together well in No.10 and in departments. It suggests a code of practice to offer guidance including what civil servants should do if they feel pressured to take a political line.

Appraisal will be a key task for the permanent secretary. He/she will construct "the framework against which departments assess their communication performance"[14] although they will not line-manage communication staff in departments. It is also envisaged that communication will "be built into the personal objectives of all senior civil servants".[15]

Departmental communication structures are addressed under Recommendation 3. While recognising that departments are very different in size, structure and communication requirements, the review group states "more needs to be done to increase the professionalism and effectiveness of communication"[16] in departments. It reiterates the view expressed in the interim report that communication needs to be integrated into policy development and service delivery. And it goes on to say that all departments should have a communication strategy that supports policy aims and objectives which should be endorsed at the highest level. Some thought is given to how communication should be structured in departments, but no template is provided because of the variable nature of the requirement. However, the permanent secretary will be responsible for ensuring whatever is put in place is effective. Particular roles are identified as critical, for example the lead civil servant in departments will be called director of communication and will have a strategic rather than tactical role. Adequate resourcing is also regarded as critical.

The review group makes specific comments on the recruitment, training and development of civil servant communicators in Recommendation 6. Recognising that a variety of backgrounds are a strength, the group recommends recruitment from outside government, between departments and from other civil service roles. The permanent secretary will be required to set overall recruitment standards and be directly involved in the recruitment of departmental directors of communication. Ministers should not be involved in recruitment, to avoid any notion of political bias and to ensure selection is based solely on competence to do the job.

Finally, on structures, Phillis recommends the disbandment of the current Government Information and Communication Service (GICS) with the new permanent secretary being "tasked with forging a new communication function across government pulling together current members of GICS and other departmental communication staff into a fully functioning communication operation".[17]

These recommendations, while accommodating the particular nature of government, will be recognisable as similar to those in large corporate organisations with devolved structures (Beard 2001) or to those organisations with endorsed branding strategies (Olins 1995). Here communication policy, strategy, oversight and coordination are overseen by a small corporate unit, but with maximum autonomy devolved to the operating units or brands. There are dangers in taking the analogy too far. The sheer size and range of its activities makes government unlike any other organisation. It is, in fact, a monolithic brand (ibid) with each department being just one facet of the same brand. Thus the NHS may be regarded as a strong, individual or endorsed brand but it is inextricably linked to the overarching government "brand". The danger for government is that damage to any particular department directly impacts on the whole of government. For example, the handling of Foot and Mouth affected the reputation of the whole of government, not just MAFF.

Phillis seems to make a major error in the allocation of titles in the final report. While great care is taken to stress the different roles of government special advisers and civil servants, the most senior special adviser based at No.10, is called the Prime Minister's director of communication. The most senior civil service appointment within department is also called "director of communication". There are grounds for confusion here, especially for a general public who has difficulty enough in divining the distinction between special advisers and civil servants.

Activities
The next group of recommendations focus on the way communication should be undertaken. Recommendation 1 re-iterates the importance of dialogue. Integral to making communication more relevant and appealing, the review group again advocates greater use of local and regional channels (Recommendation 5). The reasons for this are twofold: first local media are trusted more and, second, engagement with local communities can provide more diverse insights into the effects of proposed and actual policy "on the ground" and hence inform the policy-making process more intelligently. The final report also recommends a focus on unmediated on-line communication with a strong customer focus (Recommendation 11). One central government website is proposed that allows direct feedback via for example chatrooms and e-mail.

Although it could not be expected that the report would present a complete list of communication channels and activities, it is disappointing that this is not more expansive and that only the obvious channels are selected. All the standard strategic public relations texts (Grunig and Hunt 1984; Cutlip, Center and Broom 2000; Gregory 2000) stress the importance of a raft of communication techniques both to ensure adequate repetition of content in a variety of forms by the initiator of communication so that the range of publics is contacted, and to accommodate a variety of preferred feedback methods by different publics. Ethically this is important since difficult-to-reach groups, such as those without access to information technology and those with language and reading difficulties, can find themselves excluded from democratic processes if their preferred or essential media are not used.

Content
A key principle of the final report is to bring openness and transparency to government communication. This plugs a gap left by the interim report since it is content that has been a major concern for many people (for example,

Ingham, 2003). Recommendation 8 supports the implementation of the Freedom of Information Act (FOI) which comes into force in January 2005. The group states that the "culture of secrecy and partial disclosure....is at the route of many of the problems we have examined".[18] It goes on to say that the class exemptions and the option of a ministerial veto currently vested in the Act should not be used and that the presumption should be to disclose unless substantial harm will be caused. The review group believes openness will help rebuild trust, "encourage active citizenship by providing the public with the necessary information and data"[19] and discourage both the government and the media from spin since "the public itself will have access to material and will be able to form its own view of the accuracy of reporting".[20]

In the same vein, Recommendation 9 reinforces the importance of publicly available, independent national statistics, provided to a clear timetable and made available to public and government at the same time. It is also recommended that if ministers use departmental data, which they have access to before the official national statistics are available, they should release all the relevant data.

The system of closed lobby briefings also comes under scrutiny in Recommendation 10. The review group recommends that lobby briefings should be televised, open to any journalist and with transcripts available. Ministers should play a bigger part as the accountable, elected representatives of government and government websites should make all relevant background material available. Within this context, Phillis is adamant that journalists must be allowed to pursue a consistent line of questioning.

The proposals on content are welcome as far as they go. Access to information is critical for an informed democracy. However, information on its own is not the panacea. The availability of facts does not enfranchise those without the facilities to collate, interpret and use them. Information is not communication. Furthermore, Phillis makes no comment at all on the more difficult and potentially controversial aspects of communication where there is conflicting opinion and where policy is politically driven. For example, on immigration policy or educational reforms there is a need for greater guidance on content issues.

Moreover, the interim report recognises that civil servants have an advocacy role. While the new code of practice may provide guidance on the bounds of their role and absolve them from discussing anything "political" there is no apparent guidance on content, the nature of the language or the voracity of the non-political advocacy.

The report does not recognise some of the dangers inherent in an "on the record" televised briefings fronted by ministers. While it is good the worst aspects of a "secret" lobby system are thereby eliminated, experience in the US, for example, indicates that these can turn into either anodyne rituals or overtly campaigning sessions used as publicity platforms for the incumbent party in government. Opposition parties could make legitimate complaint that they are not being given equivalent opportunities, particularly in the run-up to an election where, it could be argued, this proposal goes against the spirit of proportional access to free broadcast airtime, a tenet of the British electoral system.

Responsibility

Finally, the review group reflects on the relationship between the government and the media. Recommendation 12 observes that while it is the media's role to question and challenge the government, it is not Her Majesty's Opposition and it should not try to fulfil that role. It notes there are declining audiences for TV and radio news, decreasing newspaper circulation and less participation in elections and conclude that "the population at large has little time for politicians or the media".[21]

Phillis calls on both parties to consider their behaviour and to judge whether it supports the objective of the review – "to help restore public trust in legitimate government communication".[22]

DISCUSSION

By addressing the key areas of structure, activity, content and responsibility, the final report tackles some of the significant issues of government communication. From an ethical viewpoint the central notion of dialogue is important. As argued in the previous chapter, published originally in *Ethical Space* Vol. 1 No.1 (Gregory 2003), Phillis is proposing a move away from the advocacy model of communication where the desire is to "win" the argument and impose a government view in the media, towards a relational model of communication where mutuality and community is served by engaging in dialogue.

In particular, the final report's recommendation on content and activities are supportive of an approach that is deontological in origin. It stresses that government and the media have a duty to work in the public interest and that the government, in particular, must open up channels of communication and provide information for the public good.

The availability of data that has agreed currency and access to relevant background information is critical to informed debate. Combine that with the ability to contribute to and initiate debate because two-way communication channels are available, and what is proposed goes some way towards the rules of ethical dialogue advocated by Habermas (1984). He states that participants in dialogue should be able to test and probe ideas, have equal freedom to initiate and continue dialogue, to set the discussion agenda and to challenge and/or explain. To do this properly they must have freedom from manipulation and equality of power. In turn, those participating in dialogue must take responsibility for ensuring they are understood, are factually accurate, are communicating in a way appropriate to those receiving the communication it and are sincere.

While it is laudable that the government is opening up communication so that the public and individuals can enter into dialogue as individuals, it has to be recognised the media will make contributions and challenges on their behalf and in the public interest. And so they should. If the media take on board Habermas's rules of ethical dialogue, progress may, indeed, be possible.

NOTES

1   *Government Communication Review Group Interim Report* (GCRGIR), avaliable online at www.gics.gov.uk/access/review/ interim-report.htm
2   ibid p 1
3   ibid p 1
4   ibid p 2
5   ibid p 2
6   ibid p 2
7   ibid p 2
8   ibid p 3
9   ibid p 3
10   ibid p 10
11   *An Independent Review of Government Communications* p 2
12   ibid p 2
13   ibid p 13
14   ibid p 14
15   ibid p 15
16   ibid p 15
17   ibid p 18
18   ibid p 23
19   ibid p 23
20   ibid p 23
21   ibid p 27
22   ibid p 6

REFERENCES

Beard, M. (2001) *Running a Public Relations Department* (2nd edition), London, Kogan Page

Grunig, J. E. and Hunt, T. (1984) *Managing Public Relations*, Fort Worth, Holt Rinehart and Winston

Cutlip, S., Center, A. and Broom, G. (2000) *Effective Public Relations* (8th edition), London, Prentice Hall International

Gregory, A. (2000) *Planning and Managing Public Relations Campaigns*, (2nd edition), London, Kogan Page

Gregory, A. (2003) "Communication and the Machine of Government", *Ethical Space: the International Journal of Communication Ethics*, Vol.1.1 pp 20-25

Olins, W. (1995) *The New Guide to Identity*, London, The Design Council

Habermas, J. (1984) *The Theory of Communicative Action I: Reason and the Rationalisation of Society*, Boston, MA, Beacon Press

Ingham, B. (2003) Evidence of Government Communications Review Group www.gcreview.gov.uk/evidence/bernardingham.doc, accessed 24 January 2004

Absolutism and the confidential controversy

Michael Foley

Michael Foley explores some of the issues relating to journalists' increasing use of confidential sources – as highlighted in the Andrew Gilligan/Dr David Kelly controversy

There is hardly a code of conduct, code of professionalism or code of ethics anywhere in the world that does not call in the strongest terms for a journalist always to maintain the anonymity of a confidential source. For instance, the National Union of Journalists of Britain and Ireland's code of conduct states categorically: "A journalist shall protect confidential sources of information." Contrast that with other clauses that contain qualifying statements such as "subject to the justification by overriding considerations of the public interest". Similarly, the International Federation of Journalists' code, which is often used as a model for journalists' codes in emerging democracies, states: "The journalist shall observe professional secrecy regarding the source of information obtained in confidence."

There are a number of reasons for the importance of protecting confidential sources. In a profession with so few rules, if any, it can be comforting to have at the centre such a strong statement of principle. Another reason might be the increasing difficulty journalists have in defending objectivity, that notion which more or less defined journalism for so long. Objectivity can be seen as a theory to get to the truth, the epistemology of journalism, which states that if you separate facts from opinion or news from views this will permit you to know the truth. Defending the anonymity of a source thus becomes a central position that sets journalists apart from other professions and gives substance to an ideology of objectivity within a practice that still has difficulties in defining itself as a profession or not.

There is legislation in a number US states giving journalists a legal protection and Sweden has had similar legislation for years. The European Court of Human Rights has ruled, in the case of a British journalist, Bill Goodwin, that protection of confidential sources is an essential means of enabling the press to perform its important function of public watchdog and should not be interfered with unless in exceptional circumstances where vital public or individual interests are at stake.

Journalists are taking an increasingly absolutist view of this position, despite the European Court of Human Rights' qualifying phrase of "unless in exceptional circumstances where vital public or individual interests are at stake". For instance, John Toner (2003), the official who serves the NUJ's ethics council, commenting on a case of a former temporary member of the union who had given evidence against a man accused of murder based on evidence given to him in confidence, said:

> *Some have argued that Nick Martin-Clark (the journalist who gave evidence) was acting in the public interest by informing on a notorious killer. We must take a broader view of the public interest than this. Sources must believe that a promise of confidentiality is as binding on a journalist as it is on a doctor, a lawyer or a priest, Any weakening in that belief will result in sources drying up and countless issues of public interest may never see the light of day.*

PROBLEMS WITH THE ABSOLUTIST POSITION

There are problems with this absolutist position. If we ignore priests, whose justifications for upholding confidentiality are theologically based, then we are left with lawyers and doctors. Both professions are highly regulated and licensed. The bodies that run both professions have the powers of the courts devolved to them, allowing them to grant and take away the right to practice. Such a scheme would be anathema to most journalists. It would have grave implications for press freedom, with the possibility of licensing and legal definitions of what and who is a journalist.

Doctors, lawyers and priests offer anonymity to ensure privacy, so that what is said can remain private. Nothing said to the practitioner will be put into the public domain. For the journalist the opposite is true. Not only will the journalist report all that is said, but will try, with all the skills at his or her disposal, to get the source to talk more and get more information, which again will be made public. As Klaidman and Beauchamp (1987: 163) say in their work, *The Virtuous Journalist*, there is a real difference between the relationship between a journalist and source compared to that between a doctor and patient or lawyer and client:

> *Confidentiality is at the heart of trust in regular reporter-source relationships. But relationships of confidentiality between reporters and sources are different from those found in other professional settings such as between lawyer and client, physicians and patients, clergy and parishioners, In these relationships, the right of confidentiality exists to protect privacy and to encourage the openness that is required to guarantee the client, patient or parishioner the full benefit of the professional's services. In the case of reporters and source, by contrast, there are non-fiduciary and even adversarial elements in the relationship, with the reporter angling to learn more than the source wants to tell and the source trying to promote a particular views and, of course, from the standpoint of the journalist, the public's interest, not the source's, should be paramount.*

One of the problems for the absolutist case is that the use of anonymous sources appears to be increasing. Day after day the media, especially newspapers, are full of quotes from "sources close to the prime minister", "industry sources" or "intelligence sources" (particularly in the reporting of the Iraq crisis) and so-called "friends" who tell all. No names are given, often only one source is quoted. Is the public to believe that the journalist is to risk imprisonment to keep the anonymity of the ubiquitous friend in celebrity news? And if they do are they to be admired as doing something central to democracy and journalism?

WHEN THE WHISTLEBLOWER IS A MANIPULATING SPIN DOCTOR
How can the public, those who are to be informed by journalism so that they can make the decision necessary in a democracy, trust journalists who offer so much information without any meaningful indication where it came from? In many, possibly most, cases the anonymous source is not a fearless whistleblower but a manipulating spin doctor, working for the rich and powerful and hiding behind a journalist's promise of anonymity. And if that is the case, who gains most by the journalists' willingness to go to prison rather than reveal a source, the source or the public? As the philosopher,

Onora O'Neill (2002: 98), commented in her BBC Reith Lecture: "I am still looking for ways to ensure that journalists do not publish stories for which there is no source at all, while pretending that there is a source to be protected."

The absolutist position, does, of course, place the journalist above the ordinary citizen. With a demand for the legal right to withhold the identity of sources of information, journalists are seeking, and in some cases getting, a right denied to others. In that case the journalist has ceased to be a citizen using the right to free expression granted to all in a professional way, but a special sort of citizen, one with rights granted by parliament or the courts, who might, of course, one day, have a view as to who can operate that right. Such a position has profound implications to what might be called alternative media. Will a citizen with a camcorder or a website be granted the same rights as a journalists if they decide to publish information from an anonymous source? Who will decide who is a journalist?

With anonymity the source holds all the cards. A decision to give anonymity has to be agreed before the information is given, so that before the journalist has heard what the source has to say, he or she has given a binding undertaking never to reveal the name, whatever the outcome. If that outcome leads to a miscarriage of justice, for instance, is that going to instil confidence into another person whose information is of great public interest, but now fears giving it to a person who would rather see a guilty person go free rather than give a name to a court?

THE CRUCIAL RIGHT OF ANONYMITY

This is not an argument for abandoning the principle of defending the right of anonymity. It is right and proper that codes of conduct state clearly and unequivocally, as the NUJ's does, that a journalist shall protect confidential sources. Codes lay down guiding imperatives and all journalists must have a strong duty to follow such codes. Such a duty ensures professionalism among journalists and also helps the public to know what journalists themselves believe are the principles of the profession. The events in Britain surrounding the death of Dr David Kelly and the ensuing inquiry of Lord Hutton raised another and quite intriguing question. Does a guarantee to maintain the anonymity of a source mean you do not try to find out who another journalist's source is?

In the many issues raised by the events surrounding the Hutton inquiry the question of a source's anonymity (namely that of Dr Kelly) was only addressed in terms of who authorised the release of his name. And the inquiry also failed to address this crucial question: If protecting the identity of an anonymous source is so central to the collective professionalism of journalists, is not the obverse of that principle that a journalist shall do everything possible to ensure a colleague's source is protected? In the case of David Kelly, that was not the case as journalists quizzed the British Ministry of Defence officials as to the identity of Dr Kelly. So now a journalist will only be able to promise that a sources' identity will be protected by an individual journalist, even though his colleagues might decide to hunt for his or her name and out the source. Some might think that is not much protection.

The problem for journalists, however, is that for the most part they are condemned to live without hard and fast rules and that all they have to guide them are ethical principles. They can adopt a legalistic Kantian allegiance to rules that tells them to follow the codes out of duty to the rules, and for no other reason, or they can adopt a more reasonable approach, that insists that they consider the consequences of their actions. As John Merrill (1989: 198) says:

> *Journalists must be flexible, or willing to moderate a basic ethical tenet in order to reach a higher ethical objective dictated by a reasoned analysis of the situation. A significant point, and it should be emphasised, is that the journalist should never capriciously or unthinkingly break an ethical rule or maxim. An exception to a principle because of a specific situation must be made only after serious thought.*

Maybe it is now time for journalists to adopt a new imperative to judge and guide their actions, trustworthiness. Are my actions, or decisions likely to increase the trust between me and my readers, viewers or listeners? Such an approach would have journalists seriously question the use of anonymous sources and ensure that they are used rarely and when used a full explanation is given as to why. With trust placed central to journalist practice fewer anonymous sources would be used and so the problem of anonymity would arise less often.

Onora O'Neill suggests that good public debate "must not only be accessible to but also assessable by its audiences" (op cit: 95). If she is right that the public's trust of the press demands that it be assessable it would mean a major change in the way journalists use sources.

REFERENCES
Klaidman, Stephen and Beauchamp, Tom L. (1987) *The Virtuous Journalist*, Oxford, Oxford
University Press
Merrill, John (1989) *The Dialectic in Journalism*, Louisiana, Louisiana State University Press
O'Neill, Onora (2002) *A Question of Trust: The BBC Reith Lectures*, Cambridge; Cambridge
University Press
Sigal, Leon (1986) "Sources Make News", *Reading the News*, Manoff, Robert Karl and
Schudson, Michael (eds), New York, Pantheon pp 9-37
Toner, John (2003) *Journalist*, July pp 18-19

Michael Foley is a senior lecturer in journalism at the Dublin Institute of
Technology

Have journalists the right to be wrong?

Richard W. Orange

Richard W Orange examines whether the Hutton inquiry's rulings deny journalists their right to be wrong

Lord Hutton's assertion in his controversial report following the David Kelly/Andrew gilligan controversy that "false accusations of fact, impugning the integrity of others, including politicians, should not be made by the media"[1], appears to leave little room for compromise or negotiation. But is it, as some have suggested, a chilling re-assessment of qualified privilege and/or a denial of a journalist's "right" to be wrong or to be misinformed?

A justification to print or broadcast damaging allegations about individuals (or companies), without establishing whether those allegations are truthful or not, is derived from the Reynolds v. Times Newspapers libel case (Court of Appeal 1998, House of Lords 1999). There is also recourse in statute law to article 10 of the Human Rights Act 1998, which deals with freedom of expression. This provision has to be weighed against article 6 (right to a fair trial), and article 8 (right to respect for privacy). The "Reynolds Defence" is an extension of common law privilege and is subject to various tests. As with the Human Rights Act, it is interpreted on a case-by-case basis.

Times Newspapers claimed the former Irish Prime Minister, Albert Reynolds, had misled his Parliament about an important judicial appointment. The resulting libel case, which went to the Court of Appeal and to the House of Lords, established additional rights for journalists. [2]

THE DUTY TO INFORM
Firstly, there was recognition in law that newspapers and broadcasters had

"a duty" to inform the public about matters that the public should know. The Lord Chief Justice, Lord Bingham, described this as the "public interest" duty. Secondly, there was recognition in law that journalists could report damaging allegations (that might later prove to be false) as long as adequate and sensible steps were taken throughout the newsgathering and publication stages. Lord Nicholls drew up a 10-point checklist in his House of Lords judgement, and left room for further additions. This can be called the "responsible journalism" test.[3]

It was Times Newspapers' failure to cite Albert Reynolds' previous explanations to colleagues of his conduct, which robbed the newspaper of a defence under the "responsible journalism" test. However, journalists have been successful in resisting libel actions using these newly-won rights. In the GKR Karate v. *Leeds Weekly News* (2000), the newspaper was sued over an article questioning the company's activities. The newspaper succeeded because the judge concluded that the reporter had taken a responsible approach while checking out the story and had acted honestly and in the public interest.[4]

The BBC raised Reynolds as part of its submission to the Hutton Inquiry. It was in direct response to this that the Judge made his views plain on the limitations of fair comment, and false accusations of fact.[5] So journalists were confronted with a statement which ostensibly instructed the media in future to "back off" any and all stories that threatened the good name of politicians unless reporters could be 100 per cent certain of the truthfulness of any and all claims.

RESPONSE OF BBC CHAIRMAN

Reaction was swift. Departing BBC chairman of governors Gavyn Davies asked: "Are his (Hutton's) conclusions on restricting the use of unverifiable sources in journalism based on sound law?"[6] Following his resignation as BBC director general, Greg Dyke said: "He does seem to suggest that it is not enough to report what a whistleblower says – you have to show it is true."[7] The *Observer* cited a BBC document that claimed the Corporation was entitled to quote Dr Kelly "whether or not" the BBC had been able to verify his views.[8] Lord Justice Lester was quoted as saying: "The media must be free to publish opinions, honestly believed to be true, from apparently reliable sources."[9]

According to the National Union of Journalists general secretary, Jeremy Dear, Lord Hutton's report was "a serious threat to the future of investigative journalism".[10] For his part, the Judge qualified his interpretation of Reynolds in an appendix to his Report. Extracts from Lord Nicholls' judgement acknowledged that investigative journalism was a vital function of the media, especially in relation to political matters. But the extract went on to say:

> *It is in the public interest that the reputation of public figures should not be debased falsely. In the case of statements of opinions on matters of public interest ... readers and viewers can make up their own minds on whether they agree or disagree with defamatory statements which are recognisable as comment and which, expressly or implicitly, indicate in general terms the facts on which they are based.*
>
> *With defamatory imputations of fact the position is different and more difficult. Those who read or hear such allegations are unlikely to have any means of knowing whether they are true or not. If a newspaper is unwilling to disclose its source, a plaintiff can be deprived of the material necessary to prove, or even allege, that the newspaper has acted recklessly in publishing what it did without further verification.* [11]

THE RELEVANCE OF REYNOLDS

Lord Hutton also cited part of Lord Hobhouse's conclusions in the Reynolds case which read: "There is no human right to disseminate information that is not true. No public interest is served by publishing or communicating misinformation." [12] The Reynolds judgement, therefore, separates comment from fact and information from misinformation. It also points out that a newspaper can be "reckless" if it runs with a story that relies on a confidential source, without making additional checks. But the difference between information and misinformation is less clear. Is it information from a source that is wrong (in which case it should be presented as comment), or is it information that the reporter has got wrong, or is it information that has been fed to a reporter from a source who is motivated by malice?

Andrew Caldecott QC, the barrister who represented Albert Reynolds at the Court of Appeal hearing and represented the BBC at the Hutton Inquiry, has pointed out that there are two "distinct species" of the Reynolds Defence. One is the reportage case, "where the newspaper is neutrally reporting a bust-up between politicians, where the paper is informing the public", and the second is the investigative Reynolds defence, "where the newspaper is exposing what it suspects or believes is misconduct".[13]

He went on: "It is very important if you are publishing anything that is defamatory to decide which of these two species of defence you are in. You should put the main story and the evidence to them (the person being criticised). It is very important. It is not enough to go through the motions."[14] So the steps taken to verify the story, the steps taken to contact the person criticised and the extent to which that person's comments, explanations or previous statements have been included in the story are important. They are among Lord Nicholls' 10-point checklist for deciding whether the newspaper has met the "duty to publish" test. Times Newspapers had not given Albert Reynolds' side of the story in sufficient detail to defend its conduct. *Leeds Weekly News* won its case because of the way its reporter had acted in pursuit of a story judged to be in the public interest, even though the article did not carry a response to allegations levelled at the company.

HUTTON'S VIEWS ON KELLY

Lord Hutton took the view that weapons scientist Dr David Kelly should not have spoken to Today's defence correspondent Andrew Gilligan and that Mr Gilligan misquoted Dr Kelly, and that aspects of Mr Gilligan's story were "unfounded". But what if Mr Gilligan had approached Number 10 for a comment – as in the *Leeds Weekly News* case – before running with the story? Would we still have been told that "false accusations of fact, impugning the integrity of others, should not be made by the media"? What if Mr Gilligan had tape-recorded his conversation with Dr Kelly? Would evidence of a conversation, irrespective of the truth of any allegations, have been enough to establish that the BBC had acted responsibly and had been right to run with the story, solely on the views of a respected "whistleblower"?

The Reynolds and GKR Karate judgements went into considerable detail to explain exactly why defamatory articles (in the public interest) enjoyed or lacked qualified privilege. The *Hutton Report* did not. It cited Lords Nicholls', Cooke's and Hobhouse's conclusions on the protection of politicians' reputations, against freedom of expression in a democratic society. But it did not run through each of Lord Nicholls' 10-tests in turn, to examine whether it was in the public interest for the story to run, albeit uncorroborated and with mistakes.

Lord Hutton has been criticised for his interpretation of libel law. Some in the NUJ and at the BBC have expressed concerns that editors will be in a much more difficult position to run with investigative exposés and critical stories in future, as a result of the Judge's findings. But the *Hutton Report* was not a libel trial. Although held at the Royal Courts of Justice, the Inquiry was a fact-finding mission rather than a judicial tribunal. On the opening day, Lord Hutton said: "It is also important that I should emphasise that this is an Inquiry to be conducted by me. It is not a trial conducted between interested parties who have conflicting cases to advance. I do not sit to decide between conflicting cases. I sit to investigate the circumstances surrounding Dr Kelly's death."

There was no cross-examination of the first batch of witnesses. Cross-examination of second batch witnesses was permitted by the Judge, but "within limits". Witnesses did not swear evidence on oath. It was made clear that oral statements to the Inquiry were protected by privilege, subject to the usual caveat re: malice. Anthony Scrivener QC, former chairman of the Bar, pointed out that the Government did not even give the Hutton Inquiry the power to require disclosure of documents or to require officials to swear that all relevant documents had been disclosed.[15] It was not in Lord Hutton's remit to rule on whether the BBC had qualified privilege under Reynolds to broadcast its story, or to award damages. The fact that he did not take such a line should not come as a surprise.

CONSERVATIVES ON REYNOLDS' 'LATITUDE'

Towards the end of the House of Commons debate on the *Hutton Report* on February 4, the Conservative shadow Attorney General, Dominic Grieve, referred to the Reynolds case, in particular its "latitude" in enabling journalists "to report sources if they believe them to be credible".[16] The frontbench MP and barrister agreed with Lord Hutton that Andrew Gilligan had misquoted Dr Kelly and accepted the Judge's consequent criticisms of the BBC. But the shadow spokesman went on to call for a reassurance that nothing in the *Hutton Report* would undermine the "clear judgement" from Reynolds in terms of freedom of expression and the use of sources. Reynolds should remain "an important protection", he said. [17]

Society of Editors executive director Bob Satchwell said: "The Hutton Report was about one piece of reporting. I have no doubt that lawyers will quote from it in future cases. But Hutton can't be used as a precedent."[18] If not a precedent then, perhaps Lord Hutton's interpretation of Reynolds is an interpretation. Lord Nicholls' 10-point checklist remains intact. Journalists can continue to claim qualified privilege for stories that are in the public interest without establishing the truth of allegations (unless they are motivated by malice). Journalists should take adequate steps to verify information, seek and include a response to allegations and ensure that interview notes are in order.

Where does the Hutton Report say that journalists act irresponsibly if they speak to people not authorised to release information? Both might be in breach of the Official Secrets Act. But the Reynolds judgement describes investigative journalism as "vital" in a democratic society. Nothing in the *Hutton Report* states that journalists should desist from obtaining information from confidential sources. Subject to Lord Nicholls' warning about presenting "defamatory imputations" as statements of fact rather than of opinion, the journalist fulfils the "public interest duty" test as long as he/she can show that his/her conduct in pursuing the story was "responsible".

More to the point, and less certain, is how libel juries will balance a politician's reputation and the public's "right to know" in the wake of the Hutton Inquiry. Time will tell.

NOTES

1   The *Hutton Report* (website: www.the-hutton-inquiry.org.uk)
2   British and Irish Legal Information Institute – Reynolds v. Times Newspapers (website: www.bailii.org)
3   Barendt, Eric and Hitchins, Lesley (2000) *Media Law: Cases Materials*, Harlow, Longman
4   *Press Gazette*, Quantum Business Publishing; Welsh, Tom and Greenwood, Walter (2003) *McNae's Essential Law for Journalists*, (17th edition) London, Butterworths
5   The *Hutton Report*
6   The *Guardian*, January 29, 2004
7   The *Independent*, January 29, 2004
8   The *Observer*, February 1, 2004
9   ibid.
10   *Press Gazette*, January 30, 2004
11   The *Hutton Report*; *Media Law: Cases and Materials*
12   The *Hutton Report*
13   Speaking at the Law for Journalists Conference, London, November 2003
14   ibid
15   The *Independent*, January 29, 2004
16   *Hansard*
17   ibid
18   Speaking at the University of Lincoln, February 10, 2004

Richard Orange is a lecturer, specialising in law and local and national government, at the University of Lincoln

The communication ethics book that has meant the most to me

Out of all the hundreds of communication ethics texts we read, one often holds a special place. Here, in the first of a series of features on this theme, academics reveal their favourites

PROFESSOR VALERIE ALIA, LEEDS METROPOLITAN UNIVERSITY

The Autobiography of Lincoln Steffens first caught my eye when I was a teenager, browsing in my Oklahoma City high school library. Having long heard my father praise and quote from Steffens' work, I decided to read it for myself. Here, I discovered a world in which journalism mattered and journalists did their utmost to make a difference. Lincoln Steffens and his companion "muckrakers" (Ida Tarbell, Ida Wells Barnett, Upton Sinclair, Jacob Riis and others) not only exposed corruption, but struggled to help change the conditions they found. *The Autobiography* is an account of a writer's growing consciousness and conscience. After all these years, through my own modest efforts at journalism and media education, it continues to inspire.

While researching my latest book (*Media Ethics and Social Change*, Edinburgh University Press, 2004) I kept being surprised at how timely Steffens' work remains, and how far ahead of many current texts. With only a change of names and dates his depictions of governments-media-public relationships, media frenzies and moral panics could easily serve today. We have much to learn, as well, from his attention to the writer's craft and artful mix of seriousness and humour.

My edition of *The Autobiography* was published by Harcourt, Brace and Company in 1931 but it was an international best-seller and there are countless other one- and two-volume versions. Although it and companion collections of Steffens' journalism (e.g. *The Shame of the Cities*) and letters are currently out of print, they are easily found at booksellers and online shops and in most public and university libraries.

CLAUDE-JEAN BERTRAND, EMERITUS PROFESSOR, PARIS 2

Published in the early 1970s, it was a short book, only 100 pages, not a celebrated classic, not a pretentiously profound volume. A survey, heavy with quotes, loaded with 144 pages of appendices. But the book did make it clear, to me at least, that media ethics meant little if it was confined to philosophy, if it did not lead directly to better media service to the public. And that such progress would not occur unless there were not only clear rules, but also practical means to enforce them — other than laws and regulations, courts and police.

I was getting interested in the "social responsibility" of media, in "press councils", quite fashionable, and in "journalism reviews" which had just been flowering all over the US. So Lee Brown's title caught my attention: *The Reluctant Revolution: On Criticizing the Press in America* (New York, David McKay, 1974).

In the post-Watergate days of "imperial media" and the "newsocracy", Brown stressed that mankind crucially needed media improvement, that improvement was predicated on criticism, that the public had to be involved. And he surveyed means of criticism in the US: councils and reviews, but also ombudsmen, accuracy forms, critical books, media columns, liaison committees and major parliamentary reports.

That triggered the development in my mind of the concept of non-governmental "media accountability systems" (M*A*S), using criticism, monitoring, feedback, debate and education. For 30 years now, I have been studying, writing and lecturing about M*A*S, eighty of them by now. To them I have devoted a website (www.presscouncils.org) and two books that have been, or are being, translated into a dozen languages. Lee Brown, thank you.

PROFESSOR ANNE GREGORY, LEEDS METROPOLITAN UNIVERSITY

Ask a public relations person to name one book on ethics and I guess they'll mention this one: *Public Relations Ethics* (1995) by Philip Seib and Kathy Fitzpatrick, Harcourt Brace. It's a slim but powerful volume which confronts some perennial industry issues head on. Relationships with the press, public relations and government and how business uses (and abuses) communication are explored in detail.

All this is rigorously underpinned with a solid examination of the various ethical traditions and the problems inherent in them, including a potent discussion on the nature of truth. However, for me, the most valuable part of the book is its practical approach to ethical decision-making models with supporting examples.

What comes through very clearly is that public relations is a complex and powerful business with profound responsibilities. Having a coherent ethical base is at the heart of the practitioner's and indeed the discipline's credibility – it allows consistency, transparency and accountability. If this profession is to counter the cynicism that surrounds it, practitioners will need to think through their own ethical approach, articulate it to their bosses and the outside world and begin to enact the role of ethical guardian in their organisations.

A little gem of a book which should be on every communicator's shelf — and embedded in their memory.

CHERIS KRAMARAE, CENTER FOR THE STUDY OF WOMEN IN SOCIETY, UNIVERSITY OF OREGON

If ethics is the study of what we ought to do — one's duty to oneself, other people, and our environment, then this study rests on our understanding of our relationships to each other and our environment. In its practical application, it also rests on the freedom to decide among alternative actions, and to have these actions taken seriously as responsible, thoughtful, and caring.

A book I have found very useful because it recognises the complexities, tensions and promises associated with communication issues involving diverse populations, concerns, and contexts is the text edited by Josina M. Makau and Ronald C. Arnett, *Communication Ethics in an Age of Diversity* (Urbana and Chicago, University of Illinois Press, 1997).

The essays have quite differing perspectives because the editors encouraged people from various situations, communities and experiences to write on ethical issues directly related to their own cultural contexts and concerns. In some cases, these issues include areas of life often neglected by traditional studies, such as intimate relationships and families, concepts of care and inclusive fairness. The essays deal with a diversity of communication contexts, from personal friendship to mass media communication.

Many people have lived in "ages of diversity" for a long time, of course, but this book acknowledges and explores some of this diversity and encourages a revisioning of much traditional communication theory, practice and scholarship. May there be many more such "diversity" books of communication ethics, including books that deal with some of the communication challenges of ecofeminism.

SARAH NIBLOCK, SENIOR LECTURER, CITY UNIVERSITY, LONDON

Teaching media ethics to would-be journalists presents enormous challenges, not least because it's an area at the intersection of theory and practice. On the one hand, we have to prepare new reporters to respond confidently and responsibly to newsroom issues according to mainstream journalism's protocols. But as educators wishing to encourage graduates to make valid and continuing contributions to ethical debates, we need to instruct in more than how to conduct a "death-knock".

I use Karen Sander's book (*Ethics & Journalism*, London, Sage 2003) in my teaching because it does something quite rare in academic texts on journalism. She synthesises a raft of contextual, institutional and global factors to show how they impact upon everyday newsroom practice. So here's relativism, and here's how it might by applied at the *Guardian*. For the student, this offers them the potential to be reflexive reporters and, one day hopefully, reflexive editors.

It's all too easy in these days of 24-hour global news and market-driven editorial values to forget that journalism was once the key mouthpiece for autonomy, objectivity and democracy. While she packs a lot into her book – it straddles textbook and research – the underlying message is the actions of journalists are deeply embedded in a long, ethical and socio-political context which we ignore at our peril.

DR IAN RICHARDS, DIRECTOR, POSTGRADUATE JOURNALISM PROGRAMME, UNIVERSITY OF SOUTH AUSTRALIA

As a young reporter working on a daily newspaper, I was often bemused by the seeming indifference of most of my colleagues to opportunities to reflect upon their calling. This lack of curiosity about journalism among those renowned for their curiosity about the world in general puzzled me. Thus I felt an instant glow of recognition when I came across "Journalists just leave" by Columbia's James Carey. The paper took its title from an observation by Arthur Caplan of the Hastings Institute to the effect that, although the institute's activities inspired most professional groups, journalists simply left at the end of a Hastings programme – and nothing more happened.

Carey pointed out that part of the problem was that neither journalists nor philosophers know how to talk about journalism ethics; that journalists are unusually vulnerable because of the very public nature of journalism; and that most models of professional ethics are problematic because in journalism the client is "the public" rather than any particular individual or group. In the process, he made a strong case for understanding journalism as a conversation, a model which has had some resonance with me ever since.

However, the aspect of the paper which had the greatest impact at that time was a section on the dilemmas which arise from journalism's situation as a private business imbued with a public trust. In particular, I was struck by Carey's insightful observation that the fundamental ethical problems of journalism originate at the deepest level of ownership but are "solved" at the level of the reporter and editor. This helped trigger an extended process of inquiry, and what happens at the interface between the media corporation and the individual journalist has intrigued me ever since.

James Carey (1987) "Journalists Just Leave: The Ethics of an Anomalous Profession", Maile-Gene, Jean Sagen (ed) *Ethics and the Media*, Iowa City, Iowa Humanities Board. Reprinted in Baird, R., Loges, W. and Rosenbaum, S. (eds) (1999) *The Media and Morality*, New York, Prometheus pp 39-54

Pointing out strengths and weaknesses

At least 100 websites deal (in English) with media ethics and media accountability systems. Claude-Jean Bertrand examines the leading sites by focusing on two from the United States: one large, the other small.

www.macalester.edu/~wpi/ethicslinks.htm
The World Press Institute, a rather pretentious name for a small outfit housed by Macalester College, a private liberal arts institution in St Paul, Minnesota, was set up 42 years ago. It is supported by a wide range of foundations, local and national media, multinational US corporations and is now directed by John Ullmann. Its mission is to "promote press freedom throughout the world" mainly by offering "a four-month journalism fellowship to 10 journalists from countries around the world" (mostly emerging democracies) and exposing them to "US journalistic practices and standards". They first study at Macalester, then travel for three months around the US, interviewing media personalities and decision-makers.

The WPI website, edited by Stephen Ward, is small but elegant and clear. Its "Global Media Ethics" section contains, first, half a dozen essays together with guidelines for contributors and feedback. The book reviews sub-section lists just one book, from 2002. Then comes a list of about 50 links to useful resources, journalism and academic organisations, stores of codes and bibliographies.

http://www.poynter.org/resource_center/
The Poynter Institute website is just the opposite of the WPI site with masses of material thrown together in such a way that the surfing visitor can never be sure of having sampled all the riches on offer..

The Poynter Institute in Florida is unique. Created in 1975 by Nelson Poynter, owner of the *St Petersburg Times,* it later took over ownership of that daily. Hence the abundant funds which it devotes to developing "excellence and integrity in the practice of the craft" by training "journalists, future journalists and teachers of journalism". Its major fields: reporting,

writing and editing (in print, broadcasting and online), media management –
and ethics. Its two major tools: seminars and a website.

The close association of the website with a daily is not the only reason
why it reminds one of a US newspaper dating from before 1982 when *USA
Today* triggered a slow revolution in packaging and layout. Its exceptionally
plentiful and diverse material looks a mess. Masses of small items (serving as
links) are crammed on every page, with too many colours, too much
underlining. That immediately makes the visitor uncomfortable.

Take the home page: it contains, on the left, a list of a dozen sections,
on the right a list of 12 columns, in the middle a list of 18 features, followed
by half a dozen "Poynter Picks" and half a dozen "Poynter News" and half
a dozen "Industry events" — plus over a half dozen other single items such
as "Create a personal page on Poynter" or "Ethics Tool: Decisions on
Deadline".

The amount of quality material on this website which is regularly
augmented and updated (some of it daily) makes it probably the best
around. But it needs restructuring so that the visitor's eye can quickly grasp
the map of the site and the full inventory of the particular area he/she wishes
to explore.

Let's move to the "Ethics" page. In the middle is a 15-page catalogue of
"Previous Stories" going back to 1994, each with useful tools (E-mail this
story/ Print this page/Add your comments to this article). On the right is
"New on Poynter", a list of links to mainly unrelated items. Then
underneath it, in small print, comes a precious list of "related resources",
ethics-oriented links to:

- "American Society of Newspaper Editors/ Poynter Ethics Tool" where,
  after registering, you can discreetly (thanks to "secure socket
  encryption") analyse a case with tools provided and obtain advice on it.
- "Poynter On Call" where, if you are a journalist "facing a tough ethical
  call on deadline" or another such problem, you can call toll-free and get
  advice from the local experts.
- "Ethics Bibliography": a comprehensive list of on-line resources and
  books.
- "Credibility Bibliography": on-line resources, articles, books polls and
  reports.
- "Codes of Ethics": just the ASNE list of US codes.
- "*New York Times* Ethics": the PDF text of the *New York Times*'s
  January 2003 Ethical Journalism: Code of Conduct for the News and

Editorial Departments.

- "Talk about Ethics": columns by Poynter's ethics experts, originally Bob Steele and since 2000 Ali Colon.
- "Poynter Ethics Journal": columns by Kelly McBride going back to 2002.
- "Journalism with a difference" (i.e. minority journalism): columns by various authors.

To my knowledge, no other media ethics website approaches this one. However, this is a US site, with the typical US focus on the individual journalist and ignorance of "media accountability systems" such as ombudsmen, press councils, journalism reviews and so on.

Reading Poynter material, you get the impression that all journalistic sins are committed by journalists, probably because they have not been taught otherwise. So media ethics consists largely in converting reporters and editors to more virtuous ways. Judging from recent scandals at the *New York Times, Washington Post, Chicago Tribune* and *USA Today,* however, it seems that such talk might not be enough. Besides, remarkable books such as *Leaving Readers Behind: The Age of Corporate Newspapering* by Gene Roberts et al. (University of Arkansas Press, 2001) have documented the decadence of journalism caused by shareholder greed.

Back to websites. To the extent that, contrary to books or journals, they are accessible by all from anywhere at any time and at no cost, it may seem useless for many of them to duplicate their efforts. Most sites with an interest in media ethics should be content to offer some original material and to provide visitors with links to a series of other specialised sites that have the resources to aim at exhaustiveness and to stay up to date. In that line of thought, the WPI may seem more reasonable than the Poynter site. But the latter, which has the financial means to be a global website open to the various approaches to media quality, actually specialises in US media only and in traditional non-controversial US media ethics. A pity.

Claude-Jean Bertrand is Professor Emeritus at the University of Paris-2 and webmaster of www.presscouncils.org

South Essex College
Further & Higher Education, Southend Campus
Luker Road Southend-on-Sea Essex SS1 1ND
Tel: 01702 220400 Fax: 01702 432320
Minicom: 01702 220642

Lightning Source UK Ltd.
Milton Keynes UK
05 November 2010

162449UK00002B/5/A

9 781905 237685